# Becoming
# Art

# Becoming
# Art

*Exploring
Cross-Cultural
Categories*

## Howard Morphy

Oxford • New York

First published in 2007 by
**Berg**
Editorial offices:
1st Floor, Angel Court, 81 St Clements Street, Oxford, OX4 1AW, UK
175 Fifth Avenue, New York, NY 10010, USA

Berg is the imprint of Oxford International Publishers Ltd.


**Library of Congress Cataloging-in-Publication Data**

Morphy, Howard.
    Becoming art : exploring cross-cultural categories / Howard Morphy.
        p. cm.
    Includes bibliographical references and index.
    ISBN-13: 978-1-84520-656-7 (cloth)
    ISBN-10: 1-84520-656-8 (cloth)
    ISBN-13: 978-1-84520-657-4 (pbk.)
    ISBN-10: 1-84520-657-6 (pbk.)
    1. Art, Yolngu.  2. Indigenous art—Historiography.  3. Art and
society.  4. Cultural awareness.  I. Title.

    N7401.M655 2007
    704.03'9915—dc22

                                                      2007033738


**British Library Cataloguing-in-Publication Data**

A catalogue record for this book is available from the British Library.

ISBN   978 1 84520 656 7 (Cloth)
       978 1 84520 657 4 (Paper)

Typeset by JS Typesetting Ltd, Porthcawl, Mid Glamorgan
Printed in the United Kingdom by Biddles Ltd, King's Lynn


**www.bergpublishers.com**

# TABLE OF CONTENTS

# LIST OF ILLUSTRATIONS

# ACKNOWLEDGEMENTS

Most of this book was written in Darwin when I was awarded a Fellowship at the North Australia Research Unit of the Australian National University, where Helen Sainsbury and Lyle Hebb created the ideal environment for a writing retreat. The research behind it has been carried out over many years and has been made possible by grants from the Australian Research Council and, earlier on, from the Australian Institute of Aboriginal and Torres Strait Islander Studies. The ideas have been developed over years of discussions with colleagues and I would like to thank in particular Wally Caruana, Jeremy Coote, Françoise Dussart, Alison French, Nelson Graburn, Louise Hamby, Ivan Karp, Cory Kratz, Nigel Lendon, Djon Mundine, Nancy Munn, Fred Myers, Morgan Perkins, Nicolas Peterson, Margo Smith, John Stanton, Luke Taylor, Margie West, Leon White and the late Anthony Forge, and Peter Ucko. In recent years I have been based at the Centre for Cross-Cultural Research of the Research School of Humanities at the Australian National University and could not have been better supported by the staff and students there. Many people have commented on draft chapters of this book in different forms. Caroline Turner, Christian Kauffman and Karen Westmacott made invaluable inputs into individual chapters. Elizabeth Coleman interrogated the argument of the whole with her philosopher's mind and continually caused me to think. Pip Deveson also read the entire manuscript with an eye for detail and clarity of argument. This book could not have been written without Frances Morphy who shared the research with me, read every chapter as it was written and then read the manuscript again as a whole. At each stage of the writing her input was critical in matters of ideas, argument and style.

It will be obvious to readers of this book that I owe an enormous debt to the Yolngu people of north-east Arnhem Land who have been hosts to Frances and me for thirty-five years. From the beginning they made it known that we were writing their history and that they had clear ideas as to what that history was. In the beginning I had the privilege to work with that generation of Yolngu intellectuals who had grown up before the arrival of the mission and who had to determine the mode of engagement with the colonial world that was beginning to encapsulate them. My main teachers were Narritjin Maymuru, Daymbalipu Mununggurr, Roy Marika, Mungurrawuy Yunupingu, Welwi Wanambi, Gawirrin Gumana, and Dula and Gambali Ngurruwutthun. Gawirrin continues to be an inspiration to the generation who have grown up since then in increasingly 'hard times'. In recent years we have been learning from their children and grandchildren, in particular Djambawa,

Bakulangay and Nuwandjali Marawili, Raymattja and Wanyubi Marika, Baluka, Galuma and Naminapu Maymuru, Dhukal and Wuyal Wirrpanda, Waka Mununggurr, and Boliny, Wukun and Ralwurranydji Wanambi. Our special thanks go to Malumin Marawili and Dhambit Wanambi for allowing us to use that special spot under the tamarind tree as our home from home at Yilpara, and to Sally Wagg for sharing her home with us at Yirrkala. I could not have received greater assistance from Will Stubbs and Andrew Blake the managers of Buku-Larrnggay Mulka Art Centre, Yirrkala and their staff.

I have received great support from many cultural institutions, in particular the National Museum of Australia, Museum Victoria, the Kluge Ruhe Aboriginal Art Museum at the University of Virginia, the Museums and Art Galleries of the Northern Territory and the Berndt Museum at the University of Western Australia. Lindy Allen, curator of the Donald Thomson Collection at Museum Victoria deserves a special mention.

# PREFACE

The ladder of art lies flat, art never improves only changes.

Margaret Preston

In this book the Yolngu people of north-east Arnhem Land are used as an exemplar of value creation processes in art. Essentially this book is about a paradox – Yolngu have always produced art but Yolngu art has only recently been recognized as art. To make sense of this paradox we have to acknowledge that there are two implicit definitions of art at play. On the one hand there is a cross-cultural definition of art that encompasses actions and objects that have something in common that can be referred to as 'art' and that places them in the analytic category of artwork. On the other hand there is designation of certain works as 'fine art' – works that are bought and sold as such in the art market and that are exhibited in art galleries and museums of fine art. The solution to the paradox is then made visible: Yolngu have always produced art but only recently has it been recognized as fine art. However, that is merely the beginning of the enquiry, since what then needs to be answered is: who defines art and fine art and how do works become included within the latter category?

I will argue that 'art' and 'fine art' are best seen to be polythetic categories as far as the substantive nature of the works that are included within them is concerned – they contain a great deal of diversity but overall there is a sense that the included works have sufficient in common across the spectrum that they form a definable category of thing. I will also argue that both categories contain substantively similar kinds of objects and can enter into each other's discourses. The works that enter the domain of fine art are on the whole ones that fit into the more general art category. The general category that I focus on is a cross-cultural one, since it is intended to apply to art wherever it is found.

The cross-cultural definition that underlies my argument is one which I developed some time ago: 'art objects are ones with aesthetic and or semantic attributes (but in most cases both), that are used for representational or presentational purposes' (Morphy 1994b: 655; Morphy and Perkins 2006: 11–17). I see it as a working definition that seems to capture the attributes of certain types of object which exist in most human societies and which reflect one of the ways in which people can act in the world – they can act through the making and use of art. Unsurprisingly it is these kinds of object that end up eventually being selected out for inclusion in the institutions of fine art, the ones that end up being marketed as fine art. Fine art is in its origins a Western category and deeply imbricated in the history of Western art since at least the Renaissance, consolidating in something close to its present form in nineteenth-century Europe (Winter 2002; Joachimides 2000). As far as its content is concerned it is a continuously changing category, usually through the inclusion of additional works and kinds of works. In its history, fine art is entangled with the development of aesthetic theory and attitudes, is connected to taste, class and hierarchy (Bourdieu 1984) and to the evolution of the art market. In this book I will argue, however, that the most distinctive feature of fine art is that it is part of a value creation process which selects what are considered to be the finest works of a particular tradition and creates the conditions for privileged viewing in selective institutions. My definition of fine art does not originate in the institutional theory of art (Dickie 1974; Danto 1964; Becker 1982), though the institutional theory addresses the present character of the world of fine art and seeks to understand the authority vested in its players. In a succinct criticism of the institutional theory of art, Christopher Janaway writes 'that it cannot be easily used, as earlier theories were to persuade us of what is peculiarly valuable about art' (1995: 59). It is to the more general concept of art that we can look in order to encompass the width of what is valued in fine art, and that width is an integral part of the dialogic historical relationship between art and fine art. Once we have understood the nature of this relationship and deconstructed the essentialism and separatism of the fine art category, we open up insights into the processes of inclusion into that category, which require us to take account of the diversity of ways in which art has been used to act in the world and the values associated with it.

Because until recently fine art has been defined by people in the West – that it is indeed in its history a Western category – it has developed a special relationship with Western art practice. Indigenous Australians produced art for thousands of years before they encountered Europeans, but it was not until they encountered Europeans that they became aware of the special select category of fine art. And in the case of Indigenous Australians they embraced it quite happily. The resistance came from the other direction (Price 1989; Errington 1998; Myers 2002). Aboriginal art has been subject to the same discourse over inclusion within the fine art gallery as other so-called 'primitive arts' and the various grounds for exclusion that have been applied to them have been applied to it (see Chapters 1 and 7). Those arguments have provided part of the background to my engagement with Aboriginal art over nearly forty years since I first became interested in the topic. During that time Aboriginal art has gained increasing recognition among Western audiences as fine art, though its entry into the category is still contested. Aboriginal art is now collected by institutions and individuals around the world, and every state art gallery in Australia has developed major collections (Figure 1). When I began research on Yolngu art in 1973 it was not being collected systematically by any state gallery and with some exceptions was not being collected by ethnographic museums either, and yet public interest in it was beginning to widen – squeezed between the exclusivity of the fine art category and the authenticity criteria of the ethnographic museums, it occupied a place captured by Nelson Graburn's phrase 'ethnic and tourist arts' (Graburn 1976).

Figure 1    Gulumbu Yunupingu at Musée du
Quai Branly. Behind her can be seen the murals
based on one of her paintings. The architect in
association with two Australian curators, Brenda
Croft of the National Gallery of Australia and
Hetti Perkins of the Art Gallery of New South
Wales, selected works from eight Indigenous
Australian artists to be incorporated within the
interior architecture of the museum. The artists
were Paddy Bedford, John Mawurndjul, Ningura
Napurrula, Lena Nyadbi, Michael Riley, Judy
Watson, Tommy Watson and Gulumbu Yunupingu.
Photograph Alastair Miller. Reproduced courtesy
of the Artist, and Buku-Larrnggay Mulka Centre,
Yirrkala, Northern Territory.

My own interest in Aboriginal art developed serendipitously. As a master's student at
University College London I developed a theoretical framework for studying indigenous art.
My supervisor Peter Ucko, while uttering encouraging words, suggested that I had better try
to apply it to a body of data. I spent several days searching, somewhat desperately, through
the shelves and filing cabinets of the library of the Royal Anthropological Institute in Bedford
Square in London. In a drawer I came across an offprint from the first volume of the *Records
of the South Australian Museum*: Sir Edward Stirling and Edgar Waite's 'Description of Toas

or Aboriginal direction signs' published in 1919. It saved my day. The article consisted of documented illustrations of some 400 objects collected by Lutheran missionary R. G. Reuther from the Lake Eyre region of Central Australia. Toas were direction signs that people set in the ground on leaving camp to let others know where they had gone. Formally they were a very diverse set of objects varying from small figurative sculptures of people and animals, to geometric designs painted on flat surfaces, to moulded lumps of clay with things fixed into them – material culture objects, plant materials, even pubic hair. In my thesis I approached Toas from the perspective of art as a form of communication: my aim was to show the ways in which such a diverse set of objects could all fulfil the same function as direction signs. I was concerned with how they were interpreted (see Morphy 1977 for my analysis).

Although I found Toas aesthetically pleasing, I did not emphasize this aspect of them in my analysis. A decade later Toas became the subject of a major exhibition at the South Australian Museum during the Adelaide Festival. This time the intention of the curators, Peter Sutton and Philip Jones, was to draw attention to their aesthetic dimension – to exhibit them as fine art (Sutton 1987). They implied that the primary function of such an intricate and exquisite set of objects was unlikely to have been as direction markers, and indeed one of the chapters in the accompanying catalogue was titled 'The great toa hoax', a trap into which I and the unfortunate Reuther had both fallen. Their conclusion in many respects was that they were intercultural objects, like the bark paintings of the Yolngu people of north-east Arnhem Land (Jones and Sutton 1986). But we are getting a little ahead of ourselves.

In order to pay my way while writing my Master's thesis I worked as a research assistant in the ethnography department of the British Museum on a project to register unregistered objects – it was called the 'no-number project' – no number no identity. While I was working there I assisted the curator of the Oceanic collection, Bryan Cranstone, to develop an exhibition on the Australian Aborigines for the soon to be opened Museum of Mankind. I was intrigued by the lack of emphasis on art and aesthetics in the exhibition and the near absence of bark paintings. The emphasis on material culture in general was a deliberate one. Bryan held the view that the main purpose of ethnography exhibitions was to inform people of the way of life of the society concerned, not to exhibit objects as art. While I have some sympathy with that perspective, the underlying assumption that art and ethnography are somehow opposed can be problematic, as I will argue later (chapter 8).[1] However, even if they had wanted to include bark paintings, the museum would have had a limited choice. A few bark paintings had entered the museum as donations, but the view was that bark paintings as objects made for sale in a post-colonial context were in some sense inauthentic and not quite the kind of thing that should be collected by an ethnographic museum. In the 1970s bark paintings were almost entirely absent from British collections.

After completing my Master's degree I was given the opportunity to go to Australia to undertake research for my doctorate. I had in fact applied for a scholarship to apply the methodology I had developed to the study of art in Vanuatu. But the condition of the scholarship awarded to me by the Australian National University was that I should study bark paintings in Arnhem Land – bark paintings as a symptom of socio-cultural change. And that was how I ended up at Yirrkala in 1973 studying Yolngu art (Morphy 1991). It soon became apparent to me that it made no sense to study bark paintings in isolation from other aspects of Yolngu art and society, and indeed the reverse was equally true. And the trajectory of their society was becoming increasingly entangled, in Thomas's (1991) sense of the word, with that of the colonial society that was encapsulating them. While bark painting certainly occupies a significant place in contemporary Yolngu society, from the Yolngu perspective this is not the result of some rupture with the past but very much in continuity with it (see Section I).

European colonization came late to north-east Arnhem Land. The first missionaries arrived in Yirrkala as late as 1935. From that perspective the process of encountering fine art has been a very rapid one. But I will also argue that history does not begin with European colonization, and the articulation of Yolngu art with the world of fine art must be understood from the perspective of their own value creation processes and the ways in which they were transformed and transforming in the colonial encounter. The richly documented record of Yolngu engagement with the outside world and my own research over a period of thirty-five years has provided me with an opportunity to look at the encounter not from the perspective of the Western art world but from a Yolngu perspective.

The encounter between Indigenous art and the fine art world has usually been written from the perspective of the Western art world. There has been a dialogue between Indigenous arts and Western art worlds but on the whole it has been written from one side. The focus has been on the artworks once they have arrived in the gallery, once they have become fine art. The idea of art by metamorphosis (Maquet 1986) – the creation of indigenous works as fine art in the Western arena – signifies the lack of agency accorded to the indigenous artist. This focus has meant that the history of the artists and objects before their discovery by the fine art world remains largely unwritten, in particular in the case of contemporary indigenous arts.

This book is about that history of Yolngu art and, as much as it is possible for me to do so, it is written from the perspective of Yolngu artists. It is about the process of their engagement with the world of fine art and argues for a relatively smooth passage of the works they produced from local contexts of production into those privileged arenas of viewing – the galleries of fine art.[2] The value creation processes in which Yolngu were engaged extended into the world of the colonial society that was in the process of encapsulating them. They saw the sale of art to outsiders as an economic opportunity but also as a means of asserting the value of their cultural production in the arenas of the encompassing society. The very fact that they have seen this process as a smooth transition in which they recognize their world in these very different arenas is a challenge to the presuppositions that kept indigenous artists for so long separated out from Western fine art discourse.

# 1 CROSS-CULTURAL CATEGORIES AND THE INCLUSION OF ABORIGINAL ART

## INTRODUCTION

The Eurocentricism of much art history of the past has created the impression that there are two kinds of art – art that is part of art history and art that is not. The implicit questions that this raises but which are seldom directly addressed are: if the objects concerned are outside the province of art history are they art at all? or if they are art in what sense are they art? and if they were absent from art history where were they present? These issues are of more than theoretical significance. Art history has long had a close relationship with the art market and with the institutions of fine art. Since the Renaissance and especially under the influence of the German idealist philosophy, art history has co-evolved with Western fine art appreciation and to a slightly lesser extent with Western art practice. This has affected the ways in which global art production has been viewed and the curatorial boxes into which non-Western art has been placed. It could be argued that art history was and is complicit in the exclusion of indigenous art from fine art galleries and museums, and its location in special places of its own, in the former Museum of Primitive Art in New York, the Quai Branly in Paris or in museums of ethnography and natural history.

However, before I am accused of singling out art history alone for opprobrium, I should say that my criticism can be equally applied to my own discipline of anthropology. Until recently most anthropologists also wrote about indigenous art as if it were a fundamentally different kind of thing from European art as it has developed in modern times – the times in which anthropology itself had emerged as a distinctive discipline in its contemporary form. Other societies did not have words for art, the objects concerned were functional items not produced for aesthetic contemplation, and so on.

The problem with the approach of both art historians and anthropologists is that they were equally embedded in the assumptions of the worlds in which they were brought up, and in the relatively recent period of historical time that preceded them. Non-Western societies were 'other' to the anthropologist's own and European art was the art historians' very own cultural heritage. They tended to share a similar conception of what 'art' was, a conception that applied to a relatively short period of the history of their own Western societies. Indeed, strictly speaking, the definition could not be applied to many of the objects that have been included as part of the canon of Western fine art, if inclusion is based on the motivations of the artists and the functional contexts for which they were intended, or indeed the response they were anticipated to engender.

Matters of definition, including the definition of art, are in many respects the subject of this book. At this stage I need only note that the view of art to which I am referring here is one that sees art as comprising objects made primarily for aesthetic contemplation and valued according to aesthetic criteria – the art of Bourdieu's *Distinction*. Anthropologists often failed to see the more general similarities between the practices of other cultures and those of their own society; and the Western art historian, influenced by taste, often failed to appreciate art that lay outside the boundaries of his or her own historical experience. Art historians, it has been argued, are often as uncomfortable with the art of their contemporary present – with the avant-garde – as they are with the art of the Barbarians and Primitives, the art that exists on the boundaries of the Western canon and beyond.

The art of hunting-and-gathering societies is well beyond the boundaries of the West. For much of the past two centuries it had a value not for what we (Europeans) have become but as a sign of what we once were. Despite their location, the cave paintings of the Dordogne were not so much part of the history of the Western canon, rather part of the prehistory of humankind. While there may be considerable merit in seeing the artists of the Dordogne as part of global heritage (and indeed seeing the creators of the rock art of Australia, 20,000 years ago in exactly the same way), there is little justification for placing contemporary Australian Aborigines in a similar position. Such an evolutionary perspective is one of the reasons why Aboriginal art has been largely invisible in art writing for much of the colonial history of Australia. Susan Lowish (2005) has written about the absence of references to Aboriginal art in the writings of art historians, in particular focusing on the writing of Bernard Smith.[1] It is only very recently, in the work of art historians such as Andrew Sayers (2001), that Aboriginal art has begun to be included in the same frame as non-Aboriginal art. And with some major exceptions anthropologists have until recently been little better at including Aboriginal art in their analyses.

The fact that Aboriginal artworks were separated out in such a fundamental way was a sign that Aboriginal art was not recognized as the same kind of object as European art. But by not including it within the same frame, art historians were reinforcing its difference and adhering to a fairly narrow conception of what art was. That definition had no qualifier attached – indeed, they were writing about 'Australian art' as if no other kind of art existed in Australia. And of course in a sense according to their definitions nothing else did. If art historians were not writing about it and anthropologists were not writing about it then no one was.

In world-art discourse there has recently been a significant shift away from the European canon toward a more encompassing conception of art, enabling very different artistic traditions to be included within the same broad frame.[2] These changes have been influenced by the need to include the relatively autonomous traditions of Asia and Latin America under the rubric of world art as much as a rethinking of the nature of Indigenous arts. This movement, however has had a particular character in Australia and other settler colonial societies. In Australia, Indigenous and non-Indigenous traditions exist side by side and have overlapping local markets. Over time it has been increasingly difficult to ignore these overlaps or to deny the Indigenous artists the right to share the same gallery spaces as non-Indigenous. The changes that have taken place have been partly the result of the persuasive actions of Indigenous artists and partly a consequence of government policy and the politics of nationhood (see Myers 2002). But they have also happened because art historians, anthropologists, and art theorists have been engaged in a process, which has created new conditions for the definition of art and has led to the development of a definition that is more encompassing of difference. And in turn the result has been in some cases the development of a closer interaction between Aboriginal and non-Aboriginal artists and a shifting of boundaries.[3]

This book is in part about how that definition of art has changed – about how Aboriginal art became art. It is more than a simplistic statement that through some form of cultural blindness Europeans did not see what was there all along. It is undeniably the case that for much of Australia's white history artists in the European tradition did look outside Australia for their sense of continuity and inspiration. They did, literally, fail to see Aboriginal art. But that was to a large extent because for the nineteenth and much of the twentieth centuries, their definition of art was narrowly focused on the works they produced placed in sequence by the values they acquired through European art history and associated with a particular way of viewing art.[4] At the level of form, many works that Europeans encountered in nineteenth-century Aboriginal art would only become acceptable in European art in the late twentieth century – sand sculptures, body arts, 'abstract' art and so on. The great irony is that when such works became the inspiration for Western art, art history projected them back in time as antecedent forms rather than as precedents for subsequent developments in European art.[5]

## CROSS-CULTURAL FRAMES

A cross-cultural definition of art needs to encompass the many differences that exist and existed between Aboriginal and European art, but it also needs to encompass the differences that exist within European art and the ways in which both art traditions have changed over time. The great challenges of a more cross-cultural definition of art is to allow what was and is different about Aboriginal art to remain despite its placement within a more inclusive category. That category cannot be European art as it was in the mid-twentieth century since that would simply be a form of appropriation, subordinating the difference of Aboriginal art to a particular Western definition. Certainly today Aboriginal art is becoming increasingly an integral part of Australian art, and it will be increasingly difficult to write about the one in isolation from the other (see McLean 1998; Eagle 2006). But the entry of Aboriginal art into the contemporary discourse on Australian art has become possible because the conception of art in Australian has changed. It has become a little de-centred, moving away from the Western canon – it is no longer as centred on 'the mutations which have occurred in styles and fashions originating overseas as they have been assimilated into conditions ... existing in Australia' (Smith, 1945: 21).

Ironically, the exercise I am involved in should not be difficult for art historians to grasp because they are, for the most part, fully aware of the diversity of motivations for works already included under the rubric of 'art history'. While I have been writing so far about European art and Aboriginal art as if they were uniform categories, both are characterized by their diversity. One of the main commissioners of 'art' in the Renaissance was the Catholic Church. Much of this was religious art and – as Bernard Smith himself has so brilliantly demonstrated – the artists of the Voyages of Discovery were hardly separable from the scientists of their day. It may indeed only be with the advent of modernism that, for a short while, the primacy of aesthetic contemplation of form became, in some people's eyes, *the* major *raison d'être* for art production.[6]

There is a sense in which a particular kind of art history may be about European art, since European art has for a period of time ring-fenced its history from the arts that surround it. But I would not be at all surprised if a more encompassing definition of art and a more global perspective on art history will challenge some of the presuppositions of that school and free it to open up alternative interpretations, orderings and influences. Certainly it is now clear that Aboriginal art was much more present in Australian art than people have allowed for. Under another label Aboriginal art was part of the visual culture of Australia. At times it strongly influenced Australian design. It continued to be practised by Aboriginal artists and continued to be rediscovered. Interestingly as Lowish (2005) points out, some of those European-Australian artists who early on were most influenced by Aboriginal art were viewed negatively at the time by a number of the art historians who wrote about their work.[7]

## ANTHROPOLOGY AND THE CROSS-CULTURAL

Anthropology is a mediating discipline concerned as much with cultural translation as with the interpretation of cultures. While in its early period it tended to translate an exotic 'them' in ways that they could be understood by a European 'us', it is now recognized that the 'them' and the 'us' need to be mutually translatable. Anthropology needs to create a meta-vocabulary – a descriptive conceptual vocabulary of culture – that facilitates cross-cultural discourse.

Anna Wierzbicka (2006) has convincingly demonstrated the cultural biases encoded in languages and argued for the need for a semantic meta-language in order to facilitate cross-cultural understanding. To achieve this she has developed her own methodology involving a natural semantic meta-language (NSM) based on a set of universal concepts which, she argues, are translatable into all of the world's languages and underlie the semantic structure. We are a long way from developing an equivalent meta-language for culture. Indeed, because of the complex nature of cultural data, of which verbal language is only a part, the formal methods of Wierzbickean semantics are unlikely to be directly applicable, even though I believe they can usefully be incorporated within the methodological and theoretical framework of anthropology. Anthropology has itself gone some way to developing through the process of its own discourse a vocabulary which enables the comparison of cultures. It has developed general categories that exist independent of the specificities of any single cultural context.

Because of the origins of modern anthropology in nineteenth-century Europe and America, those general categories reflect a historical bias toward Western cultures. Over time anthropologists have been inventing their own meta-vocabulary – more or less implicitly – for anthropological discourse by applying cross-culturally concepts of religion, kinship, marriage, gender, aesthetics, clan and so on, and refining the definitions to make them apply more widely. In practice this has involved making the terms less Eurocentric, positioning them in some inter-cultural space. (See Strang, 2006, for a relevant discussion.) Over time some words, such as 'horde' (Hiatt 1966), drop out of the anthropologist's vocabulary, while others such as 'gender' are added.

The dangers of this process are twofold. One is that the terms may come to be defined so generally that they cease to be useful. They lose touch with the intuitive core of the concept and leave only the fuzzy edges intact: which may be why marriage as defined by Gough (1959) and religion as defined by Geertz (1971), insightful as these definitions are theoretically, have not been taken up by many. The other, a more fundamental criticism, is that the very process of creating a meta-vocabulary is an imposition of Western ideology on other cultures. Rather than seeking terms which apply generally to human societies, anthropologists should be defining concepts in terms of the cultures themselves. We should not be finding marriage among the Nayars, religion among the Australian Aborigines or gender in Melanesia, but something else that comes out of those societies or regions. This is in fact a very profound issue. It is on the horns of the cultural relativist dilemma: the apparent contradiction between the fact that we are all human and yet culturally constructed as different.

The development of a meta-vocabulary for anthropology, consisting of categories that are applicable cross-culturally, can be justified on a number of different bases. The pragmatic justification is that the meta-vocabulary is simply a formalization of something that anthropologists do anyway. An anthropologist brings certain concepts with her or him into the field and uses them as an aid to analysing the data gathered from that society. The concept is then re-defined in terms of the categories and concepts of that society: so that gender in Melanesia, for example, is differently constructed or conceptualized than it is at a particular time and place in European history (see Strathern 1988). It is better that anthropologists apply these terms in a considered way that reflects, even challenges, the sense in which they are understood within the discipline than that they should apply them unreflexively and without definition.

A more theoretical answer is that the meta-vocabulary that anthropologists construct is indeed an acknowledgement of the existence of cultural categories that have general relevance. Not all cross-cultural categories are going to be universal; some may apply regionally or temporally. The cross-cultural category is in some respects a *relata* that links together phenomena which seem to have something in common, which share a family resemblance.[8] To be valid in the sense in which I am using it, however, it needs to be interrogated in the contexts where it is applied and to make sense to the people whose categories are under scrutiny. In practice such testing of the proposed category will proceed through ethnographic research, and the application of the concept will initially be intuitive. I would argue, however, that this is part of the normal method of anthropology.[9] An anthropologist undertaking fieldwork on gender, religion, kinship or marriage must interrogate the validity of those categories in the context of the society he or she is studying.

The cross-cultural category is not identical with the anthropological concept, but it is the product of anthropological investigations into the particular phenomenon concerned. Kinship in anthropology has its own history linked to a body of knowledge concerning particular kinds of social and cultural relationships between people. What is encompassed by kinship theory and the history of the study of kinship will influence the direction of anthropological enquiry. However, in order to engage in comparative analysis the anthropologist must take on board the question of what kinship is, and that is where the cross-cultural category enters into the framework. What the anthropologist includes in the comparative analysis of kinship must reflect the evolving cross-cultural category he or she has in mind.[10] It is quite possible that as a result of investigation the anthropologist concludes that no such phenomenon exists in the society concerned, though it is more than likely that something will have some relationship to the phenomenon marked by the cross-cultural category. Of course it is precisely this kind of mismatch that can result in a revision of the category itself.

It is difficult to imagine an anthropological analysis of phenomena cross-culturally or cross-temporally without the employment, at least implicitly, of the idea of a cross-cultural category. If anthropologists do not use one, then logically they are either applying a category from their own culture or they are following a topic that has previously been a field of anthropological research. In that case they are likely to be building on previous discourse on the cross-cultural nature of the phenomena concerned.

Clearly it is possible for anthropologists, but more often others, to investigate certain disciplinarily defined phenomena without reference to the categories of the societies concerned. Thus an economist might approach the economy of a particular society from the perspective of formalist economic theory without reference to the categories of the society itself. The debates between formalist and substantivist perspectives of the 1970s centred on such issues.[11] The substantive phenomena are ones that have salience in the context of the society concerned and are in dialogue with cross-cultural categories.

If we find a concept of gender or kinship useful to understanding all human societies, that means that the concept is in some respects analogous to a semantic primitive in language, a concept that is highly salient for cross-cultural discourse and analysis. I do not mean that cultural categories are independent of cognitive, biological or social processes: they articulate with them and are influenced by them but are relatively autonomous.

The universalism of cross-cultural categories must, however, always be open to question. There are concepts that are of more limited range than others, categories that apply in one part of the world or period of history but are not necessarily universal. Moreover categories exist at different levels of specificity and some of more limited range may be found nesting within more general categories. The cross-cultural category of religion contains within it many different forms. There may be concepts that are relevant to understanding Jain religion (see for example Banks 1997) that are not useful in the case of Australian religions and vice versa. The 'Dreamtime' (Morphy 1996) is an example of a term developed for understanding Aboriginal religions, one which may not apply outside Australia. Comparative anthropology involves this process of stretching and redefining concepts, rejecting their applicability in particular cases, and developing new ones when necessary: there is a dialectic between common humanity and particular ways of being human. It is the common humanity that creates the possibility of anthropology; it is the diversity of humanity that makes it necessary.

The anthropological concepts that emerge over time are fuzzy around the edges, contain phenomena linked together by a family resemblance, and comprise polythetic sets;[12] they can break apart at the edges or across the middle and ultimately prove unsustainable. There is always the danger that the more inclusive categories can mislead by placing together phenomena that are fundamentally different. The anthropological concept of religion today contains phenomena, beliefs and practices that embrace all that the nineteenth-century anthropologist Sir James Fraser included as religion and much of what he excluded from it. Fraser's evolutionary schema posited a pre-religious phase of magic and a post-religious phase of science. People of the highest 'civilization' and the lowest could be without religion. Australian Aboriginal practices were excluded from the category of religion and placed firmly in the category of magic.

Today it would be extremely difficult to write about any society and leave the box marked religion empty. The anthropological broadening of the concept, the extension of the family of practices included under the rubric of religion, has coincided in the West with a period of increasing religious tolerance. However the broadening of the concept of religion does not mean that the differences that were perceived in the past are no longer relevant. The anthropological category or, perhaps better, an anthropologically informed category, may have an impact in the world or be in harmony with more general forces for conceptual change. However, it may also be highly contested. And even if the category is generally acknowledged as embracing phenomena that should be included as examples of the same kind of thing – art, aesthetic response or religious action – it does not make any of the substantive differences between the phenomena under consideration less relevant to analysis than they were in the past. And many people may challenge the anthropological category and be offended by its embracing nature.

One of the things that anthropologists have to face is that their terms are usually also words in someone's language. The terms I have been using are ordinary words in the English language. And when they are translated they are likely to be translated into ordinary words in the language of the cultures and societies concerned, and hence are entangled with the multiplicity of contexts of their use in ordinary language. If anthropologists are broadening the meaning of the words they are employing as part of their own terminology, they are inevitably communicating to ordinary language speakers of those words that from an anthropological perspective their beliefs and practices in a particular area of life are comparable to an analogous set of beliefs and practices in a quite different cultural context. The anthropology of religion includes Islam, Buddhism, Taoism, Yolngu, Nuer or Batak religion, animistic, totemic or shamanic practices and so on, within the same framework as Christianity.

There is a difference between saying Aboriginal societies have religious beliefs and practices and saying that there is such a thing as Aboriginal religion which is the same category of thing as the Christian religion. This is not a topic I can analyse in detail here but it is one that Aboriginal Australians continually confront. Religions themselves are often defined in opposition to one another – a person is either a Christian or a Muslim, either a Catholic or a Protestant, and movement from one to another is seen as conversion. Yet many who follow Indigenous religious practices would also call themselves Christians. In their individual lives people are combining practices which others, sometimes fellow members of the 'same' Church, see as categorically distinct. The discourse over religious difference in northern Australia still includes, as it does in most other places on earth, argument over whether something is religious behaviour or not. There are occasions when some Indigenous Australians will themselves categorize beliefs and practices that fall comfortably under the anthropological rubric of religion as something else – our 'culture' or our 'law' – which in context is more neutral or expresses a difference that is relevant in their lives. Anthropological definitions are not the definitions people use themselves but are in dialogue with those, they are never passive, since they are designed to make people understand similarities and differences between themselves and others.

## ANTHROPOLOGY AS A MEDIATING DISCIPLINE

It is the idea of common humanity that makes anthropology an inherently moral discipline or rather one that is inextricably entangled with moral and ethical issues: with racism, with environmentalism, with land rights and so on. Because anthropology is by definition a form of cross-cultural discourse, a process of cultural translation, it becomes a forum for relating local issues to global processes, for showing how someone else's way of being human has an equal right to be part of the definition of common humanity as one's own, and how people's viewpoints and values need to be taken into account when coming to decisions that affect their way of life or their occupation of a space in the world. There is thus a dual aspect to cultural relativism. There is relativism that relates cultural practices to their own context and the cultural relativism that relates the practices of different cultures to a common conception of humanity. It is this that gives dynamism to the concept of cultural relativism and allows it to take into account that context itself is relative and fuzzy around the edges and that one context merges with the next. And one of the ways in which this can be done is by establishing equivalences through the creation of cross-cultural categories which enable accommodations to be made between communities occupying the same space or competing for the same resources.

The importance of cross-cultural concepts can be illustrated in the area of land rights, where anthropologists have been at the forefront of developing more universal concepts of land ownership and title. In the absence of the development of such concepts, the rights of indigenous peoples in land are likely to abrogated. In order that native title is taken into account equally with European concepts of land title in legislating for land ownership in Australia, Canada or New Zealand it is necessary that the different forms of title occupy the same conceptual space. Even then this is no guarantee that native title will be taken into account.

The development of anthropological categories is not absolutely separate from that of categories in other discourses, such as law, history and politics. In an increasingly globalized arena, larger polities extend their jurisdictions over local communities and cultures and create – by means of legislation, custom and institutional structures – their own versions of cross-cultural categories. Anthropological concepts are consciously brought to bear on concepts in these other discourses in an attempt to change their meaning. The difference ought to be that the anthropological concepts are developed from the bottom up by a process of adjusting more global concepts to the existence of regional diversity, rather than from the top down, as happens in political and some development contexts, by imposing universal categories based on international law, European philosophy or formalist economics to create a new global order. It can of course be argued that in placing native title and European title in the same frame the former has been constructed to fit the latter category in a scenario of 'enforced commensurability' (F. Morphy 2007). Indeed, the particular issue has only arisen as a consequence of European invasion. It is that invasion that has made cross-cultural categories necessary and, since anthropology's origins are more with the invading cultures than with the invaded, the categories of anthropology are surely in part instruments of colonization – or so they might be construed.

However, this is precisely the kind of arena in which the dialogic nature of anthropology can have its effect. Indigenous land rights have developed over time as part of a political process in which the right to take over the land of another people by force became increasingly unacceptable. Initially the takeover of Aboriginal land occurred without reference to Indigenous concepts of land ownership. Property rights were associated with a particular form of political economy. Hunter-gatherer societies did not have the kind of property relations that characterized European society and that were encoded in European legal systems; hence Indigenous rights did not have to be taken into account in the development of Australian land law (see Williams 1986). Over time it became very clear, partly as a result of anthropological research, that in substantive terms Aboriginal people did have close and abiding rule-governed relationships to land that were analogous to European property rights. And in areas where the land had not already been alienated from their possession the continued appropriation of it came to be seen as a denial of their human rights. The political climate changed so that it became possible to acknowledge that Indigenous Australians had concepts of land ownership which could be recognized under Australian law. However, the system of Indigenous land ownership differed in many respects from that of the colonists; in particular it involved communal title based on a spiritual relationship to land. Cross-cultural concepts of land ownership needed to be taken into account in the formulation of legislation that, in effect, enabled dual recognition of title: recognition of title under Australian law in such a way that it enabled Indigenous law to continue to operate in areas that were granted as Aboriginal land.

Arguments that at one time were used against Aboriginal ownership of land became arguments in favour of a particular form of beneficial legislation. For much of Australia's colonial history it was in the interests of the invaders to find no equivalence between native title and European title, to create a fiction of such difference that Aboriginal rights need not apply. For a long time it was said that Aboriginal people did not own the land so much as they were owned by the land. Anthropologically such a statement might have some validity, reflecting the phenomenological experience of Aboriginal people. One Yolngu expression for being born – *dhawal wuyangirr* – means to 'think of a named place'. It symbolizes the extent to which the landscape is considered to pre-exist individual human existence and create a framework into which humans fit (Morphy 1995). In the context of colonialism, however, such subtle discourse over the phenomenology of landscape can be reduced to crude argument in support of domination: in the logic of European colonialism, if Aborigines are owned by the land then the land can be taken away from them and whoever takes it then owns the Aborigines. Ownership of the land by Aborigines and ownership of Aborigines by the land belong to two largely unrelated discourses. But it is necessary that anthropologists show how both relate to a more general conception of land title so that participation in one discourse does not deny the possibility of participating in the other. By making them fit, anthropologists may be doing a disservice to Indigenous concepts but they are also forcing adjustments to European ones. And the anthropological category does not pretend to be the Indigenous category. Rather it is a means of putting the Indigenous concept and the European concept within the same frame.[13]

My discussion of cross-cultural categories so far should have alerted the reader to the idea that, from some perspectives, an anthropological category can have the effect of changing the value of the phenomenon under consideration. This is most easily seen in cases where the cross-cultural category challenges hierarchical distinctions that rank the phenomena contained within them. Under evolutionist theory in its starkest form, the sequence of magic-religion-science reflected the direction of human progress from an irrational to an increasingly rational world-view. Australian Aborigines as hunters and gatherers were taken to be representatives of early stages of the evolution of human societies and as such they were imagined to have neither science nor religion; nor, as I will argue later, art. By labelling their ritual performances, acts of worship, and spiritual beliefs as magic rather than religion, evolutionists such as Fraser were effectively positioning them below the cultures of those who invaded their lands. The terminology used did not simply point out differences between the beliefs and practices of Aborigines and Christians: it focused on a narrow area of difference to place them in separate categories. Evolutionary theory created a mask that prevented the diversity and richness of Aboriginal religious practices from being seen, appreciated and interpreted.

I am not arguing that issues of interpretation addressed by the evolutionists were insubstantial. Indeed, freed from the rigid framework of evolutionism they continue to be of relevance to anthropological theory.[14] What Tylor interpreted as faulty logic and Fraser labelled sympathetic magic re-emerges in debates over the cognitive dimension of religion, the role of mimesis in religious practice, in critiques of structuralist and symbolic interpretations of religious action and so on. However, those topics are and were relevant to the understanding of religious phenomena in general, rather than providing the basis for an evolutionary hierarchy.

The evolutionists' hierarchies were clearly multiply determined and were influenced in part by the context of colonialism and the status of the Church in nineteenth-century Europe. The division between magic, science and religion created a hierarchy that was still partly in accord with the beliefs of their Christian opponents and in accord with the objectives of missionization. Even if many of their arguments were equally applicable to Christianity, they were able to separate out their Christian colleagues from the practitioners of other religions by relegating the beliefs of the latter to the category of primitive religion and defining their practices as magic. In anthropology by the turn of the twentieth century the evolutionists' paradigm had been effectively overturned and the category of religion had been expanded to include the beliefs and practices of societies in general. The 'religious' practices of different societies were seen to have much more in common with one another when placed under the same rubric – for example to facilitate understanding of the ways in which humans approach death, misfortune and bereavement cross-culturally.

Clearly anthropologists were not the only agents in changing the perception of indigenous beliefs and practices. Indeed some Churches played a significant role. But the data of anthropology certainly was a contributing factor, and anthropological theory certainly had an impact on theological discourse. By creating a more encompassing category of religion, anthropologists encouraged people to see Aboriginal religious practices in a new light, increasing their value in other people's eyes. The broadening definition of religion often resulted in legislative changes that granted equivalent statuses to practitioners of different kinds of religion, granting them a greater equality, or at least acknowledging the relevance of their particular beliefs to the national agenda. The inclusion of 'traditional beliefs' in the question on religion in the Australian Indigenous census form is one example.

## ABORIGINAL ART AND VALUE CREATION

Art as a category is deeply entangled in value creation processes (Munn 1986).[15] The history of European art since the Enlightenment has seen the development of a super-ordinate category of fine art, the art that characteristically is exhibited in institutions for fine art. Fine art is both inside and outside art more generally defined. The general category of art contains within it a great diversity of types of products. Different categories of art can be defined in terms of their techniques and raw materials – pottery, fibre arts, painting, sculpture; or qualitative subcategory – fine art, decorative art or craft; or era or region – Mediaeval, Islamic or African art; or generic type – primitive art, folk art or outsider art.

The contents of the fine art category are not fixed and often its boundaries are blurred. 'Fine' can be added as an adjective to allow works of some non-European arts to enter its domain – Graburn's (1976) 'primitive fine art' is an example. There has been a mystique around its boundaries that has been maintained in part by the secret language of connoisseurship and the restricted code of taste (Bourdieu 1984). Fine art has maintained its exclusiveness, and in turn its value, by the continual allocation of works to other categories: to craft or industrial arts. While many institutions collected a wide range of arts they tended to curate them separately, giving fine art the highest profile and the largest budget. The boundaries 'fine art' until the end of the nineteenth century largely excluded non-Western art by placing the arts of Africa, Oceania and the Americas within the category 'primitive art', a category which often shared an adjacent space to those of Oriental and Islamic arts.

This book is primarily concerned with the boundaries between fine art and primitive art. However, discourse over fine art inevitably touches on the whole range of exclusionary criteria – for example craft versus art, or functional versus non-functional, individual genius versus skill – that can be applied to challenge the fine art status of a particular category of artworks. As Janet Berlo argues, discourse over the inclusion of non-Western art within the history of fine art has been of relevance to other areas of art including 'performance, ephemeral arts, and so called craft traditions' (Berlo 2005: 180). Indeed, as we shall see, the fact that fine art is connected closely with the avant-garde means that new forms are continually entering its province. And those new forms have an impact on the status of forms that were excluded in the past. Photography that was once outside fine art is increasingly edging its way to the centre and pulling its past with it.

So far I have been writing about value as separate from the monetary value of objects. However in the case of artworks there is a fairly close relationship between the cultural and artistic value of the object and its monetary value. Value creation processes operate both within and between categories of art. In general the highest monetary value is associated with works that fit into the Western fine art category. There is no simple ranking of value associated with other categories, but in general craftworks, pottery, glass and fibreworks are valued much lower than painting and sculpture, and folk art tends to be valued less than Oriental antiquities. Primitive art has tended to be at the middle range of the market.

Within each category there is clearly great variability in the monetary value of works, and in terms of monetary value the market as a whole comprises a series of polythetic sets. The most highly valued, most sought-after pottery will be priced far higher than the majority of fine artworks. Indeed the majority of fine artworks produced are likely to be unsaleable. The primitive art market until recently has operated in both a similar and a dissimilar way to other art markets. It was similar in that factors of supply and demand, based on judgements of quality and the scarcity of particular objects were major factors affecting price. It differed from other markets in that there was a disjunction between the sale of works by contemporary artists and the market for pre-existing works, the secondary art market. Primitive art was bought and sold as if it were a product of the past, almost as if it were Mediaeval art. Authentic primitive art was made by people who were uncontaminated by European contact, who produced work in their own tradition, free from outside influence (see Errington 1998).

Jack Maquet (1986) drew attention to the dual nature of the process of creating primitive art when he distinguished between art by destination and art by metamorphosis. In both cases he is referring to works that belong to the fine art category: fine art or primitive fine art. Art by destination was work that was made to be viewed as fine art in the restricted sense of European and American artworlds. Art by metamorphosis concerned objects that had been made with quite a different purpose in mind – to fit in functional contexts within the producer's own society – and that were subsequently transformed into art through the process of recognition and de-contextualization associated with the Western art gallery. The primary creators of art by metamorphosis are not the original producers, but the artists, art collectors, art dealers and art galleries of the West. As far as the Western primitive art market is concerned this vitiates the need for a cross-cultural category of art – an object's original significance in the culture of production is irrelevant to its transformation into primitive fine art (see Price 1989, Vogel 1988 and Errington 1998 for relevant discussion). Maquet concludes that 'few art objects by destination were ever made in pre-Renaissance Europe or in non-literate societies' (Maquet 1986: 22).

The way in which indigenous works became defined at a distance, on the basis of criteria determined by a secondary or tertiary market, separated contemporary indigenous artists from the value creation process associated with the sale of the previous generation's art, creating a disjunction that separated their past from the present. It made their past into someone else's past – that of the Western art market that defined the conditions of their existence. They were of course free to produce fine artworks, but those would need to be fine art as it was being produced as part of the continuing Western fine art canon.

And this is where the fine art market articulated with the avant-garde to conspire against geographically diverse contemporary traditions, as it did against the development of alternative modernisms. The avant-garde, particularly under the hegemony of modernism, in part determined what was the acceptable fine art production of the moment, and this was linked to the temporal sequences of European art history. Contemporary art had to be produced in its own time – in the 1930s Impressionism could no longer be avant-garde, in the 1960s Cubism belonged to the past. The African artist who continued to produce works along traditional lines was almost certainly going to be producing work behind the times, since the European tradition had placed indigenous art logically prior to the present. If he continued to produce art in that form then it would be relegated to tourist art or folk art and would be sold through lesser markets at lower prices. Of course the market was not as neat as that since it was hard to define the cut-off point between authentic primitive art and the inauthentic present. In many contexts the artists were distant from the market and it was possible to disguise the conditions of contact and hence the degree of contamination. But this ironically worked against innovation and individuality which were almost a requirement of contemporary fine art production in the West.[16] The authentic work of primitive art had to be a fine example of its time identifiable in place and time. By the middle of the twentieth century there was a limit to the number of new forms of primitive art that could be discovered. Perhaps the only option to keep working within a tradition was to produce works as if they belonged to the past, works that could masquerade as the authentic past. And with appropriate addition of patina, they might just be accepted as such (see Steiner 1994 and 1995: 160–2).

The history of Aboriginal art has been a little different from most so-called 'primitive' art: from the arts of Africa, Oceania and the Americas. Aboriginal art as we shall see was largely on the periphery of developments in world art until the second half of the twentieth century. The metamorphosis of Aboriginal art from ethnographic object to Primitive art was delayed. While there have been exceptional moments when Aboriginal art engaged the interest of the national and international artworlds, for the most part Aboriginal art was relegated to a footnote in world art. Australia was a tiny continent relative to the Island Pacific in the surrealists' map of the world published in 1929.[17] Even within Australia few non-Indigenous artists took an interest in the forms produced by Indigenous Australian artists. Even works that passionately focused on the aesthetic power of Aboriginal art tended to place them at the beginning of time, as in Karel Kupka's *The Dawn of Art* and Louis Allen's *Time Before Morning*. Irresistibly romantic labels perhaps, but ones that projected Aboriginal artists into the past. Ironically, perhaps because of its late recognition, the metamorphosis of Aboriginal art into fine art has been more in the hands of the artists themselves and closer to the original point of production than in the case of most other Indigenous arts. Aboriginal art was almost bypassed by the process of primitivization, since few works by Aboriginal artists gained the status of primitive fine art. Aboriginal artists have in recent years been an integral part of the value creation processes associated with their art both within their own societies and in the national and global arenas into which it has moved.

Until recently art historians have tended to focus on the domain of fine art, indirectly reinforcing the established canon, adding value to the works that were included within it and enlarging the field of discourse in a field that remained restricted. They neglected the study of non-Western art, in particular the so-called primitive arts, and certainly avoided studying them in the context of the producing societies. The exclusion had something in common with the separation of magic from religion or, to employ a related distinction, 'primitive religion' and advanced religion. Art history developed contemporaneously with anthropology and both disciplines were strongly influenced in the nineteenth century by evolutionary theory and a hierarchy of value that positioned European civilization at the apex of human history. Primitive art was seen as logically prior to the fine arts of civilization. From the nineteenth century on, in part influenced by German idealist philosophy, fine art became separated from art in general as a particular kind of aesthetic activity. To quote Irene Winter,

> By the early nineteenth century, aesthetic responses were asked to meet certain conditions: they had to include the exercise of judgment with respect to beauty; and they had to be effected in a state of 'disinterested contemplation', in which the work itself was experienced divorced from any context, utility or prior concept. Aesthetics, in this way, insisted upon a category of works designated as 'fine art', that could be considered as such, distinct from works called artifacts, the utility of which form a significant part of its identity. (2002: 2)

The definition of fine art became doubly Eurocentric. It developed out of a particular discourse in European philosophy, and its exemplary works were those of the European canon, the sets of works that led to the refinement of judgements of beauty. Non-Western arts were excluded from the fine art category and de facto non-Western artworks were not the product of the same aesthetic sensibilities. Primitive art was not fine and in some respects it was being edged out of the category of art at all. To an extent, objects of primitive art were being defined as art only in the context of Western societies. Their potential as art was recognized by European artists who saw that they had something in common with their own practice, but it was doubted whether the people who produced them were motivated by the same sensibilities.

The study of non-Western, in particular indigenous, art in context became the province of anthropologists who were for the most part outside the domain of value creation in fine art. I suspect that Mariett Westermann (2005: xi) is largely correct when she writes '"Art" in anthropology is often taken in the original Western sense of the Latin term *ars*, making by prized skill'. This may explain why anthropologists have not taken up the cudgels in the arena of fine art to the extent they did in the case of religion. Anthropologists may have themselves been victims of the hegemony of the fine art category, that in many ways divorced art from function and context and for a while located the aesthetic response in 'disinterested contemplation'.

Anthropologists tended to emphasize the functionality of art objects, their meaning in social context, and their value as items of exchange. Perhaps overliterally they looked for words that could be translated directly as art and in many cases failed to find them (see Van Damme 1997). They may also have been offended by the fact that the objects displayed as primitive art were removed from their functional context displayed on gallery walls for aesthetic contemplation, supported by a fine art ideology in which the form of the object spoke for itself and spoke to the universal aesthetic sensibilities of the audience. To many anthropologists this reflected little more than an appropriation of the material culture of the indigenous world to satisfying the tastes of a Western elite.[18] The ideas that guided the Western viewers 'unmediated' response owed more to the Western imagination than to the intended effect in the society of origin (see Price 1989; Errington 1998). Ethnographic museums also found themselves in competition with art galleries, which could pay more for works elevated into the category of primitive art, even if they did not yet quite breach the walls of the fine art galleries. The value creation process that moved them in that direction moved them out of the range of affordability.

For much of its history, anthropology has maintained a distance between the anthropologist's own world and the worlds of its subjects. That distance helped to maintain the primitive-/fine art divide. Anthropologists neglected the ways in which indigenous societies early on became involved in trade, gained knowledge of other representational systems, incorporated new techniques of manufacture and made use of introduced material culture (see Thomas 1991). To an extent, anthropologists shared a similar concept of authenticity to that of the art market. And like the art market they viewed societies in the early days of colonization as if they had not changed. Of necessity both anthropologists and dealers extended the period of first contact, allowing for the society to be observed and for authentic objects to be collected. They were interested in dramatic evidence of social change and instances where aesthetic systems tended to collapse in the face of missionization: where art ceased to be produced and singing traditions associated with male initiation and religious cults stopped being performed. But the slow incremental changes that occurred in other contexts, resulting from processes of adjustment that were often themselves linked to modes of resistance, were easily overlooked and, when noticed, were interpreted as a slow process of cultural loss.

When anthropologists began to take seriously the engagement of indigenous societies in the post-colonial world, they became aware of how often those societies had taken an active role in engaging with outsiders (see Graburn 1976; Thomas 1991). They were able to see how quickly people learnt to take part in trade relations, how rapidly they learned the languages of the colonizers, how much interest they displayed in their religious practices. Art objects were often among the earlier trade items and resulted in an intensification of local art-producing industries, which often had as much consequence on the internal dynamics of the society as it did on the external relations (see Thomas 1991).

## CONCLUSION

There appears to be no a priori reason why a particular conception of what art is should become the de facto category to which all other arts are compared in order to determine the degree to which they are art. But this is what happened with Western fine art occupying the superordinate category. As a consequence other arts were often defined by 'lesser' terms such as 'craft' (Maquet, 1986) or 'prize skill' (Westermann, 2005), or given functional labels such as 'ritual object' or given no definition at all (Gell 1998), as if being art were only a secondary aspect of their existence.

As a result, the aesthetic and expressive dimension of art objects in their societies of production has been overlooked or deemed irrelevant. People have been unable to analyse the relationship between art production in different cultural contexts. Synergies between artistic processes often enable artists to transcend particular cultural contexts and insert their works into different cultural frames without leaving their own culture behind. Under the narrow definition of art as fine art, context is almost irrelevant to determining the value of the objects as works of art. That value comes from their formal properties alone. Yet inevitably that means valuing one set of evaluative criteria, those associated with Western fine art, above other sets. Indigenous art objects from this perspective become almost another kind of found object.

For there to be an anthropological analysis of art, it does not matter whether an object is labelled 'art' or not. The anthropologist is interested in analysing material objects, or cultural forms, according to their use, meaning, significance and value in their social and cultural context(s) (see Morphy and Perkins 2006: 15ff.). An anthropologist is interested initially in the categories of the society under study. Often the categories into which objects fall are not marked lexically – there is no generic term which refers specifically to art objects (Van Damme, 1997). However the meta-categories can be derived from observation and the use of language in context.

One of the most characteristic kinds of object that Yolngu produce today is the bark painting. There is no single word for bark painting as such. A bark painting may be referred to as _nuwayak_ 'bark', analogous to a Western artist referring to his or her painting as a canvas. It can also be referred to as a *miny'tji*. In this context *miny'tji* means painting. However *miny'tji* also covers 'colour' and 'design'. The design on a dress, the blazon on a car door, the pattern of the plumage on a _lindirritj_ (rainbow lorikeet), can all alike be referred to as *miny'tji*. The meaning of miny'tji encompasses all natural and cultural designs. This makes sense according to Yolngu metaphysics: design is the sign of the identity of an object or person or thing, and in a sense no design whether 'cultural' or 'natural' is accidental. All design to Yolngu is significant form – but some forms are more significant than others. Yolngu for example can refer to the most sacred paintings as _likanpuy_, *djalkiri* or _madayinbuy_ *miny'tji*, in contrast to ordinary paintings, *wakinngu miny'tji*.[19]

Another category of 'art' object produced by Yolngu is wooden carvings or sculptures in abstract or figurative form, often intricately carved and painted. The bodies are sometimes bound with feather-string, and adorned with pendants of feathers, string and beeswax. These objects can be referred to as *dharpa* (wood), and like bark they can have *miny'tji* on them. The more elaborate objects with feather-string and tassels carved in hardwood are likely to be *rangga* (sacred objects) and each *rangga* will have its own set of names, some of which link it to other objects in sets – the set of ceremonial digging sticks – *wapitja* – for example. However, many names are exclusive to particular objects and refer to their different parts or different dimensions of their Ancestral significance. One name, for example, will reference the use of the digging stick by a particular ancestor in a particular place. The beautiful wooden sculptures that Yolngu sometimes produce for sale are simply referred to as *dharpa* or by the kind of subject that they represent, *mokuy* ('spirit being') or *wayin* ('bird, animal').

Looking at art or aesthetic forms more broadly, Yolngu employ a set of terms that distinguish between singing or perhaps music, dancing and painting. Singing is referred to as *manikay*, dancing as *bunggul* and painting as *miny'tji*. And not surprisingly both *bunggul* and *manikay* can be applied to the songs and dances of birds and animals. Yolngu have an extensive vocabulary for talking about artworks. They also, as we shall see later, have an aesthetic vocabulary that is applied across artforms (see Morphy 1992). The terminology does not coincide precisely with that employed in Western art, but that vocabulary too is extensive, diverse, comprised of overlapping terminologies, and changing and contested. Yolngu terminology reflects the phenomenal world as Yolngu apprehend it, for example, associating design in nature with design in art – both alike are *miny'tji*. Yolngu terminology also articulates with the spiritual and ritual ordering of the world categorizing objects and performances by their level of sacredness, whether they are *djalkiri* (foundational) or *garma* (public ceremonial) or *wakinngu* (mundane).

In the context of Yolngu society, Aboriginal art is not fine art as it was most narrowly defined in Western art. It was not designed to be placed on gallery walls and put on pedestals for aesthetic contemplation. However, if in analysing objects in Aboriginal society it becomes clear that they have much in common with objects that are included under the broader Western rubric of art which includes fine art, then the question of the relationships between the objects concerned in the two contexts becomes relevant. And in exploring the relationships between the Aboriginal and Western artworks in their own cultural contexts, the reason why Aboriginal art can move into the more general categories of Australian art or World art becomes apparent – it is indeed because the arts concerned have something in common: there is a cross-cultural category of art.

The Western category of fine art and the narrowness of its definition meant that for a long time art historians and anthropologists neglected to study the aesthetic and expressive dimension of objects in indigenous contexts. They also neglected to study the formal systems involved, the techniques of production, the training of artists and so on. However, when they began to turn to these aspects of artworks toward the middle of the twentieth century, they discovered that the aesthetic, expressive and iconographic dimensions of objects were central to understanding the form of the object, the purposes for which it was used and the effect it had. Their analyses showed how much overlap there was between art in different cultural contexts. It became less surprising that European artists had been able to use the forms of 'Primitive' art to free themselves from the constraints of their own tradition. They had intuited a relationship, a family resemblance, between the objects they 'found' or 'discovered' and their own art practice. Even though they inserted their own interpretations of the motivations of the original artists and provided a cultural context that owed more to the Western imagination of the other than the reality of the art in its social context, they did bring the forms of much indigenous art into discourse with World art.

Today the fine art market has become one of the contexts for Aboriginal art. Aboriginal artists are producing art for sale and entering the art market in analogous ways to those of non-Indigenous producers. Yet in many cases they continue to produce paintings in indigenous contexts for quite different purposes. Today, the same work could be produced by a Yolngu artist as a body painting in a circumcision ceremony (Figure 2) and then on a

Figure 2  Painting the initiates at Yilpara in 2001. Boys of the Dhuwa moiety being painted with *miny'tji* by Wuyal and Dhukal Wirrpanda, Wukun Wanambi and Wanyubi Marika as part of their circumcision ceremony. Photograph Howard Morphy.

painting destined for the Queensland Art Gallery.[20] The very fact that the same painting can be produced as art by destination for the Western art market, that in the past could only be created as art by metamorphosis, challenges the presupposition upon which the fine art category was once based. It has resulted in the de facto acceptance of 'traditional' Aboriginal art as fine art in Australia, and its widening global appeal has posed a challenge to the more narrowly defined Western category. Of course, it can be argued that these works of 'art by destination' are different from art produced for internal consumption, but the artists would see them as works of equivalent value and identical origin, so though part of the intention behind their production is different, it is not clear why or if that difference is significant.[21]

Many of the presuppositions that previously excluded Aboriginal art from the fine art category – that the works did not involve individual creativity, that aesthetic criteria were not involved in their production and so on – can be seen to be false in the contemporary context. Reciprocally, the entanglement of art with different functional contexts in Indigenous societies encourages the recognition of the fact that Western fine art is not that different. The myth or ideology of disinterested engagement for aesthetic contemplation divorced Western fine art from the many practical contexts it occupies – as a commodity, an embellishment, a definer of status or a marker of place. In other words, comprising works that are themselves often deeply imbricated in the politics and economy of the society that produced them.

In Western society, fine art exists in dialogue with the broader domain of artistic activity. The boundaries have never been rigid ones, particular works or kinds of works have always shifted categories, new kinds of artworks are always being brought into the fine art category, and categories are sometimes problematized, as the decorative arts challenges the separation of art from craft. In many ways the category of fine art is not a category of objects but a way of viewing objects that are prized exemplars of aesthetic value or, in the case of some more recent works (following from Dada and Duchamp), conceptual significance. Art by intention is nothing more than the illusory surface edge of the category, the idea that the category is somehow produced by the agency of artists in the present. The reality is that over time the majority of artworks were produced with other venues in mind and it is impossible to anticipate precisely which works produced in any particular present will eventually become accepted as the finest expressions of aesthetic sensibility or fit some other criteria of artistic significance.

My conclusion is really that fine art is a process rather than a category. At any one point in time it categorizes a section of a mobile continuum in which certain works are selected out for greater reverence than others. There is, however, no reason to value any one criterion over another to rank the sets of objects globally and hierarchically. In Yolngu art the criteria for selecting certain works over others and ordering them in sequences must include their spiritual value, their closeness to the sacred. Yet when we look at the art in detail we will find many overlaps between the objects of other places and times, including contemporary

Western art. In the case of Yolngu art the attributes that inspire aesthetic contemplation in the art gallery are the same attributes that convey a sense of spiritual power in the context of Yolngu epistemology.

However one interprets the impact of the insertion of Aboriginal art into the shifting sands of the global fine art market, it has made a difference to Yolngu artists and it has added a major context for their art production. This book investigates value creation simultaneously in two areas: the local frame of the production of Aboriginal art including the production of art for sale to the global market, and the global frame of the collection, curation, exhibition and marketing of Aboriginal art as fine art. If art exists in both local and global contexts, then it would seem methodologically sound to employ a concept of art that applies in both rather than to use the definition of one to encompass or exclude the other. Thus the question of defining art cross-culturally intersects with the question of value creation.

# SECTION I
# A SHORT HISTORY OF YOLNGU ART

There has until recently been a tendency to approach the arts of non-Western cultures synchronically rather than as part of dynamic regional trajectories. The classic approach was to define regional styles and undertake a formal analysis of the objects in collections to isolate diagnostic features of style. Often the objects were treated synchronically even if they were collected over a considerable period of time. The perspective owes much to a view that 'traditional' societies were relatively unchanging prior to European colonization. Hence if one developed a data set of objects collected prior to the disruption of colonization, it could be treated as a whole for analytic purposes. It is also the case that until recently there have been relatively few longitudinal studies of Indigenous societies by anthropologists. There have been exceptional studies of change in artforms for example, by Richard and Sally Price (1999), but on the whole change in Indigenous art has been addressed more by archaeologists (Taçon et al. 1996) and some art historians (e.g. Kubler 1985). The ahistorical approach of much anthropological writing creates a mismatch between it and art history. Anthropologists have failed to observe the dynamics of local art systems as they engage with processes of social change associated with colonialism or globalization. Yet it is precisely in the context of change that the dynamics of local systems are revealed as the societies respond and adjust to new circumstances. And it is the dynamics of local art systems that enable local traditions to make a contribution to global art processes. The initial encounter between Indigenous artists and European colonists was an unequal one. In many cases the nature of contact and the imposition of alien rule resulted in a breakdown in the process of cultural transmission and cultural production. However, in many other cases the breakdown was more in the mind of the outside observer than in any evidence of discontinuities in local traditions.

In certain kinds of colonial encounter, indigenous artistic practices have been able to maintain their strength throughout processes of engagement with an encroaching post-colonial world. In such cases it is possible to see how Indigenous artforms have developed their own ways of articulating with global artworlds, becoming integrated without losing their relative autonomy. They depend upon a complex intersection of circumstance and time. Some encounters are more brutal than others. That is circumstance. And global art-worlds have, until recently, been resistant to the inclusion of indigenous arts in the global category of fine art. And that is time.

In the chapters in this section, I explore the dynamics of Yolngu art in the context of the articulation between Yolngu society and European Australian colonists. By adopting a diachronic perspective I hope to show how the local Yolngu artworld adjusted to new art contexts that developed during the process of their colonization. In the first two chapters I look at the recent history of Yolngu art – from the time of intensive colonization in the mid-1920s. I use three sources of data – archival data, material culture collections made by outsiders (in particular missionaries and anthropologists), and my own fieldwork over a period of some 30 years. I give prominence to collections in part because of my belief that they provide a means of connecting the present with the past. They provide a perspective on change over time and hence on the dynamics of material culture systems. The making of collections was also an integral part of the colonial process, so that collections also provide insights into the impact of colonization on the material production of a society and a dialogic perspective on the interactions between the colonists and the colonized; they reveal how they learnt about each other and how they engaged in transactions. The making of collections is of course the salient arena for the process by which Yolngu material culture became art. My aim in these chapters is to provide an overview rather than a definitive history. I have written elsewhere a detailed ethnography of Yolngu art using ethnographic data and historical resources and do not intend to repeat that here (Morphy 1991).

Looking at Yolngu art in terms of its articulation with the encompassing Euro-Australian world enables one to see the process of the engagement and also to challenge some of the presuppositions that have been the product of keeping the Indigenous and non-Indigenous worlds separate. The chapters that follow the historical ones will consider issues that are central to art history's project: innovation in aesthetic and representational process, an artist's reflection on a different tradition from his own, and the extent to which the idea of art history is itself relevant to understanding art practice across cultures.

# 2 THE HISTORY BEGINS

Yolngu art became recognized as art in the wider world through the process of its commercialization. Yolngu society only opened up to the Euro-Australian world in the 1920s and 1930s – before then the art of the region was virtually unknown. There are probably no hidden collections of it waiting to be discovered in the basements of some European Museum. The people who passionately believed in Yolngu art were in many respects the same people who marketed it, collected it, bought it and sold it, organized exhibitions of it and wrote about it. There were at the beginning many who rejected it as art and who needed to be persuaded. There are some today who remain unpersuaded, who resist its inclusion in art gallery spaces, who still argue that it is ethnography not primitive art and not part of a larger category of contemporary Australian art. In reality the Yolngu situation is probably no different in many respects from that obtaining on the North West Coast of America in the mid-nineteenth century, in New Ireland at the beginning of the twentieth century, and in countless other places where missionaries, traders and anthropologists for a while saw something 'like art' in the societies concerned. Yolngu artists engaged with the process of production for the outside world and became involved with it as artists had in the Pacific, Africa and the Americas, on countless occasions before – as Nicholas Thomas (1991) has so elegantly demonstrated. The difference in the Yolngu case is only a matter of timing. Yolngu art became art in the world outside at a moment when the categorizations of the Europe-American art world were beginning to be challenged. In the cases of many colonial societies, the response to their art was more often than not delayed, awaiting discovery and metamorphosis into art by actors in the global arena, by artists and collectors in Europe and America. Meanwhile local forces –missionaries and government officials – conspired to interrupt production by banning the Potlatch (Cole 1995), or by burning the 'idols' (Seip 1999: 269). Pacific and Native American artists were always having their works pushed into the primitive category, reinvented as something else, somewhere else, by someone else.

Time or timing has also been important in another respect. In the 1930s Australia was just beginning to come out of an era in which Aborigines had been excluded from Australian society. The rights of Aboriginal people had been gradually eroded away. The Aboriginal population was still thought to be dying out, and welfare policy aimed at smoothing the pillow of a dying race. The 1930s saw the beginnings of a slow process of change. Punitive expeditions were no longer a legitimate response to problems, welfare policies began to improve. Yolngu were fortunate in who their missionaries were and they were fortunate that their population had remained strong. After the Second World War there was a steady movement toward including Indigenous Australians more equally in Australian society. The key events are well known and need not be discussed in detail here, but comprised such things as the granting of award wages, being counted in the census and eventually, for some people, land rights and the recognition of native title (see Attwood 2003 for a detailed analysis).

One of the consequences of inclusion was that Indigenous Australians began to have an increasing role in the imaginary of the Australian state, and Aborigines became a more central theme of Australian political discourse. Aboriginal imagery began to proliferate and Aboriginal identity became very loosely associated with Australian identity (Lattas 1991; Von Sturmer 1989). Certainly until the 1960s the main thrust of policy was assimilation, directed toward the absorption of Aborigines into the mainstream population. And much of the Aboriginal imagery was the product of non-Aboriginal Australians and emphasized a primitive, almost caricature world, disconnected from the present (Black 1964). However, the changes that did occur gradually opened the space for greater Indigenous agency in Australia's cultural and political life.

The 1970s saw a further shift of emphasis with government policy moving more toward integration and self-determination. Aboriginal people had the right to the same benefits as other Australians and shared with other Australians the right to determine the direction of their lives. These changes were introduced by the Whitlam Labor Government of 1972–75, but many were implemented by the subsequent Liberal-Country Party coalition government. As far as Aboriginal artists were concerned the timing of these changes in policy – the move to inclusion – meant that they were able to benefit from the changing cultural policies that developed under the Whitlam Government. The most important change that occurred in cultural policy was the creation of an arts-funding body, the Australia Council, in 1973.

The Australia Council was made up of a series of boards based on particular artforms – literature, visual arts and so on. In addition an Aboriginal Arts Board was created with a brief to cover all Indigenous artforms. As well as operating as a granting body, the Aboriginal Arts Board indirectly facilitated the marketing of Aboriginal arts through policy advice and strategic support of Aboriginal-arts cooperatives. Fred Myers (2002) has provided a comprehensive analysis of the Aboriginal Arts Board and the various government instrumentalities that were created to facilitate the marketing of Aboriginal art. While his analysis is centred on a very particular art movement – that of Western Desert acrylic paintings – much of what he writes about the institutional structures and the individuals involved in policy development is relevant to the Yolngu case. The Aboriginal Arts Board provided Indigenous artists with opportunities that they did not have previously to obtain resources to help with their own art practice. The coincidences of timing again worked in favour of Yolngu art. The previous decades had seen an increasing appreciation of the art traditions of northern Australia – in particular Western and Eastern Arnhem Land and Melville and Bathurst Island. The change of government policy had gone a long way toward overturning 'the great Australian silence' (Stanner 1979). Aboriginal people and Aboriginal issues were becoming a more significant part of the Australian political agenda and Indigenous imagery was becoming again a component of Australia's national identity.

The timing and place of Yolngu entry into artworlds other than their own has to an extent worked in their favour. Yolngu entered the market at the beginning of a period of change in Western conceptions of art. They entered the dialogue from a place that could be constructed as remote and 'primitive' in the Western imagination yet was, in geopolitical terms, becoming increasingly proximate. Yolngu, as members of a hunter-gatherer society encapsulated in a developed first-world state, have had the advantage of local markets that often do not exist elsewhere. Placement and timing have meant that in the Yolngu case the adjustments that have occurred have been in many ways coordinated with internal and external change in ways that have not often happened elsewhere. The process could so easily have been very different.

## EUROPEAN CONTACT

The earliest documented account of Yolngu contact with Europeans was the unhappy encounter between a group of Yolngu and the crew of Mathew Flinders's boat the *Investigator* on 22 January 1803.[1] Flinders had just visited Chasm Island in the Gulf of Carpentaria between Groote Eylandt and the mainland, where William Westall, the artist who accompanied him, recorded the rock paintings that they discovered there. These included one of a Macassan prau with a line of people stretched out along the mast. The subject of the painting was significant since, unknown to Flinders, this indeed was the time of year when boats from South Sulawesi came to the Arnhem Land coast to trade with the Yolngu people, and use their labour in the gathering and preparation of bêche-de-mer. The Macassan fleet had been coming for over a century, and leaders of Yolngu clans had established close relations with some of the Macassan sea captains (*bunggawa*) who returned each year. Yolngu were used to dealing with outsiders.

Flinders's crew landed on Morgan Island in the north of Blue Mud Bay close to the coastline. A number of Aboriginal people paddled to the island in bark canoes. They came to meet the strangers and apparently advanced toward them with spears raised. Mr Whitewood was wounded trying to take one of the spears. Contrary to Flinders's instructions the shore party subsequently fired at the Yolngu, killing at least two of them. Yolngu today, without a second's reflection, interpret the Yolngu advance on Flinders's men as a greeting ceremony. Indeed since they would have been anticipating the arrival of people from overseas – Macassans – that interpretation is quite credible. The following day William Westall returned to the shore and found a body washed up on the beach. He drew a poignant and highly realistic sketch (Figure 3). The dead man is recognizably from one of the clans who live in the area today, and on his arm is a woven band of the kind that adult Yolngu always wore. The encounter reveals Yolngu society at the point of European colonization as linked to the outside world through Macassan contact, not isolated in the way that Flinders presumed.

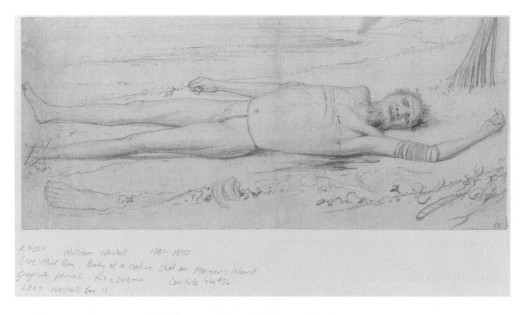

Figure 3    *Blue Mud Bay, Body of a Native Shot on Morgan's Island*, by William Westall (1781–1850). William Westall's sketch of the body of an Aborigine shot on Morgan Island, in January 1803, is deeply moving and somewhat ambiguous – the accompanying severed foot hints at his dissection at the hands of the explorers. The drawing appears to be a close likeness of the person who died, recognizable today as a Yolngu from the Blue Mud Bay area. The woven armbands are a sign of his status and relationship with others. Reproduced with permission of the National Library of Australia, Canberra.

And we see one of the roles of art in the early nineteenth-century West – the artist/scientist of the voyages of discovery.

After Flinders's departure, Yolngu were left to their own ways for another hundred years before they next encountered Europeans. They lived in the far north-eastern corner of Arnhem Land, in 'untamed territory' as the writers of popular books would describe it. They lived beyond the colonial frontier effectively until the establishment of the mission station of Yirrkala in 1935. But gradually in the preceding decades European colonization had moved closer in stages with the occasional police or prospecting party and the occasional sortie by pastoralists moving in from the south-west. Yolngu remember these earlier border skirmishes but they are largely absent from official records.

The most traumatic massacre occurred around 1911 on the riverbank at Gängan.[2] A number of Yolngu clans were gathered for the performance of a Ngärra ceremony. The Ngärra is the most restricted of all Yolngu ceremonies. It involves the making and revelation of sacred objects in the men's ceremonial ground. The ceremony culminates in a great communal immersion in the river, where men women and children gather together in an act of joyous purification. On this occasion the ceremony went terribly wrong. An armed party led by Europeans – some say a police party, others say stockmen – came to Gängan. They seized the bundles of spears and broke them and then, after bludgeoning the ceremonial leader to death, opened fire on the other men. The women and children who were camped separately fled the area and one or two men escaped to spread the word.

Gawirrin Gumana, a leading artist, community leader and ordained minister of the Uniting Church lives at Gängan today in his old age. It was his father Birrikitji Gumana (c.1890–1982) who told him about the events that took place there. Birrikitji was away at the time on Trial Bay working with a group of men making a dugout canoe. They heard about the killings and Birrikitji returned to his country to see for himself. He described coming to the riverbank where the bodies of the dead had been left. Freshwater crocodiles and other scavengers had eaten most of the bodies. But their ceremonial armbands remained behind; and that was how he was able to determine at first who had died.

This story shows how little relations with Europeans had progressed in the hundred years since Flinders's visit. However, it also shows powerfully the relationship between material culture and memory in a hunter-gather society viewed for so long by Europeans as being materially impoverished. The canoe was being made at Trial Bay, and today people will be able to point out the exact place where Birrikitji was nearly one hundred years ago. People know where to find the stands of canoe trees and they know the network of relationships and the rights of ownership associated with them (see Dunlop 1981a). The spears were in bundles because of the ceremonial event – the people were bound together by their sharing of spears, but it made them vulnerable to attack. And the armbands are mnemonics of people, as well as signs of the sacred nature of the performance in which they were taking part.

These armbands were not the everyday ones that Westall drew on the dead man's arm. Ceremonial armbands are elaborate constructions made of possum-fur string, feathers and beeswax and bound in complex ways. The armbands are associated with particular sacred objects, which are themselves manifestations of ancestral beings. Such armbands are worn by participants in a Ngärra ceremony and initiates at circumcision, and create an association between the person and the ancestral being concerned. The armbands left behind marked the identities of those who had died. Identity, linking people with places and with ancestral beings, lies at the heart of Yolngu art, as we shall see.

## MISSION TIMES

The Gängan massacre signalled the beginning of more intensive contact with outsiders. The Macassans no longer visited the Arnhem Land coast: they had been effectively prevented from visiting the shores by the imposition of a regime of high taxation. Their final voyage was in 1907. However, visits by Japanese pearlers and European adventurers increased, culminating in the killing of the crew of a Japanese boat in 1933, at Caledon Bay. A police party set out to investigate the deaths. The police made a detour via Woodah Island, close to where the Yolngu man was shot by Flinders's men all those years before. A group of women were rounded up and chained together, and left in the charge of Constable McColl. The group included Djaparri, the wife of Dhäkiyarr and daughter of one of the men who had died at Gängän. Dhäkiyarr speared McColl and freed the women.[3]

The police planned to mount an armed expedition into eastern Arnhem Land to find the culprits and 'tame' the people. However, the time of official vengeance expeditions had passed and a national outcry resulted in a very different solution. The government decided to allow a mission station to be set up in the region and sent anthropologist Donald Thomson to enquire into the grievances of the Aborigines and to find a peaceful solution (see Thomson 2005). Within two years the mission settlement of Yirrkala was established on the Gove Peninsula, and over the next decade Yolngu gradually made it the centre of their regional lives. Many Yolngu, however, continued to spend much of the year living as hunter-gatherers in their own estates.

The mission station of Yirrkala was in fact the second mission station in Yolngu country. The first was established at Milingimbi in 1923, in the far west of the Yolngu-speaking region. Compared with many denominations in other parts of Australia, the Methodist Overseas Mission set up a very benign regime in eastern Arnhem Land. The founding missionaries – T. T. Webb at Milingimbi, and Wilbur Chaseling at Yirrkala – both showed great interest in Yolngu society and tolerated Aboriginal religious practice (see Morphy 2005a). They set in train a regime that for the most part was concerned to protect Aboriginal rights and interests. They also aimed to prepare Yolngu through education to be able to engage with the wider economy and develop self-sufficient communities.

From the beginning of the establishment of the mission, Yolngu opened up a trade in artefacts and material culture. T. T. Webb saw the sale of artefacts having multiple purposes: it provided a source of income for the mission to enable the purchase of commodities such as tobacco, flour and sugar; it taught people the value of labour; and finally it showed congregations in the south of Australia that Yolngu had skills as artists and craftsmen which demonstrated their equality as human beings. Thus from the beginning art was entangled in the value creation processes of the mission both internally and externally. Internally, it was designed to show Yolngu the value of labour in both a moral and an economic sense. Externally, it was a way of supporting the mission economy but also of influencing the attitude of congregations in favour of the Aborigines.

Wilbur Chaseling at Yirrkala had a similar philosophy to Webb's and he immediately engaged Yolngu in art and craft production. Within a year of his arrival Chaseling was dispatching large collections of artefacts to museums in the south-east of Australia. We have very few accounts that explain how the market for Yolngu art and material culture developed so rapidly – the museum records are simply the accounts for the transactions, and little attempt was made to ensure that the collections were documented. However, as a marketing exercise it was remarkably successful, with the main museums in Melbourne, Sydney and Brisbane all acquiring collections. Webb also made a superb collection for the Basel Ethnographic Museum in 1934.

Milingimbi became the base for two anthropologists, Lloyd Warner and Donald Thomson, whose aims partially overlapped with those of the missionaries – even if one of them, Donald Thomson, developed a fairly antagonistic relationship with them. Warner spent nearly two years at Milingimbi between 1926 and 1928. He made extensive collections of art and material culture but wrote little about either in detail (see Hamby 2007). He wrote in depth about Yolngu religion and symbolism, yet the poetics of Yolngu performance remained in the background. However, the depth of his analysis shows the immense attention he paid to Yolngu exegesis of ritual forms, and the title of his book, *A Black Civilization*, reflects the impact that Yolngu culture had on him (Warner 1958).

Donald Thomson wrote relatively little about Yolngu society, and his contribution as anthropologist was little regarded at the time of his death. However in the local arena of eastern Arnhem Land his impact had been considerable. Thomson was an activist and an adventurer; he was also an inveterate collector and a superb photographer.[4] As an activist he wrote strongly in favour of Aboriginal rights, and in the early 1940s he engaged Yolngu in the Australian war effort by establishing a coast-watching patrol made up of the fiercest fighters on his genealogies. His greatest achievements as an ethnographer – his photographs and his collection of Yolngu art and material culture – have only been appreciated since his death.

Thomson's collection of Yolngu art and material culture was built up over nearly a decade from the beginning of his research in1935 to the end of the Coastal patrol in 1943. Thomson's collection remained literally under wraps until his death in 1971. He kept it away from the Australian Research Council, who paid for most of it to be made, and it was never exhibited. Although he employed research assistants to work on the collection, he published little on it. Yet when it was opened up after his death it revealed a compendious inventory of the material culture of north-east Arnhem Land meticulously documented and in excellent condition (Figure 4). Many of the objects appeared as if they had just been made.

It is quite difficult to assess the place of Thomson's collection in the history of Yolngu art. By the time of Thomson's death Yolngu art was already beginning to achieve widespread recognition, and yet the collection he made was still largely unknown. So it could be argued that it made no contribution at all. However this would be to fail to see the importance of local processes in the developing articulation between Yolngu society and the outside world. The view from outside, after Europeans have 'discovered' a particular art, nearly always masks the agency of Indigenous artists. Thomson's collection illustrates the way in which Yolngu engaged with a developing market economy and it reveals the richness of Yolngu material culture at the time of colonization. It is also the case that since his death the collection itself has not only had an impact on Yolngu society, which has enthusiastically reconnected with it, but also become an integral component of the value creation process associated with Yolngu art and society. Thomson's collection has become the subject of many research projects, exhibitions and publications and it recently inspired a successful feature film, Rolph de Heer's *Ten Canoes* (Hamby 2007). However we are getting ahead of ourselves.

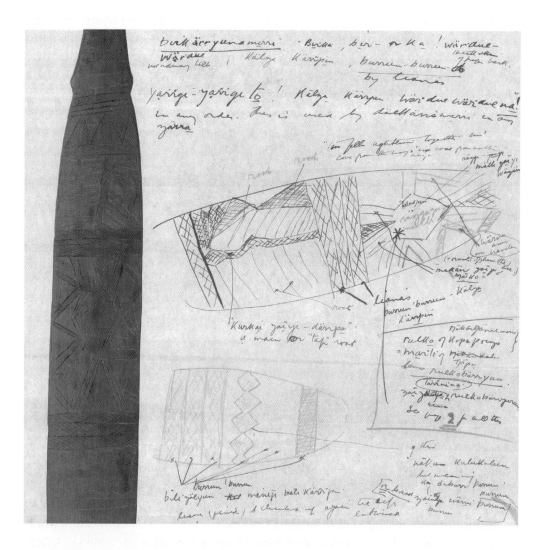

Figure 4    Djimbarr'yun's paddle. On the left is a detail of a paddle
incised with designs representing an ancestral paperbark tree, made
by Djimbarr'yun Ngurruwutthun for Donald Thomson in 1942, and
on the right is an extract from Thomson's fieldnotes. In these he
commented: 'This paddle with its intricate, interesting and finally
beautiful mintji, was collected at Trial Bay on 11/6/42 ... The whole
represents not so much an actual barrakula, a paperbark tree, so much
as a symbolical representation. Or a material personification (words fail
me – rationalisation, projection?) of native ideas, this time in mythology
but coloured by their experience of the tree.' DT 841, The Donald
Thomson Collection on loan to Museum Victoria from The University of
Melbourne.

I have been writing so far as if the art industry was introduced from outside. However, this gives a false perspective on the history of Arnhem Land art from within. Missionaries such as Webb and Chaseling were able to build collections for Australian and overseas institutions so rapidly because Yolngu were already involved in the production of material culture for exchange. Trade of material objects was integral to the structure of Yolngu society, as Thomson demonstrated in his one major publication *Economic Structure and the Ceremonial Exchange Cycle in Arnhem Land* (1949). Trade clearly occurred over several hundred years with the Macassans, and the rich incorporation of Macassan-derived material culture in Yolngu mortuary rituals suggests that artistic expression was a major component of Yolngu interaction with Macassans (McIntosh 1996). And finally Yolngu traded with European collectors at the edges of their country for some time before the establishment of mission stations in their own lands.

## ART IN YOLNGU SOCIETY

Donald Thomson's collections reveal a richness in Yolngu material culture that provides an essential background to understanding the success of Yolngu artists today. It includes a fine collection of bark paintings, but, as with the collections made by Warner and Webb at Milingimbi, they make up a small percentage of the collection as a whole. Thomson's collection shows that virtually every artefact produced in Yolngu society can be produced in an unembellished or an embellished form. While some additions are purely decorative, most have elements of meaning. The embellishment of objects connects the mundane contexts of everyday life to the more restricted context of ceremonial performance – art usually has reference to the sacred and to the relationships between people and place. 'Art' can be added to any object.

Art in the sense I am using it refers to aesthetic and semantic dimensions of objects that Yolngu refer to as *miny'tji*. They are the same attributes of objects that Europeans would single out if they were looking to segregate or identify a set of Yolngu objects as art objects or identify decorated as opposed to undecorated objects – in other words they have a family resemblance with the European category of art. The same *miny'tji*, in the sense of 'design', can occur on different surfaces or be incorporated into the form of an object in many different ways – Yolngu 'art' production is a dynamic system that adapts form and content to context. The same design can occur as the subject of a bark painting or body painting or be engraved on the stem of a previously undecorated pipe (*lunginy*) and so on. The object is transformed by the design – Yolngu art is a form of purposive action, albeit a pleasurable one.

The status of the surface or object painted or carved varies in relationship to the purpose of the art. In the case of a bark painting the bark is primarily a canvas on which to produce a painting for whatever purpose is intended – to reveal a design to initiates, to pass knowledge on to another person, to create an item of exchange or, today, to make a work for sale to the art market. A painting on the human body connects the person directly with the ancestral

Figure 5   Lunginy, an engraved smoking pipe. The Donald Thomson
Collection, on loan to Museum Victoria from The University of
Melbourne

being associated with it and has transformative powers. An engraving on a pipe (*lunginy*) changes the status of the pipe and the tobacco smoked in it. The effect of adding the design to the object may indeed be to make it aesthetically more pleasing, certainly it adds meaning to the object, but as we shall see it does so for a particular purpose (Figure 5). It is able to fulfil that purpose because of the kind of thing art is in Yolngu society.

North-east Arnhem Land is a rich environment for hunters and gatherers, and Yolngu had an extensive material culture. Yolngu were semi-sedentary for large parts of the year. In the wet season they lived in substantial bark dwellings to protect themselves from the torrential rains. They were a coastal people and had a number of different types of boat according to different environments – dugout canoes for the bays and open seas, bark canoes for the shoreline and waterways and specialist bark boats for the inland swamps. Yolngu had many different varieties of spear for different hunting activities, baskets for every kind of function, from holding water to storing honey to transporting yams. A different fishtrap existed for each major waterway, employing different techniques according to environment and ancestral law. Yolngu made different varieties of string and cord according to the function required, from the thick turtle-hunter's rope to the fine string for netbags and hafting weapons.

The artistic elaboration of material culture can be seen to occur in two distinct ways: on the one hand the elaboration of the form of material objects themselves and on the other the embellishment of the objects by the addition of a painted design. The division is not between functional and non-functional objects but is associated with functional specialization.

## ELABORATED FORMS

I can consider here only a few brief examples of the ways in which the forms of artefacts are elaborated. Spears (*gara*), digging sticks (*wapitja*) and baskets (*bathi*) are in Yolngu society the archetypal objects. They are associated with the gendered division of Yolngu society; spears are primarily associated with men and baskets and digging sticks primarily with women.[5] Digging sticks will vary mainly on the basis of the hardness and durability of the wood from which they are made, and the sharpness of the point. As we have noted, spears and baskets come in many varieties. At the apex of the category are highly complex forms that occur mainly in ceremonial contexts.

The elaborated form of spear is the hook spear (*baṯi*). A *baṯi* is characterized by an intricately carved wooden head in which a sequence of barbs (hooks) are carved on either one side or both sides of the head (Figure 6). The sequence of barbs may be interrupted by

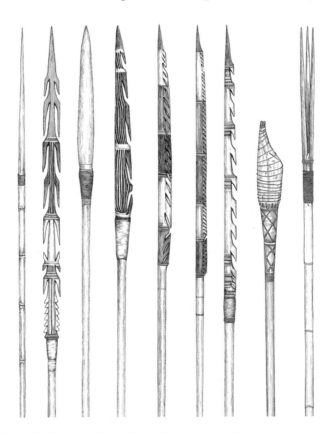

Figure 6   Spearhead compilation. Five ceremonial hook spears, with their carved wooden barbs, are illustrated with other spear types. Pen and ink line drawing by Joan E. Clark. The Donald Thomson Collection. Reproduced with the permission of Mrs D. M. Thomson and Museum Victoria.

another element – a square or a wedge-shaped barb – as opposed to a pointed one. The head can be carved either with the spear shaft out of a continuous piece of wood or separately from the shaft and subsequently hafted to it. Spears may be painted with designs that vary on the basis of clan. These *bati* are primarily used on ceremonial occasions. They are the standard spear used by dancers in ceremonies enacting any activity in which an ordinary spear would be used. They are used to demarcate ceremonial space. Rattled together in bundles, they add to the drama of ritual performance, and they are a valuable item of ceremonial exchange. Functionally they can be a lethal weapon but that is not their primary purpose. However, they are used for ritual punishment at the end of a *makarrata* ceremony.

In a *makarrata* a person who has been accused of a particular crime – usually involvement in a death – has to face up to a barrage of spears thrown by his adversaries. Assuming he succeeds in avoiding the spears and that the participants want to resolve the dispute, the person concerned will offer his leg for spearing. The *bati* may then either lightly cut the flesh or be pushed deeply into the leg and broken off, resulting in a serious wound. *Bati* designs are unique to each clan and are associated with ancestral beings connected to a particular area of country. The surface form of the spear and the designs painted on the body of the spearhead are sufficient to identify the place.

Sacred dilly bags (*bathi*) are the basketry equivalent of the hook spear. These baskets are the joint production of men and women. The bags are shaped like the everyday cylindrical tightly woven bag worn over the shoulder and head and used to carry food or personal items, ochres, beeswax and so on. The sacred bags will have tufts of feathers woven in bands or covering much of the surface and are also likely to have designs sewn onto the surface. They will be completed by the addition of a number of feather tassels or arms (*wana*). *Bathi* are brought out at certain stages in ceremonial performances at times of heightened drama and spectacle. In a burial ceremony they may be carried by dancers who are re-enacting the journey of ancestral beings searching for the spirit of the deceased. Or they may be grasped in the mouth of a dancer performing the aggressive dance of the ancestral crocodile or shark expressing anger at those who might have caused the death. In this case the bag becomes a focal point for the emotions of the participants. On another occasion the bag may be brought out at a circumcision ceremony after the initiate's chest has been painted with clan designs (Figure 7). The boy will be decorated with head ornaments, armbands and a breast girdle of feather-string. He will be lifted on the shoulders of his mother's brother before being carried to the ceremonial ground. The *bathi*, with its tassels flowing, is hung over the boy's shoulder as he is danced forward in triumphant splendour. Ceremonial dilly bags and spears can also be worn by clan leaders at the height of a dispute when declaiming to the community. Such occasions are rare and are associated with moments of great tension in the community. These cause the majority of people to adopt a very low profile.

The identity of the bag is multiply determined: the designs woven into it, the particular combination of feathers, and the form of the *wana* all point toward the owning clan.[6] The *bathi,* like the paintings on the boy's chest, are designed to mark out his spiritual kinship

Figure 7 Yirritja-moiety boys prepared for circumcision. The *dhapi* or circumcision ceremony at Yilpara in 2001 combined both a Dhuwa-moiety and a Yirritja-moiety ceremony. Here we can see the Yirritja-moiety boys in their ceremonial regalia prior to being carried to the ceremony ground. The two boys on the left are painted with a design associated with the ancestral snake at Baraltja. Photograph Howard Morphy.

– linking him to groups of his own moiety. The feather string that is used on dilly bags and the sacred armbands, and the string that is wrapped around the sacred objects are all preserved and over time become part of the history of ceremonies past. Feather string that is used in ceremonies may be wound into a tassel that moves from an armband to a sacred dilly bag, sharing out the substance of the sacred.

The digging stick, which in everyday life has the least formal variation, undergoes the most transformations in ceremonial context. Digging sticks exist both as the core of many of the most sacred objects, forming the core around which the object is constructed, and as ceremonial staffs in their own right. Digging sticks can be decorated in many different ways: designs can be engraved on their bodies; the body of the digging sticks can be bound and designs woven into the resulting surface, which is then painted with ochres; some segments may be bound with feather string or possum-fur string; and then just as with the *bathi*, feather and beeswax pendants may be attached to the object and hang down from the top or middle section.

Ceremonial staffs can be used in re-enactments to represent the digging sticks that ancestral beings used as walking sticks, or used for digging up wild yams, prising out yellow ochre or opening a beehive, for cutting heads in mourning and prising paper bark from the trunk of a tree – anything, in other words, for which ordinary digging sticks can be used. In their elaborated form they can stand for the ancestral being itself; the digging sticks of Nyapililngu or the Djang'kawu sisters are the women themselves or parts of their bodies (Figure 8). The most important of these digging sticks are better conceived of as ceremonial poles – placed in the ground, in a room, a shelter or a ceremonial ground, they mark a ceremonial space. And just as is the case with the *bathi*, each refers to a particular ancestral being – each is the digging stick that a particular ancestral being used to perform his or her creative acts.

Figure 8   *Nyapililngu*, 1969. Artist Narritjin Maymuru. National Museum of Australia, Canberra. The carving was one of a series produced by Narritjin as ceremonial posts for mortuary rituals associated with his brother Nanyin's death and burial. The sculpture represents the ancestral woman in the form of a digging stick, the digging stick that she used in her creative acts (see Morphy 1991). The designs on her body refer to the landscape at Djarrakpi associated with her life. The spikes hanging from either side of the figure (the *wana*, or arms of Nyapililngu) are bones used by women to cut their heads in mourning. After the ceremonies were over, the sculptures were sold to Jim Davidson and subsequently transferred to the National Gallery of Victoria in Melbourne and the National Museum in Canberra. A third has recently been gifted back to Buku-Larrnggay Art Centre at Yirrkala. Copyright the artist's family. Reproduced courtesy of Buku-Larrnggay Mulka Art Centre.

## ADDING DESIGNS

The second way of embellishing objects is by adding a design to an ordinary artefact rather than making an extraordinary one.[7] This is usually done by applying paint or painting a design on the object, although it might involve engraving a design on the surface. The Thomson collection is full of objects with designs painted on them: canoe paddles, clubs, pipes, spear-throwers and so on.[8] There were many reasons why objects were painted, including for pleasure. Paintings that comprised a single colour wash of white or red paint, or occasionally yellow, must be differentiated from more complex designs. White is commonly used as a form of mask to protect people from pollution, and objects from contamination. Red, on the other hand, is a colour of renewal. Objects or people who are being brought back fully into life are likely to be painted in red ochre once the purification rituals have finished. For example, if a car is used to transport a body for burial, the car will be smoked and washed before being painted with red ochre as a sign that it is ready to be used again. Yolngu use red ochre in a house opening several months after a person has died or in painting trees or a veranda where a deceased person used to sit.

More detailed paintings comprising clan-owned designs are painted for a different reason. In Thomson's time one of the reasons for painting designs on an object was to restrict its use to a particular group of people, to give maximum authority to the clan who owned the design. A clan design painted on a tobacco pipe would restrict its circulation to initiated men who had access to knowledge of the design or people who were related to that clan. A design painted on a canoe would be an attempt to control who used that canoe. Painted designs can also be used to transform an everyday object like a paddle into an object that can be used with greater effect in a ceremonial dance. Many Yolngu dances involve the re-enactment of sea voyages by ancestral beings and the painted paddles distinguish the clans who come together for the performance.

Today, paintings are rarely done to restrict the use of something – though the fact that a vehicle may have carried a sacred object is sufficient to restrict its use for some time after-ward. The most commonly painted objects today are motor vehicles, which quite often have clan's designs, or figurative representations of totemic beings, painted on their doors. Vehicles in many ways occupy the conceptual space occupied in the past by dugout canoes, and the clan specific sets of names that were once applied to canoes are today the names of motor vehicles. Indeed, the name is sometimes painted on the doors in place of the clan design.

Painting in these contexts marks the ancestral identity of the object and, in many respects, the human body can be treated in the same ways. Variants of the designs that are painted on material culture objects are used as body paintings. The categorization of Yolngu paint-ings is extremely complex and I have discussed it in detail elsewhere (Morphy 1991). Here I will refer to one major distinction between two categories of body painting: boldly outlined clan designs without cross-hatching that mark the ancestral identity of the performers, and the more elaborated version of the designs that shine brilliantly with the cross-hatched infill (*l̲ikanpuy* or *ma̲dayinpuy miny'tji*). The latter paintings often include one or more figurative representations. The generalized design is usually painted on the bodies of men who move from restricted into open contexts – these are designs associated with the viewing of the clan's sacred objects. Today they are most often worn when a more restricted dance performance is included in a mortuary ritual for a senior person. The main context for body painting today is on the chests of boys at their *dhapi* (circumcision ceremony). People are also painted after they have recovered from a serious or life-threatening illness, and men are painted after they have been through a restricted ceremony.

In Thomson's time a further context for body painting was after death and prior to burial. Painting the chests of the deceased had largely ceased by the mid-1960s. This may have been out of deference to the missionaries, but was also a response to a number of other factors, including a shift to burying the body in a coffin. Since that time Yolngu have used a series of alternatives to mark the sacred identity of the body. Until the 1980s the coffin lid was painted with a similar design to that which would have been painted on the body. In recent years a number of alternative means of marking the body's identity have been developed: these include placing bark paintings beside the body, wrapping the body in painted cloth or printed batik designs, or even on one occasion commissioning shrouds with images of paintings printed onto them. Yolngu mortuary rituals are a major site of creativity.

The main explicit purpose of body painting is to mark the ancestral identity of the person and to associate that person with the power of a particular ancestral being. Body paintings are part of the clan's ancestral inheritance. They are the designs ancestral beings wore on their bodies when they took part in ceremonies that celebrate their land-transforming acts. The designs encode these events in their form, and indeed their form is of ancestral origin. For example, a diamond design associated with a particular area of land was burnt into the body of an ancestral clapping stick as a fire spread through a ceremonial ground. The form of the painting associated with this event will include variants of the diamond designs as well as other elements that cover the story as a whole and relate it to the topography of the landscape.

The generalized outline of a clan design painted on the bodies of dancers who have just emerged from the men's ceremonial ground – for example, a diamond pattern or a circle with radiating lines – will represent the group as a whole. In a ceremony that shows the ancestral floodwaters of a group of clans coming together at a confluence of two or more rivers, each of the clans is likely to have a design that differs in minor ways from every other one, representing its own tributary, its own body of floodwater.

The more detailed individual body paintings that are made at circumcision or that were painted on a dead person's body or a coffin lid have a more specific function. In the case of circumcision they identify the initiate with a particular ancestral being associated with his clan's country or a related country. Life is a process of accumulating ancestral identity, and circumcision is one stage in a male life where that is accomplished. The boy may be given a new name associated with the painting. In the performance different manifestations of the ancestral world are brought together. The armbands that the boy wears and the dilly bag that he carries are likely to reference the same ancestral beings as the painting on his chest, and the sequence of the songs that are sung and the dances that are performed will move him into that ancestor's domain.

Mortuary rituals involve a series of parallel and coordinated enactments of the life and spiritual identity of the dead person and are designed to move the spirit toward its final destination. The body painting or its equivalent marks a phase of the spirit's journey and marks the spiritual kinship to the Ancestors that the person has become closest to in his or her life. The painting almost literally transports the person's soul, and yet at the same time the person gives power to the ancestral domain. In death, persons will carry something of that image with them and it will be in the memories of the people who succeed them. In the Yolngu world there is a dialogue between the living and the spirit world mediated by the dead who pass from one to the other. And the actions of the living in producing powerful paintings, in dancing with energy, and singing with strength simultaneously help the mortal soul of the deceased and contribute to the power of the ancestral domain.

## CONTINUITY AND CHANGE IN YOLNGU ART

In Thomson's time art was imbricated in the body of Yolngu material culture as a whole. Art brought the mundane world in touch with the sacred. Art and ceremony remain a central part of Yolngu life today. There have, however, been significant shifts in the forms of art and contexts of ritual – but not a diminishing of them. In many respects Yolngu art still brings the sacred into contact with everyday life, even if the everyday is sometimes that of the international art world or the Australian politico-juridical system.

Over time the diversity of Yolngu material culture has been reduced and simplified. This is mainly a consequence of a changing economy and the replacement of traditional material culture by introduced items. While Yolngu still hunt, fish and gather extensively they use different equipment. Fishing still involves spears but the prongs are made of iron fencing wire not stingray barbs. Women gather yams as much as ever but they will dig them up using metal digging sticks and carry them back in plastic bags or buckets rather than using *bathi* of woven fibre. Spears are seldom used in hunting and though Yolngu settlements and camps remain well armed with them, the diversity of form is less. Guns have largely replaced spears in hunting large game. People no longer make dugout canoes but use manufactured boats with outboard motors. People still make harpoons for turtle and dugong, but the ropes will be purchased, no longer made by themselves. The knowledge to make the diverse types of baskets still exists and Yolngu women make them for sale, but they are more likely to be used by European women to carry things in, if used at all.

The ceremonial objects and ceremonial regalia of Thomson's time are still a feature of Yolngu ritual life. Hook spears (*bati*) are still manufactured for ceremonies, the feather *bathi* remain prized items and a circumcision ceremony remains a spectacle of colour. Ceremonial *wapitja* will be brought out on major occasions and returned to safe keeping after the event.

Sacred objects and ceremonial posts are still manufactured in restricted contexts, and are still central to the internal economy and part of a network of exchange and obligation that connects people across north-east Arnhem Land.

In the broadest sense much of the contemporary Yolngu economy is centred on ceremonial activities and the fulfilment of ritual obligations. Burial and circumcision ceremonies last for several days and often for as long as two or more weeks. A major ceremony may involve 200–300 people although not all will be present for the whole occasion. Mortuary rituals are usually held at homeland centres in the dead person's estate or an estate closely associated with that person. The homelands are up to 250 kilometres away from the main population centre of Yirrkala and have to be reached by dirt road or by aircraft. The core resident populations of the homelands range from 25 to 150, though population mobility results in major fluctuations in community size. Thus the logistics of organizing and provisioning Yolngu mortuary rituals are considerable and the expense absorbs most of people's income for the duration. Today the cultural production of ceremonial performance has a market value in the outside world – the same people who produce carvings and paintings for sale and perform ceremonies at the opening of exhibitions in southern cities are the leading performers in the rituals of their own society. Yet external market factors hardly enter the internal ritual economy, and paintings, ceremonial poles and sacred objects are still produced to fulfil ritual obligations. Indeed the money earned from the sale of artworks will often be used to support ceremonial activity through the purchase of food and materials such as cloth. Ritual experts will be fed and provisioned as would have happened in the past, but they will not be paid for their labour and expertise. Women who make the sacred feathered dilly bags used in rituals are paid something for the considerable labour involved in their production, but that payment has no relation to what the market value of the object might be. Indeed such objects are never made for sale today.[9]

The contexts for Yolngu ceremonial performances have widened. While Yolngu still perform ceremonies for internal consumption, they also occupy the ritual spaces that are created at the points of articulation between Yolngu and the outside world (see Morphy 1983 and 2006a). Yolngu perform ceremonies to farewell missionaries and other people who have made a contribution to their lives. Yolngu perform ceremonies to welcome politicians and visiting dignitaries. Yolngu dress up in traditional splendour for graduation ceremonies and some Church events, including the ordination of Yolngu ministers. And when hearings of important legal cases connected with land rights or native title are held, Yolngu will make the court their own through welcoming ceremonies and the display of sacred digging sticks and other ceremonial paraphernalia. The details of the performance will be mapped out to fit the occasion. When it is thought appropriate, dignitaries may be shown sacred objects and be invited to enter restricted spaces.

# 3 BARK PAINTING AND THE EMERGENCE OF YOLNGU FINE ART

The major shift over time in art production has been away from embellished material culture objects toward bark paintings and other objects produced primarily for sale. Other objects include hollow-log coffins, softwood carvings, woven baskets and bags, *yiḏaki* (commonly known as didgeridoo) and occasionally some functional items such as spears and spear throwers. My main focus will be on bark paintings, since until recently they have dominated in the fine art market.[1] However, today hollow-log coffins have joined bark paintings as a major component of the market for Yolngu fine art.

Bark paintings were originally a minor component of Yolngu material culture. However, we do not know how minor. There were a number of Indigenous contexts in which bark paintings were produced. They were made for certain restricted men's ceremonies and displayed with other sacred objects in the shelter built for that purpose on the ceremonial ground. Bark paintings were used to show designs to people who had a right to them and as a means of passing on knowledge. The walls of bark huts were occasionally painted with designs. However, these designs were generally not ceremonial designs but 'informal' paintings of human figures and animals. Lloyd Warner collected a few paintings of the kind that were displayed on the ceremonial ground and Thomson collected some fifty paintings from different Yolngu artists. Painting on bark was one of the contexts in which elaborated clan paintings (*ḻikanbuy miny'tji*) were produced (Figure 9). Such paintings could also be produced on other surfaces, and the most frequent surface was probably the human body.[2] However, clan paintings could also be painted on human skulls (Thomson 1939b), on certain ceremonial objects, on bark coffins and on sacred posts. Indeed, to understand Yolngu paintings one has to look beyond the particular painting or painted object and see them as instances of an ancestral design associated with a particular place (see chapter 2).

Yolngu country is divided into estate areas associated with the action of a particular ancestral being or set of ancestral beings. Yathikpa on Blue Mud Bay, for example, is a place belonging to the Maḏarrpa clan associated with *Bäru*, the Ancestral Crocodile (Figure 10). *Bäru* was originally human in form but transformed into a crocodile as a result of a fight in ancestral times with his wife Dhamilingu, blue-tongued lizard. She set fire to the bark hut in which he slept and in his agony he leapt up from the ground, with flaming sheets of bark burning into his body, and dived into the sea to quench the flames. The fire continued burning beneath the waves and can be seen today manifest in the fields of waving sea grass beneath the surface of the water. Each event in the narrative has an expression in

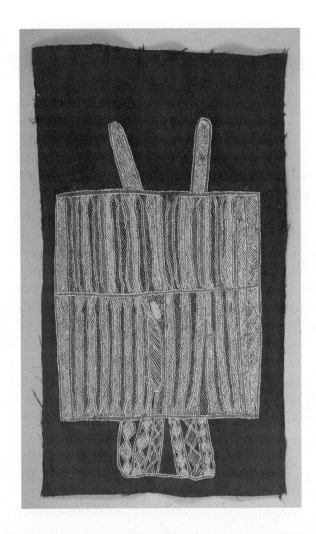

Figure 9   *Fish Trap at Baraltja*, 1942. Bark painting by
Mundukuḻ, collected by Donald Thomson at Caledon Bay
on 17 September 1942, while he commanded the Special
Reconnaissance Unit of Eastern Arnhem Land 'warriors'
to monitor Japanese activity. Mundukuḻ was the father of
Gumbaniya Marawili (see Figure 10). The painting represents
the mouth of the Baraltja River associated with the ancestral
snake Burrut'tji or Mundukuḻ. (See also a similar painting
on the chest of the boy at the left in Figure 7, who is a
classificatory grandson of the artist.) The background design
represents the form of an ancestral fishtrap, made out of the
snake's ribs and the flow of brackish water through the river
mouth during the wet season (see also Figure 30). The Donald
Thomson Collection on loan to Museum Victoria from
The University of Melbourne. Copyright the artist's family.
Reproduced courtesy of Buku-Larrnggay Mulka Art Centre.

the form of the landscape. The source of the original fire can be seen hidden in the jungle, and the feet and tail of *bäru* are transformed into rocks and a sandbar jutting out into the water. The marks of the fire can be seen to this day burnt into the back of every estuarine crocodile. This pattern, represented as a connected chain of diamonds, is the underlying design element of Madarrpa paintings. The paintings as a whole are produced by organizing sets of the design to fit in with the ancestral landscape, with the land-transforming events that occurred. The core meaning of the design will switch according to focus: it might be the crocodile's back or the fire, or the turbulent waters of the bay and so on. In every case it signifies the Madarrpa clan itself and its sacred-origin story. Variation can be built into the design by including the ceremonial ground that belongs to that country or outline forms of sacred objects associated with particular places. In a later chapter we will see how paintings are produced that express the ancestral dimension of the Yathikpa landscape. At this stage

Figure 10 *Bäru at Yathikpa.* Section of a painting by Gumbaniya Marawili of the Madarrpa clan (born circa 1933), representing the crocodile ancestor Bäru at Yathikpa. The background pattern represents fire and the waters off shore. Australian National Maritime Museum, Sydney. Copyright the artist. Reproduced courtesy of Buku-Larrnggay Mulka Art Centre.

I only need to point out that the paintings associated with each place are generated from the ancestral events that occurred there. Each Yolngu painting can be related to a template associated with place that is identified with a particular geometric pattern, which in its detail is unique to a particular place.[3]

It is possible to see now how Yolngu can produce designs from a particular place that vary according to the surface available. The core geometric design can be reproduced on a matchbox-sized object if required – incised into clapsticks or on the stem of a pipe – or as a body painting, or on a coffin lid or a hollow-log coffin. According to the size of the surface the painting may include other elements – the ceremonial ground, a figurative representation of a crocodile or one of the other beings connected to the place and involved in the events that took place there. Bark is simply another form of 'canvas' – a surface that can vary in size from the top of a skull to the surface of a large hollow-log coffin.

Over time as the Yolngu economy changed, ochres on bark became increasingly the most common medium for painting. The change occurred both as the inventory of material culture was reduced and as the demand for bark paintings for sale increased. Unsurprisingly the change of focus of Yolngu collections in museums has moved in an almost parallel way. Bark paintings were a minor part of early collections and with carvings and hollow-log coffins, have become the major part of contemporary collections. In turn these, together with some figurative carvings, comprise virtually the entire collections made by art galleries.[4]

I can only provide a brief account of the development of Yolngu bark paintings here and will concentrate on dynamic elements of the process that occurred. We have already touched on the beginnings of this process (in chapter 2) with the involvement of missionaries and anthropologists in the early development of the market. The focus of the early collectors – Thomson, Warner and Webb – was on obtaining a representative sample of Yolngu material culture. The objects on the whole displayed superb craftsmanship and finely worked and painted designs. Interestingly the bark paintings collected by Thomson represented the *likanbuy* clan paintings, the sacred designs – painted on the chests of initiates and the bodies of the dead – which alluded to the form of sacred objects and are subject to strictures of clan ownership and control. Formally and in technique and composition many of the paintings are similar to the fine artworks produced today for sale to museums and collectors around the world. Chaseling's paintings are different.

The majority of Chaseling's paintings do not include clan designs and have a high figurative content. The quality of a lot of the work is quite rough and cross-hatching though present is reduced in area. A few paintings can be linked to clan stories and to the ancestral world, but many seem to be collections of animals of the land and sea (Figure 11). Chaseling's collections also include scenes from mission life and contact themes – horses, cattle, boats and even planes. When I began to work with Yolngu artists in 1973 some forty years after Chaseling first commissioned paintings, Mungurrawuy Yunupingu, one of the leading artists, was quite clear as to why the paintings had the form they did. Mungurrawuy had produced many paintings for Chaseling and he labelled them 'anyhow' paintings. His

Figure 11 *Porpoise and Turtles*, 1937. Artist unknown, collected by the Rev. Wilbur Chaseling 1937. Many of the paintings collected by Chaseling comprise figurative representations of creatures of the land and sea. The absence of clan designs makes it difficult for Yolngu to identify the artist or clan of the painting. Chaseling did not record the artists' names, hence many of Chaseling's paintings remain by an 'unknown artist'. Museum Victoria. Copyright the artist's family. Reproduced courtesy of Buku-Larrnggay Mulka Art Centre.

explanation was that when they asked Chaseling what paintings he wanted he replied 'paint them anyhow'. The question still arises as to where the forms came from.

Yolngu had a variety of different genres of painting. As well as the sacred paintings, people painted figurative representations on hollow-log coffins and certain other categories of figurative painting. Although we do not have any examples of Yolngu paintings on the walls of bark huts, we do know that they painted them; and, in the surrounding areas, we know that such paintings usually comprised secular subjects – animals and human figures. The public nature of the wet-season huts meant it would have been inappropriate to paint sacred designs on the wall where all could see them.

I do not intend to be dismissive about the 'anyhow' paintings even though they were not valued by Yolngu as highly as the sacred art. They provide an interesting and diverse set of paintings, which provided the context for expressing Yolngu figurative iconography. As a category of painting they have continued into the present, and are referred to as 'hunting stories' or *wakinngu* (mundane). They are sometimes produced as bark paintings. More usually they are reproduced as figurative forms incised and painted into the bodies of softwood carvings of animals produced primarily though not exclusively for the tourist market. The most common context for such subject matter today, however, is in the prints produced at Yirrkala by women artists. These frequently include scenes from daily life and contact themes such teachers at the Literacy Production Centre or a football match (Figure 12).

We can trace, in Yolngu response to the demand for paintings, the emergence of two motivating themes that have continued to the present. Yolngu used paintings as a means

Figure 12   *Indigenous Jobs in Remote Areas*, 2000. Artist Marrnyula Mununggurr. The print was produced by Marrnyula as a commission and represents Indigenous and non-Indigenous Australians working together using new technology. Photograph Howard Morphy. Copyright the artist. Reproduced courtesy of Buku-Larrnggay Mulka Art Centre.

of showing others the values of their way of life and the core structures of their society, and they used them as a source of income, as a means of engaging with the economy of the encompassing world. We can also see that Yolngu had to adjust early on to the demands of that outside world and to the consequences it had on their society and way of life. In particular they had to make choices about the transmission and control of knowledge in a transformed context in which their own society would need to articulate with alien institutions and practices. Yolngu society was engaging in an adjustment process and art was to take a central role in that process.

Within five years of the establishment of Yirrkala mission, the outbreak of the Second World War and the establishment of military bases on their doorstep further disrupted the Yolngu world. Yolngu engaged in the war in a number of different ways, as members of Donald Thomson's coastal patrol, helping with unloading at the airbase and taking part in rescue operations. As far as art was concerned, the war opened up for a short period of time a local market. The origins of the softwood carving tradition can be traced back to that time as people turned to making souvenirs – carvings of animals, human figures, dugout canoes and so on – for the military.

Soon after the war's end anthropology again took a hand in the direction of Yolngu art. In 1946/47 Ronald and Catherine Berndt based themselves at Yirrkala for a year's intensive field work, and in 1948 Charles Mountford spent several months there as leader of the American-Australian Scientific Expedition to Arnhem Land sponsored by the National Geographic Society (Mountford 1956). The Berndts and Mountford were almost as formidable as Thomson in their role as collectors and were passionate advocates for Aboriginal art. The Berndts were certainly more professional as anthropologists than Mountford, but all helped to develop the market for Aboriginal art. The role of such collectors in creating a market should not be underestimated.

The Berndts and Mountford had overlapping aims. Ronald Berndt used the collection of art and material culture as a central component of his methodology. He commissioned several hundred paintings as part of his research and documented them in immense detail (Figure 13). In addition to bark paintings Berndt collected works using crayons on butcher's paper (see Hutcherson 1995). Bark can only be used as a medium for painting until the early dry season. As the dry season develops it becomes impossible to prise bark from the trees. He arranged for his father to send him supplies of butcher's paper from Adelaide together with coloured crayons. Yolngu adapted immediately to the medium and to the array of introduced pigments, producing a series of works that Berndt toward the end of his life saw as the pride of his collection. Many of the paintings that Berndt commissioned were the sacred designs that were used in different indigenous contexts. The collection includes few of Chaseling's 'anyhow' category. Berndt also used paintings as an innovative method of eliciting ethnographic material. Each week he would introduce a particular theme – ceremonial life, marital relations, spirit conception, mapping clan countries – and sets of paintings were produced by artists reflecting those themes.[5] The works used Yolngu

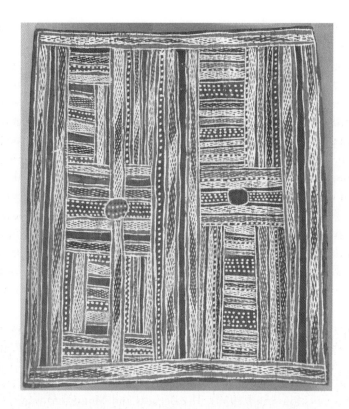

Figure 13   *Gulbingoi Rock (lorikeets) and Garingan Rock*, 1946.
Artist Mawalan Marika. This painting was collected by Ronald
Berndt in 1946 and represents the place where the Djan'kawu
sisters landed at the end of their long sea journey from Buralku
(see Berndt 1952). The painting represents the Rirratjingu-clan
design associated with the actions of the Djan'kawu sisters in the
Yalangbara region. One set of meanings refer to the alternating
patterns of light and shade in the sand dunes as time passes,
another to the movement of shifting sands. The ancestral women
used their digging sticks to create wells, which can be seen as the
circles. Reproduced courtesy of the Berndt Museum, University
of Western Australia. Copyright the artist's family. Reproduced
courtesy of Buku-Larrnggay Mulka Art Centre.

iconography to produce exegetical discourses on the topic concerned. And some of these
paintings too can be seen as antecedents of the innovative printmaking tradition that began
in the 1980s.

Mountford's relationship with Yolngu artists was less intensive. He led a large team of
researchers comprising archaeologists, zoologists, botanists and biological anthropologists
(see for example Mountford 1956). The paintings he collected included many that would
have fitted well within the Chaseling collections, but he also collected a large number of clan

paintings. The Berndts and Mountford wrote ill of each other, but both in their different ways contributed significantly to an increasing knowledge of and interest in the art from Yirrkala. Mountford's expedition generated considerable publicity at the time. The fact that it was sponsored by the National Geographical Society resulted in images of Yolngu art and art from other areas of Arnhem Land being distributed overseas as well as in Australia.[6] The Berndts and Mountford both published books on Arnhem Land art and included many works from Yirrkala.[7] And in 1949 the Berndts, Elkin and McCarthy helped to organize a major exhibition in the art gallery in the David Jones store in Sydney, following on from an earlier exhibition at the same Gallery in 1941 (Figure 14).[8]

The exhibitions at David Jones were important ones, since the Gallery was at the same time at the forefront of introducing modernism to Australian audiences (see Stephen 2006). David Jones developed a close relationship with the Museum of Modern Art in New York, and following the Second World War began to take on travelling exhibitions from MoMA, including the 1945 'What is modern painting?' Stephen has shown how this relationship developed out of an earlier exhibition that moved in the opposite direction. 'Art of Australia'

Figure 14   The 1941 David Jones Exhibition, 11–22 August 1941.
Australian Museum Archives, AMS351; V7958. Photographer
G. C. Clutton.

was toured by MoMA through North America in 1941. This exhibition was curated by Theodore Sizer, the director of Yale Art Museum. Stephen notes that Sizer had grasped 'the modernist appeal of Aboriginal art and gave it an unprecedented place in the exhibition, which proved extraordinarily popular, with twenty-nine American cities electing to take the show' (Stephen 2006: 582).

The interest in Aboriginal art in the aftermath of the Second World War and its tentative connection to modernism may have been a factor influencing the destination of the Arnhem Land paintings collected by Mountford – almost by accident, they became the first works of Aboriginal art to breach the art gallery walls in Australia.[9] The exhibition was sponsored by the Commonwealth Government and some of the paintings were gifted to the main State art galleries. A large collection from the exhibition also ended up overseas in the collection of the Smithsonian Institution in Washington.

## INTO THE ART GALLERY

In retrospect, the interest shown by a few anthropologists and the marketing endeavours of the missionaries had a significant impact on the profile of Aboriginal art from Arnhem Land in the decade following the Second World War. More exhibitions were organized at the David Jones Gallery in Sydney; design competitions were held for the commercialization of Aboriginal art in the form of textiles; Aboriginal art featured in the 1956 Melbourne Olympics with use of images recorded by Mountford at Oenpelli on the 1948 expedition. The Methodist Missions at Milingimbi under the superintendentship of Edgar Wells, and at Yirrkala under the management of Doug Tuffin, continued to market art and establish connections with collectors in the southern States. Arguably, however, the turning point for the recognition of Arnhem Land art, and Yolngu art in particular, occurred in the late 1950s and early 1960s.

The collections of Warner, Thomson and Berndt were made as part of their anthropological research and Mountford's collections as part of a natural history expedition. At this time Australian art galleries remained resistant to adding Aboriginal art to their collections. In 1958, however, the Art Gallery of New South Wales became proactive in the Aboriginal art market (discussed in detail in Chapter 8). Dr Stuart Scougall, a Sydney-based orthopaedic surgeon with an interest in Aboriginal health, began to collect Aboriginal art in 1956. He persuaded Tony Tuckson, the Deputy Director of the Art Gallery of New South Wales to join him in a series of expeditions to Arnhem Land. Tuckson himself had become inspired by Aboriginal art as a result of the David Jones exhibition in 1949. The initial collections they made were of Tiwi art from Melville and Bathurst Islands, and included an impressive set of *pukumani* poles – carved and painted ironwood poles placed around the grave during mortuary rituals.[10] However, they subsequently made two visits to Yirrkala in 1959 and 1960 when they commissioned a series of bark paintings and carved and painted figures representing ancestral beings. Tuckson, a distinguished artist himself, found inspiration for his own work in the works of the Indigenous artists he collected, and his

Figure 15 *The Djan'kawu Creation Story: Sisters Giving Birth*, 1959. Artist Mawalan Marika. The graphic figurative image of the sisters giving birth to the Yolngu clans is referenced in more abstract ways in the other panels of the painting. Reproduced courtesy of the Art Gallery of New South Wales. Copyright the artist's family and DACS 2007. Reproduced courtesy of Buku-Larrnggay Mulka Art Centre.

collection comprised a series of outstanding works. Formally they are in direct continuity with the collections made by Berndt, but many are considerably larger in scale (Figure 15).

Scougall's and Tuckson's motivations were to place the works in the Art Gallery of New South Wales as opposed to an ethnographic museum. They intended that the works should be seen as art rather than ethnography. While in a later chapter I will argue that the distinction itself is problematic – art and ethnography should not be seen as opposed but complementary perspectives on artworks – my present concern is to stress that the collection methods that they adopted differed little from those of Berndt and Mountford.[11] Scougall, Tuckson and their accompanying team produced a meticulously documented collection that placed the artworks well within their cultural context.

Almost overlapping with Scougall's and Tuckson's endeavour was the effort of Karel Kupka, a Swiss artist and anthropologist influenced by the surrealist movement who developed a passion for Aboriginal art. He undertook a series of expeditions to Arnhem Land in the 1950s and 1960s developing collections for the Ethnographic Museum in Basel and the Musée National des Arts d'Afrique et d'Océanie in Paris. Kupka was initially motivated by a primitivist agenda. He saw the art of Arnhem Land as representing one of the last regions in the world of primitive art that was uncontaminated by European civilization. Inspired by André Breton, he was looking for a primitive art that came directly from the soul and expressed the emotions of primeval man. Kupka is also sometimes celebrated as a person who approached Aboriginal art from the perspective of its formal qualities as opposed to its cultural meaning – fine art as opposed to ethnography. In this respect Kupka and Tuckson can be placed in the same frame.

Kupka's positioning of Aboriginal art at the dawn of human history certainly antagonized Australian anthropologists such as Berndt, Stanner and Elkin who came from a tradition that rejected the evolutionist paradigm. Australian anthropologists were concerned to stress the contemporary and autonomous nature of Aboriginal society and rejected any arguments that positioned Aboriginal society as an earlier stage of human evolution. However, in terms of methods and approaches to collecting, and the destination of the objects concerned, Kupka, Tuckson and Scougall, Mountford and Ronald Berndt were involved in similar tasks and there were overlaps in their approaches to Aboriginal art.

Despite its title and the preface by Breton that positions it in relation to a particular ideology of Western art practice, Kupka's *The Dawn of Art* provides a rich documentation of Yolngu art in context. Kupka's original collection was sponsored by the Ethnographic Museum in Basel. He was as interested as any of his predecessors in documenting Yolngu art and placing it in the context of their society. He provided a more detailed perspective on the technical and aesthetic practice of Yolngu bark painting than did Berndt, but less detail on the ceremonial context and the aesthetics of song poetry associated with the paintings. Kupka wrote up his research for a doctorate in anthropology at the University of Paris, and his thesis is essentially a documented catalogue and ethnographic contextualization of Yolngu artworks. The works he collected, like those collected by the Berndts and Mountford, all ended up initially in ethnographic museums or museums of ethnographic art.

Kupka, Tuckson and Scougall, the Berndts and Mountford all believed passionately in the visual power of Aboriginal art. Their research and writings complement each other's and together they have provided extraordinarily rich and well documented collections of art. In addition, all were interested in the role of the individual artist in Aboriginal society and were concerned to attribute works to particular artists, though Mountford was much less systematic than the others in this respect.[12] All followed a similar method of documenting paintings, one that came out of the organization and structure of Yolngu society. Paintings were attributed to moiety and clan as well as to individual artist. Documentation was recorded from the artist himself or a senior member of the clan, and comprised a detailed decoding of the iconography of the paintings, relating them to Yolngu mythology and ceremonial performance. Such a format for documenting Yolngu art has almost become standard and though it can be challenged, and generalizing it to other Aboriginal societies problematized – it has its origins in the discourse between the Yolngu artists and the original collectors and recorders of their art.[13] Today Yolngu will insist on foregrounding the moiety division into Dhuwa and Yirritja as a preliminary to presenting the face of their society to the world.

The early 1960s also saw the beginning of the development of specialist art dealers focused on Arnhem Land in general, but strongly emphasizing the art of north-east Arnhem Land. Dorothy Bennett (1915–2003), who accompanied Scougall to Arnhem Land as his secretary, began her dealership in 1962 and continued selling Aboriginal art until shortly before her death at the age of 89. The other pioneering dealer was Jim Davidson, a Melbourne-based businessman with interests in the Pacific region. He developed an interest in Aboriginal culture and offered his services to the Federal Government to help in the marketing of Aboriginal art. Beginning in 1962 Davidson would make annual visits to Arnhem Land, in particular to Oenpelli, Milingimbi and Yirrkala, to collect paintings for sale to his clientele. He organized exhibitions to coincide with Indigenous events such as the Moomba Festival, and sold artworks from his home. He made a down payment on the works at the time of purchase and brought an additional payment to the artists the following year after they had been sold. When we began working at Yirrkala in 1973, visits by Davidson were eagerly anticipated by some of the senior artists.

Bennett and Davidson both documented the paintings they collected, Davidson in considerably more detail and with greater accuracy than Bennett. Davidson established close relationships with a number of Yolngu artists including Mungurrawuy Yunupingu, Yanggariny Wunungmurra and Narritjin Maymuru. These artists welcomed his return visits and would prepare barks especially for his arrival. Both Bennett and Davidson established links with overseas collectors and facilitated the export of Aboriginal art. Bennett developed the Barnett collection, while Davidson helped build the two major American collections that developed from the mid-1960s – that of Ed Ruhe, a professor of English at the University of Kansas (see Morphy and Smith Boles, 1999), and Louis Allen, a California businessman (Allen, 1975). Davidson developed close relationships with the missionaries in charge of the marketing of art. He got on well with Edgar Wells, after the latter had moved to Yirrkala, and with Doug Tuffin and Alan Fiddock.

The dealers and the missionaries documented the works they acquired in a way similar to that followed by the anthropologists and curators, though with a little less regard to accuracy in some cases. Davidson became a conduit linking the artists of Yirrkala with the major private collectors. He documented the paintings for collectors and entered into extensive correspondence with them. He wrote of conversations he had with the artists while commissioning their work, and answered the questions posed by the collectors as best he could. Although both Louis Allen and Ed Ruhe visited north-east Arnhem Land on occasions to pursue their own research, the basic documentation of their collections was undertaken by Davidson and the mission.

Thus by the early 1960s the basic groundwork for the marketing of Yolngu art had been established. Artists from Yirrkala had made considerable contacts with the outside world, and had attracted the attention of passionate collectors who believed in their art. The collectors approached the art from different perspectives, but always as aesthetically pleasing and culturally meaningful objects. The collections were beginning to spread around the world to Paris, New York, Washington and Basel. Major collections had been acquired by Australian state museums, and the walls of a major art gallery – the Art Gallery of New South Wales – had been breached for the first time by Aboriginal art. Influential people in the Western artworld had begun to say strong things about the art: Tony Tuckson in Australia, and André Breton in France. Major books had already been published and the first overseas private collectors had begun to acquire works. A dealership system was emerging which found support at the local level through mission staff. All this had been accomplished within 25 years of the establishment of Yirrkala mission.

However, it is worth pausing to reflect on how thin the thread was that connected all of these events together. The development of knowledge about and interest in Yolngu art was serendipitous. Elsewhere in Australia missionaries were not so supportive of Aboriginal art enterprises. In some areas, art production was banned for long periods as a heathen practice (the Tiwi Islands and Oenpelli for example). Indeed, in neighbouring western Arnhem Land the Anglican Church, at the time of the establishment of Yirrkala and for long afterward, showed little interest in promoting Aboriginal art. What if they, instead of the Methodists, had been awarded the missionary franchise for north-east Arnhem Land? How was it that, at a time when anthropology was showing little interest in art and material culture, virtually all the anthropologists working in north-east Arnhem Land went against the trend, building collections of art and material culture and including art centrally in their writings? What would have happened if Stuart Scougall's interest in boomerang leg, a supposed bone deformity of Indigenous Australians, had not led him into Arnhem Land and facilitated his interest in Aboriginal art. It is unlikely that either Tony Tuckson or Dorothy Bennett would have travelled there, and so the first opportunity for Aboriginal art to enter the Art Gallery of New South Wales would have been lost and the first dealer in Yolngu art might never have visited the region.

I put these questions in part to acknowledge the achievements of those few passionate individuals who challenged the viewpoints of their times. Had some of those steps not occurred things might have been different, and the local trajectory of Yolngu art would not have been precisely the same. Aboriginal art might have had to wait a few more years to break into the national and international art worlds. However, the slender thread is not as fragile as it can be made to seem. Three factors need to be taken into account: one is the relatively limited space of north-east Arnhem Land itself, a second is the determination of Yolngu in all eras to continue practicing their art, and the third is the beginnings of a change in attitude toward Indigenous art that can be discerned in Australia and Europe after the Second World War.

In the 1930s and 1940s there were only around 3,000 Yolngu people spread among three main settlements or living in their clan estates. North-east Arnhem Land at any one time provided only a limited space for a relatively few individuals from outside. Yolngu were the focus of interest of many people, and it is very likely that had one set of anthropologists or collectors not arrived to occupy the space allowed, others would have replaced them. Outsiders were attracted to north-east Arnhem Land because it was viewed as one of the last places to be opened up and, for their different reasons, those looking for 'uncontaminated' pre-European artforms or traditional ceremonial practices were likely to find their way there.

Secondly, the colonial conditions had changed. Euro-Australians were becoming more responsive to Aboriginal concerns. There was a change in the climate of opinion in the southern states of Australia that made people more interested in Aboriginal art and culture. The very fact that north-east Arnhem Land was pacified by the Methodist Overseas Missionary Society and an anthropologist, rather than as a consequence of a police punitive expedition, was a sign of that change. The era of what Stanner (1979) referred to as the Great Australian Silence – the absence of Aboriginal people from national discourse – was close to an end. The slow turning of the Australian artworld toward Aboriginal art and culture had had its effect: a few 'Australian' artists such as Margaret Preston were being influenced by Aboriginal art;[14] a nationalist literary movement – the Jindyworobaks – was seeking inspiration from Indigenous artforms; Australian craft was being influenced by Aboriginal design; and Aboriginal-inspired musical forms such as the ballet *Corroboree* were being produced. There had been signs of an increase in the number of exhibitions of Aboriginal art and commercial galleries such as David Jones were prepared to put on exhibitions for sale.[15] All of these factors combined to make the post-war period one of those moments when Aboriginal art for a while struck the nation's consciousness. However, the other major factor in ensuring that Yolngu art would have the opportunity to be seen by wider audiences was the agency of the artists themselves. In order to appreciate this, we need to view history so far from the perspective of Yolngu artists and to see the ways in which they engaged their art practice with a changing world.

## THE ART OF PERSUASION

From the beginning of the mission era, Yolngu were responsive to the opportunities presented by collectors of their art. For both collectors and Yolngu, there were two distinct aspects to their engagement: an exchange of information and an exchange of goods. The particular emphases of these exchanges varied from individual to individual and over time. Missionaries such as Webb and Chaseling saw value in Yolngu art as a commodity that would enable Aboriginal people to acquire desired goods – tobacco, sugar and tea – and thus to encourage them to remain at the mission station. They also saw art and craft as a means of demonstrating to their congregations the substantial skills of Aboriginal people.

Anthropologists such as Thomson and Berndt saw Aboriginal art and material culture as a source of information about Aboriginal society. They also saw it as a commodity that would eventually find its place in museum collections. They paid for the works in exactly the same way as the missionaries did by exchanging it for desired goods, which included tobacco but also items such as cloth and knives. As the trade developed, other motivations were added on the collectors' side including the desire to collect art as opposed to information and the wish to demonstrate Yolngu rights to their country.

The objectives of the collectors became more complex over time and also tended to merge, though not all shared precisely the same objectives. There are early signs that the interests of the Methodist missionaries overlapped with those of the anthropologists. Webb and Chaseling valued many aspects of Yolngu culture – hence knowledge exchange, learning about Yolngu culture, was among their motivations (see Morphy 2005a). Later on missionaries such as Edgar Wells and his wife Anne produced precisely the same kind of detailed documentation as did anthropologists (A. Wells 1971). The missionaries also became increasingly entangled in the Yolngu struggle for their rights – rights in land and the right to be provided with good educational and health facilities (see for example E. Wells 1982). And from the beginning that too was part of the anthropologists' agenda. Donald Thomson wrote pamphlets on Yolngu rights and Ronald Berndt became a major player in the first land-rights case – the Gove case – brought by the people of Yirrkala. The argument in favour of recognizing Yolngu art became part of the agenda of all concerned. Anthropologists, missionaries and art gallery curators, with slightly different emphases, all argued for Yolngu art to be recognized on an equal basis with Western art.

Yolngu motivations influenced the ways in which the collectors saw their art – its political dimension, for example – and created the synergies that have just been discussed. The collectors were a diverse bunch. Many of the people with whom Yolngu interacted were bitter rivals – almost all the anthropologists wrote ill of each other's work and were united in turn by their opposition to the missionaries. Similar divisions existed among the mission staff. The dealers were openly dismissive of one another. Yet these rivalries hardly affected the interface between Yolngu and these outsiders, reflecting in many respects how much those outsiders had in common with one another. That 'in common' was produced by Yolngu agency in large measure.

We have only indirect evidence of Yolngu motivations for working with the collectors early on. Yolngu did not write accounts of their reasons for engagement and anthropologists and missionaries neglected to record them. In the case of Yirrkala, we do have oral histories recorded by Nancy Williams (1976) and myself from some of the artists who produced paintings for Chaseling, Mountford and the Berndts. We also begin to have very good documentation of Yolngu motivations from the 1950s, not too long after the trade began.

From their writings we know that Warner and Thompson developed close relationships with individual Yolngu.[16] The relationships were intellectual as well as affective. Thomson writes of the intellectual discourses he carried on with Yolngu while he camped with them on bark platforms above the Arafura swamp in the wet season as they hunted for magpie geese. Plagued by unimaginable swarms of mosquitoes, Thomson elaborated on the principles of Linnaean taxonomy to demonstrate that Europeans, like Yolngu, had complex ways of classifying the natural world. And Chaseling details the theological discussions he had with Yolngu at Yirrkala soon after his arrival (Morphy 2005a). The rich and detailed documentation of Thomson's collections provides evidence of Yolngu willingness to teach an interested outsider about their way of life, and its intellectual underpinnings, as subsequent generations of researchers have discovered (see Figure 4).

Yolngu continue to incorporate outsiders into their society, allocating them a place in the kinship universe, adopting them into their families, making them relatives to particular Yolngu and to each other. Indeed this inclusion of outsiders, up to a point, is a general characteristic of Australian Aboriginal societies (see Morphy 1983) and in Arnhem Land long predates European colonization.

For several hundred years, coastal Yolngu had maintained close and continuing contact with outsiders – the Macassan traders from eastern Indonesia who arrived each year with the coming of the wet season. Yolngu incorporated many elements of Macassan life in their ceremonial song cycles and ritual practice. Indeed some Yolngu rituals are a partial ethno-history of Macassan contact.[17] Yolngu exchanged trade goods with the Macassans – tobacco, cloth and rice – similar goods to ones they subsequently exchanged with Euro-Australians (Macknight 1976). Thus the incoming European-Australians, without realizing it, fitted into a pre-existing pattern of trade and exchange that involved an exchange of knowledge. While the case is hard to prove, it is generally thought that Yolngu learnt from the Macassans the techniques of manufacturing dugout canoes and the technology of hunting large sea animals with harpoons. Cloth that was obtained from the Macassans became a highly valued commodity within Yolngu society. Cloth entered the ritual sphere: it continues to be used in burial ceremonies to wrap or conceal the body; it is used to manufacture laplaps for ceremonial dancing; and torn into decorative strips it can be substituted for feather string and woven as adornment into the bodies of sacred dilly bags.

By the 1950s we begin to have strong evidence of the complexity of Yolngu motivations. Certainly people entered the production of art and craft for financial return, certainly they responded to consumer demand, producing the 'anyhow' paintings for Chaseling and carving wooden figures for the military during the war. But they were also using art to teach incomers and others from the wider society from which they came about their way of life and to assert the value of that way of life – Yolngu used art as a means of persuasion and a form of political action.

The detailed documentation of the paintings collected by Thomson, Mountford and the Berndts is indirect evidence of the use of art in teaching outsiders about the values of Yolngu society. Art was used as a means of knowledge transmission within Yolngu society and it also worked well with a larger audience. From the beginning of the mission, Yolngu invited mission staff to their ceremonial performances and early on began to create rituals of inclusion. Similar rituals had been held over the centuries to celebrate the arrival and departure of the Macassan fleet.

Three events that occurred between 1957 and 1963 illustrate the way Yolngu used art in interaction with outsiders. These events have been described in detail elsewhere and I will only refer to them briefly here. In 1957, people from Yirrkala and the neighbouring Yolngu settlement of Elcho Island (Galiwin'ku) created the Elcho Island Memorial outside the local church. The memorial comprised a series of elaborately carved and painted wooden sacred objects together with a number of bark paintings. These were set in concrete outside the church. The motivations for the Elcho Island Memorial were very complex (Figure 16).[18] It was aimed at the internal restructuring of Yolngu society and constituted an attempt to create regional unity, almost to create a more open society, by publicly exhibiting objects that were previously restricted to the men's ceremonial ground. The intention was not in any way to devalue the objects, but to place them in wider circulation as a way of adapting Yolngu society in the face of change instituted from the outside. But it was also directed to the

Figure 16   The Elcho Island Memorial. Photograph Ronald Berndt, 1958. Courtesy of The University of Western Australia Berndt Museum of Anthropology. Catalogue number: P1455.

outside. At the opening of the Memorial the leaders put forward a series of demands to the missionaries and government ranging from respect for their rights in land to the provision of better school and health services and a request not to interfere with the traditional system of marriage. The participants saw themselves as offering something of value to Europeans – opening up the ritual heart of their society – as a gesture of goodwill and an assertion of value (Berndt 1962: 39, 75).[19] Berndt labels the event, quite aptly, as an Adjustment Movement. It was almost a cargo cult in reverse.

The second event is the making of the Yirrkala Church Panels (Figure 17). Edgar Wells had previously been superintendent at Milingimbi, and while there had developed a great interest in Aboriginal art. On his arrival at Yirrkala he decided to build a new church. He discussed the design of the church with Yolngu elders. One of them, Narritjin Maymuru, suggested that the church should include panels of Yolngu paintings in addition to Christian iconography. It was then that the idea of the Church Panels was born. The Yirrkala Church Panels comprise two great sheets of Masonite designed to be placed floor to ceiling either side of the altar (see A. Wells 1971). The panels were divided on the basis of moiety: a Dhuwa moiety and a Yirritja-moiety panel. Each panel included the sacred paintings (*likanbuy miny'tji*) associated with the lands of the clans who had moved to live in Yirrkala.

Figure 17   The Yirrkala Church Panels. Photograph courtesy Ron Croxford.

The paintings were ordered in part on a geographic basis with the southern clans at the top and the northern clans toward the bottom.

From an artistic perspective the Church Panels can be seen as the culmination of a period of great creativity beginning with the collections made by Ronald Berndt and leading up to the Tuckson and Scougall visits. The crayon drawings collected by Berndt, in particular, engaged the Yolngu artists who took part. In the process of carrying out his ethnographic research Berndt collected a geographically structured mythological map of the Yolngu world. The artists of the main clans of the region each produced paintings of their clan territories. In addition Berndt worked with Yolngu to produce a regional map of place names covering the area from Blue Mud Bay in the south to Goulburn Island in the West.[20] In some cases individuals produced maps that comprised a series of adjacent clan estates represented through the iconography of their sacred art. The Berndt collection was an analogue of the restricted men's ceremonies in which clans perform in sequence the dances and songs connected with their estates. The precedent for composite paintings also existed in the hollow-log coffins that sometimes included a number of paintings from different clans.

Scougall and Tuckson likewise created the analogue of the ceremonial ground or, more likely, it was created for them by Yolngu as a condition of their work. Artists would come each day to work on their paintings, sometimes collaborating with one another. Scougall and Tuckson encouraged Yolngu to produce paintings on large barks, which allowed them to include a number of different episodes of the same myth on a single canvas. Again the innovation was not a profound one: it was an incremental step that produced impressive results. Yolngu had always combined myth segments in ceremonial performance; for example, each boy at a circumcision ceremony might be painted with a different segment of a particular myth or some segments would be danced and sung while others would be painted (Morphy 1984 and 1994a). Berndt's collection also contains a number of what I have referred to as episodic paintings. But the paintings collected by Tuckson and Scougall were exceptional in their overall scale. They certainly paved the way for the grand conception of the Church Panels.

Another important contextual factor behind the Church Panels was the growing Yolngu awareness that other people were showing an interest in their land. By the time of Scougall and Tuckson's visits, Yolngu had become aware of geologists from a French mining company prospecting on their land. While the church was being built their concern increased. Yolngu had not been consulted about any mineral prospecting and neither had the local missionaries (see E. Wells, 1982). Yolngu began to contact authorities in Darwin and protested that they did not want their land to be mined. The decision to place the paintings in the church was partly to demonstrate their long-term and spiritual relationship to the land. It was also a statement about the equivalence of Yolngu and Christian religion – a continuation of the dialogue that they had been having since the arrival of the missionaries at Yirrkala (Morphy 2005a). This dialogue was soon to move away from the local context to engage with national politicians.

JULY 1964                                          THREE SHILLINGS

# *Walkabout*

AUSTRALIA'S WAY OF LIFE MAGAZINE

*special*
*features*
*inside*

ANATOMY OF OUR THEATRE • TWO NEW COLUMNS

MACQUARIE STREET • LAKE-MOUTH OF THE MURRAY

PHOTOGRAPHIC PIONEERS • BUS-TOUR MARATHON

Figure 18   Dancing for the Elizabethan Theatre Trust. Cover
of *Walkabout Magazine*. Photograph Davydd Beal.

In 1962, the same year as the Church Panels were made, a group of Yolngu dancers joined Aboriginal performers from Western Arnhem Land on a tour of theatres in Sydney and Melbourne organized by the Elizabethan Theatre Trust (Figure 18). The performance naturally emphasized the exotic nature of the dancers and could be interpreted as positioning Yolngu in the past (see Magowan 2000). However, the party included leaders such as Narritjin Maymuru, the instigator of the Church Panels, and Roy Marika, both of whom were later to play a major role in the struggle for land rights. The visit provided Narritjin with the opportunity to hold, in Sydney, one of the first solo exhibitions of work by an

Aboriginal artist. The group visited the Art Gallery of New South Wales and saw Aboriginal artworks exhibited side by side with European ones. Years later Narritjin recalled the impact that this had on him as an acknowledgement of equality. The existence of the Art Gallery of New South Wales as an institution was to him a sign of the high value that art had in European society. From a Yolngu perspective the tour provided the opportunity to familiarize themselves with Australian society in the urban south of the country and make contacts that would subsequently prove useful. Their positive reception also made them aware of the power of cultural performance.

The following year the Church Panels began indirectly to achieve one of their objectives. Yolngu concerns about mining resulted in the visit to Yirrkala of two Labor members of Parliament, Kim Beazley senior and Gordon Bryant. After showing the visitors the panels in the church, Yolngu leaders let them know that they were sending a petition to Parliament to seek protection of their rights in land. Impressed by the panels, Beazley suggested that they send the petition in the form of a bark painting.

The Bark Petition is in fact not one but two documents, each with the same text (Figure 19). The petitions comprised two sheets of bark with paintings of totemic animals and geometric designs as a frieze around the edges, with a typewritten text fixed in the centre. The paintings represent respectively designs of the Dhuwa and Yirritja moieties. They have often been written about as if they were the product of a number of artists working together despite the fact that they appear to be the work of a single hand. And indeed both petitions were the work of Narritjin Maymuru.[21] The petitions requested that no lease should be granted to any mining company until the concerns of the people of Yirrkala had been properly investigated. It stated that Yolngu had used the land from time immemorial, that it sustained their life and that the land contained many sacred sites.

In the long term the Bark Petition had its effect; in the short term the Yolngu lost out. The petition did result in a Parliamentary Commission of Enquiry into the situation – however, the lease was granted to the mining company. In 1971 the Yolngu people took the Commonwealth Government and the mining company – Nabalco – to court in what has become known as the Gove Land Rights case. That too they lost. But in his judgment Justice Blackburn implied that the law was out of step with the reality of Indigenous rights in land, and in 1976 the Commonwealth Government passed the *Aboriginal Land Rights (Northern Territory) Act* which granted the possibility of title over unalienated Crown Land to Aboriginal people living in the Northern Territory. As a result, Yolngu became owners in Australian law of most of their traditional lands – it was too late for the clans immediately affected by the mining lease. The mine went ahead with devastating impact on their lives and on those of other Yolngu resident at Yirrkala.

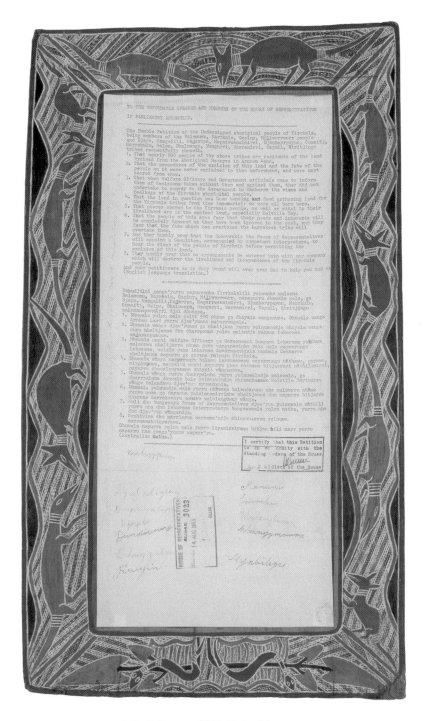

Figure 19   The Yirrkala Bark Petition, 1963. 59.1 x 34 cm.
Parliament House, Canberra. Reproduced by permission of
Buku-Larrnggay Mulka Art Centre.

# 4 DIALOGUE AND CHANGE

From the discussion so far we can identify a theme that recurs throughout the recorded history of Yolngu society – Yolngu create a dialogic relationship with the outsiders who enter their country. The dialogue can be seen in the initial interactions with missionaries and anthropologists in which the two parties exchange information about their way of life, social organisation and system of values. Yolngu create analogues between the events and structures of their own society and those of the encompassing society and attempt to make them fit together in particular contexts. They see analogies between their institutions and those of outsiders – between the ceremonial ground and the court of law, between the meeting of Yolngu elders at a *Ngärra* ceremony and the institution of Parliament, between paintings and written documents, and so on. And they have been remarkably successful in getting outsiders to engage with their propositions. For example, in the Australian Parliament in Canberra, the Bark Petition as an icon of Indigenous rights is displayed next to the Magna Carta.

These exchanges are always oriented toward gaining an understanding of other people's points of view. One of the outcomes of this dialogue has been in the area of education, where Yolngu have developed a model of what they refer to as 'two-way education' (see Marika-Mununggiritj, 1999). This model was developed in the period following the implementation of a government policy of self-management in the 1970s. It was developed by Yolngu and non-Yolngu teachers at Yirrkala School as an elaboration of bilingual education. Two-way education basically views Yolngu and mainstream Australian educational systems, and the bodies of knowledge associated with them, as being relatively autonomous and complementary. It is necessary to learn both ways and find ways in which the two can be combined to advantage.

Yolngu consider that this orientation toward dialogue and knowledge exchange as something that has always been part of their relationship with outsiders. Their view is that they established relationships of exchange and mutual recognition with the Macassan visitors and that they invited the first missionaries into their land on their own terms as means of creating peace. The speed with which they engaged with the first missionaries and anthropologists and the trajectory that has developed from that moment suggests that this may have been the case. On the other hand there is also evidence for much tenser and aggressive interaction with outsiders. Certainly today the idea of creating a dialogue for mutual engagement is explicit in Yolngu dealings with outsiders. And they attempt to create a dialogue through the use of their own cultural forms and by trying to engage outsiders in Yolngu metaphors that concern communication and understanding.

In October 2005 I attended a meeting at Yilpara called to discuss regional economic development. Yilpara is the largest of the region's homelands with a stable population of some 160 people. The meeting comprised a group of people representing the southern Yolngu clans, who refer to themselves collectively as Djalkiripuyngu,[1] and people representing different departments of the Federal and Territory governments. The meeting was seen to be an important one since government was emphasizing the need for Yolngu to develop a self-sustaining regional economy.

Remote Yolngu settlements such as Yilpara were being threatened by a government policy which saw them as unsustainable. The Federal Government's aim was to reduce welfare dependency and improve the cost-effectiveness of service provision. Yolngu, too, wished to reduce their dependence on government but they were determined not to move away from their own lands. They are living on their own estates to which they have strong emotional and religious ties and for which they feel a great sense of responsibility. But they are also there because of the negative impact the mining town of Nhulunbuy has had on the health and well-being of the population. People living at the homelands believe that they are healthier, and that their young people have a greater sense of responsibility and lead more disciplined lives; the community is drug- and alcohol-free, and hunting and gathering provides a major food resource – in short they believe that there is a much better future for people living at a settlement such as Yilpara. They also have evidence that the area has considerable economic potential in areas that fit in with their way of life and skills. Yilpara is one of the major art and craft producing communities, situated in an area of major marine resources, in a rich and largely unspoilt natural environment with considerable tourist potential.

The European visitors were representatives of government departments concerned with tourism, economic development, education and infrastructure, as well as representatives of funding bodies. As is now an established convention, the visitors were greeted with a welcoming ceremony (Figure 20). They were invited to sit down under the shade of a traditional timber-framed open shelter, roofed with palm leaves. The Yolngu singers gathered outside the entrance of the shelter. Led by Djambawa Marawili and accompanied by a *yidaki* they sang powerfully. The group moved forward in unison, the sound swelling as they moved into the shelter. The sound built up into a crescendo with the rippling of clapsticks. The singing was punctuated by an aggressive almost roaring intervention from two of the singers with mouths opened wide and tongues flickering. Finally a set of power names was intoned.

Ngulpurr Marawili, who was chairing the meeting and was the designated official translator, began the proceedings by explaining why that particular song was performed.[2] The song was from the river mouth at Baraltja one of the nearby *djalkiri* places.[3] We will encounter paintings of Baraltja in the next chapter (see Figure 30 but see also Figure 9). Baraltja is the place of Mundukul, the great ancestral snake of the Yirritja moiety. Mundukul is associated with the seasonal cycle and the movement of water. Yolngu country is marked by dramatic

Figure 20  Burut'tji welcomes the visitors. Djambawa Marrawili leads
the group of singers. Photograph Howard Morphy.

seasonal variation. During the wet season from November or December to March or April
the country is inundated. The rivers flow strongly, overflowing their banks, spreading out
into the wetlands, creating great inland lakes and finally pouring out of the river mouths and
creating great plumes of fresh water far out into the bays. With the onset of the dry season
the process is reversed. The rivers dry up and the freshwater retreats – it retreats so far that,
deep inland, salt begins to flavour the fresh water. Mundukul moves with the flowing water.
In the coastal wetlands as the rains begin, Mundukul tastes the waters. He tastes the salt
water and, taking it deep into his throat, he spits it high into the air. His tongue flickers and
he creates lightning. Standing up high at Baraltja, spitting water across country and sending
lighting into the sky, Mundukul communicates with other Yirritja moiety snakes associated
with other river systems across north-east Arnhem Land. Mundukul's connection to places
where fresh and salt water meet is significant. The coming together of fresh and salt water

is thought to be highly generative. It is an important metaphor of connection, between people, places and seasons – it is the inland meeting the sea, it represents intermarrying clans, it marks the passage of the seasons. Places where salt water and fresh water mix are seen to be spiritually powerful and the waters when they mix are the Yolngu 'fountain head of knowledge' (see Morphy and Morphy, 2006).

Ngulpurr spoke briefly to the assembled company, most of whom did not have this background knowledge, but the message he conveyed was clear. He said that the message of the song was an important one and that the snake at Baraltja was a being who communicated to different groups of people – exchanging ideas with other groups. He said that the snake in tasting the waters – in swallowing the water and spitting it out – was taking in the knowledge of other groups and then passing it on for them to swallow in turn. He said that they had come together like the snakes to swallow each other's knowledge so that they would understand one another better and be able to work together.

## THE DYNAMICS OF CHANGE IN YOLNGU ART

The production of art for sale required certain cultural adjustments, one of which being the need to respond to an external market, and the other the internal consequences of producing art for new contexts of use and display.

There is no requirement to regard the first as problematic. The market is at times overly concerned with change in Indigenous art, yet at the same time almost requires it. Western art markets are suspicious of intervention and market response, since the prevailing ideology emphasizes the free expression and the individual genius of the artist. Indeed, there are many pressures that can adversely affect the nature of Indigenous art production, but those include the imposition of conservatism and a rejection of change and innovation at least as much as by encouragement of innovation. I am not concerned here to make judgements about changes that have occurred in Yolngu art but simply to document them. But I do emphasize two facts. Yolngu art has always been diverse, dynamic and changing, despite an ideology of conservatism, and Yolngu have on the whole been the main agents of change. There are as many examples of resistance to change in the history of Yolngu art as there are of innovations.

Yolngu in many cases had to find solutions to changes contingent on the opening up of their art to new contexts. These solutions can be framed as problematic in a market obsessed with a particular concept of authenticity.[4] I will address only two issues here: the creation of permanent artworks in a society that, with some exceptions, had produced works of short duration; and the opening out of previously restricted works to women. But first I will provide a brief reflection on the changes that have occurred in Yolngu art.

### INNOVATIONS IN YOLNGU ART

I have written elsewhere about changes in Yolngu art since 'mission times' and different characteristics of paintings produced at different periods of time (Morphy 1991). Writing about change in Yolngu art is very like writing about change in other bodies of art. Yolngu art is very diverse; there are differences across the Yolngu-speaking region and great varia tions between artists. Yolngu art is a system of practice in which it is possible to produce new works all the time in different media and for different purposes. Yolngu ideology is that change is constrained by the ancestral nature of the art – by the fact that the patterns that were created in the past influence the form of art in the present and must influence its form in the future. Yolngu artistic practice creates a balance between possibility and constraint. I will argue in a later chapter that Yolngu conservatism – if that means adherence to a particular tradition – is not that different from the Western perspective of seeing art having a place in a history of forms. Innovation can be understood as part of the trajectory of formal practice in Yolngu art – stemming from Yolngu art as a particular way of seeing, understanding and acting in the world. And that history of acting in the world has always been responsive to new contexts and new possibilities. Innovation is influenced by how art, as a means of acting in the world, is used.

I will only give a few illustrative examples of changes here, picking up some that connect to the history that I have outlined so far. Change in art concerns changes in techniques and media of production, stylistic changes and changes in subject matter and content. Over time there will be complex interrelationship between the various factors but also degrees of relative autonomy. Change over a period of 70 years is inevitably determined by multiple factors and is complex. It is a response to both internal and external pressures.

In the technical sphere, the art of bark painting has changed little since Thomson's time. The main changes that have occurred can be seen as substitutions. Sheets of bark are, as they always have been, cut and pulled away from the trunk of stringy bark trees (Although the implements have changed, the technique of removal has not.) The fibrous outer surface is removed and the bark is flattened by heating it over a fire. The inner surface is then sanded down ready for the first covering with red ochre, which acts as a primer. The four pigments that are used are the same as in Thomson's time, red and yellow ochre, manganese for black and white pipe clay. The main difference is in the fixative used. Since the 1960s commercial wood glue has been substituted for local fixatives such as orchid juices and seagull eggs. The brush used for the cross-hatching remains the *marrwat*, a brush made of long strands of human hair that is loaded with pigment and then drawn in a fluid motion across the surface of the bark. Commercial brushes are used to cover broad areas and to delineate the underlying geometric and figurative forms of the painting. For many years the barks were held flat by two split sticks bound at either end of the bark (an innovation that coincided with the production of bark paintings for sale). The sticks were an invention of the 1950s. Since 2000, these have been replaced in many cases by a metal frame that is fitted to the back of the bark at the art centre once the painting is completed.

Most of the changes that have occurred in the technical domain, although I have labelled them substitutions, have more or less subtle consequences, since technique is only relatively autonomous of other aspects of art production. The replacement of orchid juices by wood glue, depending on the quantity used, is the most dramatic. The use of glue tends to make the surface of the bark shinier and the pigment appear harder. The changed visual effect is in synergy with Yolngu aesthetics. The effect is to enhance the brilliance of the surface of the painting – to make it shine (see chapter 5 and Morphy 1992).[5] The replacement of the sticks at either end of the bark with a frame discreetly placed at the back has also encouraged a change in the form of the paintings. In the past it was necessary to paint a frame around the edge of the bark to define the boundaries of the painting, since nothing could be painted under the place where the sticks crossed at top and bottom. Artists now often paint to the edge of the bark, creating a distinctive boundary or absence of boundary to the work. The art market has responded positively to this innovation and consequently the majority of Yolngu fine artworks are presently produced without borders.

Another area of change has been in the scale of paintings produced. Until the 1960s the majority of bark paintings were small-scale – seldom more than a metre in height and 60 centimetres across, and usually smaller. Large barks were added to the repertoire at the time of Tuckson and Scougall's visit (see Figure 15). These had been produced in the past and indeed one of the largest ever is in the Donald Thomson collection, produced collaboratively by Wonggu Mununggurr and his sons in 1943. Thus the potential for large-scale works existed and, encouraged by Tuckson and Scougall's interest, the dimension of bark paintings doubled for the time of their visit. These larger barks were magnificent works of art and they also allowed the artists to represent a series of episodes of the same myth on a single bark. It is easy to see how the interaction of Yolngu with the market produced the larger barks. Europeans were interested in the story behind the painting – in seeing the myth as a narrative rather than as a series of separate episodes. Art galleries also demand works of different scales and the idea of works on a grander scale almost certainly appealed to Tuckson.

After Tuckson and Scougall, the scale of barks became reduced again. An occasional large bark was produced, by Munggurrawuy Yunupingu, Narritjin Maymuru, Mawalan and Mathaman Marika, and Mithinari Gurruwiwi, among others, but on the whole they were scaled back down in size. There were both technical and market reasons for this. Technically it is much harder to obtain large sheets of bark than smaller ones. While large sheets of a quality suitable for roofing a bark hut can easily be obtained, they are likely to split in places and thus be unsuitable for painting. However market factors were significant. Yirrkala and other Arnhem Land communities remained remote from the rest of Australia until the 1970s. There was only a small local market for art and most artworks had to be shipped to the southern States. The logistics of packing and shipping large bark paintings at the time would have been considerable. Moreover, the larger barks would have been more expensive and much harder to sell in the conditions of the time. The institutional market – though growing – was relatively small, and private collectors preferred the smaller barks.

By the 1980s circumstances changed, making it possible once again to produce large barks. The production of large barks was in part stimulated by two commissions, one from the National Gallery of Victoria and the other from the American collector John W. Kluge. The art centre facilitated the collecting of large barks and the use of vehicles made it much easier to collect barks of maximum length from the trunks of large straight stringybarks. In the past the high part of the tree had to be reached by a tree-branch ladder placed precariously against the bark. Today a four wheel drive vehicle can be driven beside the tree. The roof can be used initially as a ladder and then as the means of transporting large sheets back to the settlement for painting. The improvement of freight services from northern Australia also means that it is as easy to transport large bark paintings securely as it is bundles of smaller ones. The production of large bark paintings fits in with the desire of the late twentieth- and early twenty-first-century market demand for large artworks to occupy the spaces on gallery walls. The large barks enable the artists to compete with artists working on large canvases.[6]

While there have been some changes in the technique and scale of Yirrkala bark paintings, those changes have been initiated within the community, often against a background of considered resistance. Doug Tuffin told me that Narritjin Maymuru refused to participate in the initial large-bark project since he felt that the scale of the paintings was out of proportion to that of the human body – which, he argued, was the primary surface for sacred clan paintings. His resistance did not last long and he subsequently produced many large barks. However, conscious resistance is one of the reasons why artists from Yirrkala continue to use traditional materials. With the success of the acrylic movement in Central Australia and elsewhere, Yolngu artists have at times been under pressure to paint in acrylics on canvas or ochres on art paper. Indeed, the enthusiasm with which Yolngu artists engaged with Ron Berndt's 'experiment' with crayons on butcher's paper suggests that they might have welcomed the new medium, especially during seasons when the bark cannot be prised off the trees. The artist's council that governs Buku Larrnggay Mulka art centre, however, has insisted that works sold though the art centre should be produced using traditional techniques and local materials. On the other hand, an avenue for innovation has been opened up in another area of the art centre's activity, the print workshop.

Yirrkala artists have been at the forefront of Indigenous involvement in printmaking. Narritjin Maymuru was the first senior artist to work in the medium when, as a Creative Arts Fellow at the Australian National University in 1978, he worked with the teacher and artist Jorg Schmeisser on a number of etchings. While Narritjin himself did not follow up the practice, many Yirrkala artists have become successful printmakers. Buku Larrnggay Mulka has a permanent print workshop and gallery. And the rules for the print workshop are different from those of the main art centre, allowing for a full range of colour choices and encouraging innovation in form and experimentation in the techniques employed.

In turning to style and content, I will focus on the relationship between the figurative and geometric components of Yolngu art. It would be possible to produce an analysis which saw the history of the art made for the market as a dialectic between figurative and geometric forms. In Chaseling's time, Yolngu responded to his request for paintings by producing a large series of paintings with a high figurative content, whereas recently, in response to the art market's appreciation of more abstract forms, Yolngu art made for sale has a significantly reduced figurative content. However, such a perspective fails to take account of two important factors – the relative autonomy of the internal and external contexts for the production of art for consumption, and the fact that the geometric and figurative components of Yolngu art are better seen not as two separate 'styles' but as components of a single artistic system, at the heart of which lies the relationship between representation and abstraction. By approaching the changing forms of Yolngu art produced for sale from these perspectives, we can see how artists continue to produce new artworks over time for use in both internal and external contexts.

Yolngu art has responded to the market and to suggestions and pressures from the market in different ways at different times. We have seen how Chaseling's request for 'anyhow' paintings produced an early series of innovative paintings. Those paintings came out of a Yolngu tradition of informal art – the art of the bark hut – and built on the figurative component of the sacred art. Paintings in that genre continue to be produced into the present. Until the 1970s, paintings with a high figurative content dominated the market for Aboriginal art. These were easier to sell because the market wanted bark paintings that were easily interpreted and that represented Indigenous subjects – public ceremonies, myths of transformation and illustrations of ceremonial activity. However, Yolngu continued to produce sacred clan paintings for sale, usually with figurative representation but sometimes as apparently purely abstract forms. And in ceremonial contexts the diversity of the art was as it had always been. In many respects the internal contexts provide a reservoir of potential for the commercial art.

The paintings of Chaseling's collections belong to a particular time. Some paintings are produced today that are the equivalent of 'anyhow' paintings, in that they illustrate secular themes not connected to a clan's sacred art, but stylistically such paintings are quite different from those of Chaseling's time. For example, the forms of the figurative representations have changed, and the background is now generally infilled with cross-hatching. However, it is still possible to see paintings produced today that are formally very similar to those collected by Donald Thomson 70 years ago (compare Figures 7 and 9 for example). Unsurprisingly these are geometric paintings comprising largely of clan designs – paintings that the European art market today would classify as abstract. Inevitably I need to qualify what I mean by 'formally very similar'. The basic pattern and scale of the artwork is similar and from a Yolngu perspective it is recognizable as belonging to a particular clan – Rirratjingu, Manggalili, Maḏarrpa, and so on.

However, qualitative aspects of particular images may differ according to the material used and the technical accomplishment and aesthetic sense of the individual artist. Again this is something that applies in the case of abstract art in general. The particular value of the work is going to depend on its historical position and on the individuality of its expression.

The form of a Yolngu clan design can be reproduced using different techniques, which create different effects. The geometric design associated with fire comprises a basic diamond that varies slightly from clan to clan. That design will appear very different according to whether it is painted on a body, engraved into a wooden clapstick or sewn with string on the surface of a basket. When painted the effect will vary depending on whether it is outlined in white, or yellow, or red on a person's body, whether or not it is infilled with cross-hatching and the particular combination of ochres that are used. The quality it conveys will differ according to the nature of the pigment, the fineness of the cross-hatching and the sense of proportion. Control and awareness of these factors are part of Yolngu artistic practice and this sensibility creates continuities in the trajectory of Yolngu art. Thus geometric clan designs have been produced since European colonization, and probably for centuries before that, but each time they are reproduced there is the possibility of uniqueness.

The Rirratjingu clan design associated with Yalangbara references the creative acts of the Djan'kawu sisters, two female creative ancestral beings. It has been reproduced many times as the background pattern for paintings from that estate. In 1946 Ronald Berndt collected a number of paintings in which this was the dominant design, many of them by Mawalan Marika (see Figure 13). Sixty years later his daughter Banduk Marika won the bark-painting prize at the National Aboriginal and Torres Straits Islander Arts Award with a painting on a similar theme. A year later Banduk produced a screen print of the same design (Figure 21). The pattern in each case is structurally similar but the effect varies.

However, although the form of the geometric art appears to be stable over a considerable period of time, it is in reality the springboard for creativity and diversity in Yolngu art. First, as we have seen, the geometric art itself has the potential to vary greatly in its impact and in a sense – like all abstract art – it is responsive to the subtleties of artistic practice and to the parameters of possible variation.[7] The geometric art also has a historical position both in its engagement with external audiences and internally. The art world's response to Yolngu geometric art varies according to its own fashions and perceptions and presuppositions. At times abstract geometric Indigenous Australian paintings from Arnhem Land have been by far the hardest to sell. Until the 1970s, as noted above, the broad market for Indigenous Australian art responded better to the figurative component in the art than to the geometric. This is partly because abstraction in Yolngu art needs to be appreciated in its own terms before it is related to European abstract art. Otherwise there is a danger of misinterpretation, of seeing Yolngu abstraction as derivative or decorative. It gains its power once it is seen in its own historical position. Fortunately, geometric art has continued to be integral to Yolngu artistic practice internally while the dialogue with the outside world has developed in stages.

There is a recursive element in Yolngu art. It includes the narratives that are associated with particular places, the themes of Yolngu art and society, and certain designs that are specific to particular clans and ancestral beings. The ancestral template that underlies sets of paintings from a particular place is ever-present as a sign of the identity and creativity

Figure 21    *The Djan'kawu sisters at Yalangbara.*
Artist Bandak Marika. Copyright the artist.
Photograph Will Stubbs. Reproduced with
the permission of Buku-Larrnggay Mulka Art
Centre, Yirrkala.

of the ancestral being in that place. (For a detailed discussion of the idea of template see Morphy 1991.) At the most elementary level the geometric art operates as a code for the figurative art – it condenses the ancestral creation stories and their interrelationships into a core mnemonic that can generate a series of alternative images. The diamond clan design discussed earlier, for example, is associated with the Maḏarrpa clan's story of the origin of fire, and any element of that origin story can be represented in a Maḏarrpa painting through figurative representations – the crocodile on its nest or bringing fire into the sea, the dugong hunters' boat being immolated in the fire, and so on. This relationship between the figurative and the geometric elements has been the engine for creativity in Yolngu art.

However, the relationship between the figurative and geometric also operates at a conceptual level. Contemporary Yolngu art exploits the boundaries between figuration and abstraction as a means of conveying the metaphysical underpinnings of the artists' world-view. Yolngu view the world in terms of its ancestral (*wangarr*) creation and ancestral precedence. A central distinction is made between 'inside' and 'outside' forms and knowledge, between surface appearance and an underlying ancestral reality. The way in which this metaphysic is played out in Yolngu art is explored in some detail in the next Chapter.

## ADJUSTING ART – REMODELLING SOCIETY

The engagement with the outside world has had many consequences on the position art occupies in Yolngu society. Internally there are considerable continuities with the past in the role of art, but it has also provided a medium for the transformation as well of the Yolngu way of life. We have seen how art has been deployed in new contexts, not simply the art gallery and the museum but in the ritual and ceremonial spaces that are created through interactions between Yolngu and Australian society – including graduation ceremonies, court cases, and welcoming ceremonies for dignitaries. Yolngu do not neatly separate the functional purposes of rituals from the performative – art from political action. Their presence at the opening of art exhibitions is not simply to entertain or add dignity to the occasion, but a chance to make that arena their own. Yolngu use ceremonial performance as a means of setting the agenda or conveying an important message. In his artist's statement for an exhibition of his works as part of the 2006 Sydney Biennale, Djambawa Marawili was quoted as saying he wanted the public to realize that these works were 'not just pretty things' (see Figures 29, 30, 31). The ceremonial performance that Yolngu used to open the exhibition was connected to Mungurru the great Yirritja-moiety currents that flow into the north of Blue Mud Bay and to *Bäru* the crocodile ancestor. The performance was deliberately chosen to emphasize Yolngu concerns about their rights in the intertidal zone. Djambawa was conscious that the warehouse in which his works were exhibited jutted out into Sydney harbour, and he could not help making a passing reference to the fate of the Indigenous people who had once occupied the harbour's shore.

The contemporary artworld often demands themed exhibitions from Indigenous and non-Indigenous artists – it is one of the contradictions of modernism's separation of form from content that titles are still a requirement. Aboriginal artworks are often conceived of with multiple purposes in mind. The *Aboriginal Memorial* in the National Gallery of Australia is an excellent example; another is the Saltwater paintings. One of the major projects developed by Buku-Larrnggay Mulka Art Centre was the Saltwater Collection. This was acquired by the National Maritime Museum, after being exhibited around Australia. The collection was originally conceived of as a way of making a statement about Yolngu rights in sea – a form of political action in continuity with the bark petition (Buku-Larrngay Mulka 1999). Djambawa initiated the project after Yolngu found that a sacred site associated with the Crocodile Ancestor *Bäru* had been defiled by barramundi fishermen who had left behind a severed crocodile's head. The collection comprises a set of large bark paintings that represent clan ownership of the sea along the eastern Arnhem Land coast.

The expansion of Yolngu art outward through its use in political action and engagement with the outside world has been associated with an opening up of Yolngu art within the society itself. At the time of Thomson's and Warner's research, clan paintings of the kind that Banduk produced for the Aboriginal Arts Award were mainly the province of men. Such paintings would have been revealed to older women, were certainly painted on the dead bodies of clanswomen as well as men, but as a rule they were painted exclusively by men in semi-restricted contexts, and when they moved into public arenas were masked by smudging. Up until the time of the Tuckson and Scougall expeditions, painters producing works for museums would often create a separate ceremonial space away from women and children where they could produce paintings without them being seen. The opening up of paintings occurred gradually and in harmony with the expansion of the art market. It soon became apparent that it was not possible to open up Yolngu art to the outside world and keep it closed internally. Moreover, women gradually became involved in the painting business. It began in the 1960s with the daughters of senior artists helping their fathers with the cross-hatching of bark paintings. Banduk's sister Dhuwarrwarr was among the first, taught by her father Mawalan. Eventually those women began to produce the entire paintings themselves. And by 1973 women would occasionally produce paintings in ritual contexts.

I have argued elsewhere that the process was a considered one and that many other factors were operating to change aspects of the relationships between men and women. The Elcho Island Adjustment Movement provides another example where Yolngu took action to – in Ken Maddock's phrase – remodel their society. In that case, objects that had previously been restricted were brought out into the open. The manufacture of art for sale became a context in which Yolngu could restructure their society in a crucial arena or domain of interaction with the outside world. The manufacture of art for sale began to take on functions that had previously been carried out in other institutional contexts. Changes in the context of art were indeed required as the material culture and economy of Yolngu society changed. Art that had been dispersed throughout the material world in painted and decorated objects became concentrated in paintings. When people spent longer periods based at Yirrkala mission away from their country, paintings – together with ritual performance and song cycles – became both the means by which they maintained contact with their country and one of the main ways in which knowledge of the country was maintained. When they returned to their country with the outstation movement of the 1970s, they knew the country partly though art. Today painting for sale has become one of the main contexts for knowledge transmission.

Yolngu society has also undergone a major economic transformation, moving away from a hunter-gather economy into a mixed economy in which hunting and gathering continues to provide a significant component of the diet but is only one of a range of productive activities in which people engage. As hunters and gatherers, women's labour was at a premium, since many of the more time-consuming tasks of food gathering and craft production were undertaken by them. While hunting and fishing has continued undiminished, there have been substitutions in many areas of women's production: gathered foods have been largely replaced by introduced foods, and material-culture objects replaced by purchased items.

Fibre work continues as a craft activity for sale and for the manufacture of ritual objects, but a string carrying bag is more likely to be used for carrying things by a purchaser in Sydney than by a Yolngu. Women's participation in artwork thus enables them to take part in a major area of contemporary economic activity and one that is highly valued as a cultural activity.

Painting for sale has become one of the main contexts for value creation in Yolngu art – internally as well as externally. The process of training remains highly disciplined; the rules of practice that the younger artists have to learn are treated as seriously as ever. Younger clan members still spend many years as apprentices helping their fathers, mothers or brothers to produce paintings by infilling the designs with cross-hatching under the meticulous observation of their teachers. Successful artists are rewarded with high prices for their artworks, and dedicated apprentices share those rewards by accompanying them to the opening of exhibitions and taking part in Yolngu-directed opening performances.

Today's Yolngu artists have grown up in a community in which becoming an artist is an objective in both of the worlds in which they live. The skills that are recognized by the fine art world are also recognized within the community. While not all Yolngu ceremonial or community leaders are artists, those leaders who *are* artists are also the people who are called upon to paint in ritual contexts and to prepare the objects used in ceremonies. And as I have shown elsewhere, the aesthetics of ritual performance is integral to its success both as spectacle and in creating a sense of spiritual uplift (Morphy 1994a).

## CONCLUSION

Ceremonial performance, art production and the art industry have become the focal points of Yolngu cultural life. Internally, ceremonial activity, especially funerals, takes as much – if not more – time as it did in the past. This is in part because the logistics of provisioning large numbers of people has become easier in the post-hunter-gatherer economy, and partly because they have *had* to devote more time to it. The mining town of Nhulunbuy has had a catastrophic impact on the health of Yolngu people living nearby and has greatly increased the death rate, in particular among young people. Funerals have become a focal point of Yolngu life and there has been an intensification of ceremonial activity around them. Funerals have expanded and incorporated aspects of other rituals.

Externally, art has become a means to engage culturally with the world outside. It is an arena in which they express their values, to argue for their cause. Bridging the internal and external worlds is the economic significance of art and craft production. With hunting and gathering, art has for long been the main component of the productive economy of the homeland communities where most art is made. Internally, the economy remains re-distributive. The returns to a leading artist are rapidly dispersed among the members of his or her kin group. Art is an important factor in the economic survival of those communities, hence the role of art as a central component of an economy is more significant in contemp-orary Yolngu society than in the mainstream.

Art has a central role in community life. It is a focal point of cultural intensity in contemporary Yolngu life; it is also the arena in which change and transformation are likely to occur. The increased role of women in art production is one sign of that, having consequences on the authority they have in public affairs. There is an emphasis on art as a means of communicating Yolngu values and knowledge – both internally through teaching the younger generations through painting and externally through exhibitions and as a medium for disseminating Yolngu knowledge. Art is seen by non-Yolngu as something desirable. As well as being aesthetically pleasing, Yolngu art is today seen by many in the world outside as a way of learning about Yolngu society, a means of appreciating their knowledge of the environment, as an access to a more spiritual perspective on the relations between people and land. One consequence is that many ideas for developing a future regional economy build on Yolngu art or add value to it – educational and environmental tourism, or ranger programmes adapted to maintaining a cultural landscape. As well as being a focal point of Yolngu identity in the outside world, art is also seen as a potential area for diversification, for separating out some of those multiple factors that determine the present production and impact of Yolngu art – the skills, the knowledge, the technical system, the history of engagement with outsiders – to create new forms of articulation with the non-Yolngu world.

# SECTION II

# ENGAGING WITH ART HISTORY

The previous three chapters constitute a movement toward the present day following the Yolngu people's encounter with the Western world, and through that their engagement with wider worlds of art. They had not previously been entirely isolated from the diversity of other people's art, encountering differences as they crossed boundaries within Australia and interacted with visitors from eastern Indonesia. My analysis suggests that from the Yolngu perspective the process of moving their art into more global contexts has been remarkably smooth. On the whole it has happened without their becoming directly engaged with Western art discourse about the kind of objects they produce. Yolngu artists have not agonized over whether they produce contemporary fine art or primitive art, although as soon as they became aware of the connotations of the word 'primitive' they rejected it as having nothing to do with their way of life. They have accepted the equivalence of their art to that of other Australians, and unproblematically accepted museums and art galleries as venues for housing their art.

However, while the movement of their art into global arenas was largely directed by their own motivations – using it to assert the value of their way of life, seizing economic opportunities, creating opportunities to widen their engagement with and knowledge of the world outside – this movement was part of a process of change that made them players in new arenas, actors in new frames. Even if they were unaware of it, the work that they produced created definitional problems and provided a challenge to established institutional categories – and as part of this process their work became subject to analysis by art historians, anthropologists and others. Indeed, the history as I have presented it so far is not a simple descriptive account, if ever such a thing were possible, but an analysis influenced by my disciplinary background. Increasingly Yolngu themselves will be involved in that discourse, which will in turn influence the ways in which they see their art.

In the next set of chapters I will be analysing Yolngu art explicitly from the perspective of certain general questions in the comparative analysis of art. In Chapter 5, I focus on the issue of representation and vision, analysing how Yolngu represent, express and conceive the land and seascape of coastal Arnhem Land. In doing so I approach their art through a problematic that can be applied to many other artistic systems, periods or styles. Chapter 6 presents the response of two Yolngu artists to the art of another culture, that of the Abelam of Papua New Guinea, and their interpretation of it; the chapter thereby challenges the presuppositions that non-Western artists are locked in their own traditions and are somehow unable to adopt an analytic perspective on cultural forms other than their own. It is one of surprisingly few analyses of this type to have been attempted. The chapter also enables me to look at another key concept in the analysis of art style from a cross-cultural perspective. Finally in this section, chapter 7 examines Yolngu discourse about art from a comparative perspective, focusing on how Yolngu conceive of the relationships between different paintings over time. The chapter reveals ontological differences between Yolngu and Western concepts of art, in particular with reference to the role of individual creativity and the production of difference. However, I also argue that a more detailed examination problematizes the degree of difference and reveals synergies between the two viewpoints, enabling a better understanding of how Yolngu art can operate in both internal and external frames.

# 5 VISUALITY AND REPRESENTATION IN YOLNGU ART

European art history has taken the relationship between painting and vision as one of its central questions.[1] The origins of this tradition can be traced back at least to classical times where one criterion of excellence in painting or sculpture was seen to be in the closeness with which it replicated the actual appearance of things. The creation of the illusion of reality has long been a theme of European art and some have argued that art history was for too long concerned with the ways in which that illusion was created. The late Ernst Gombrich's (1958) brilliant analysis of European illusionist systems of representation, referred to by Bryson (1986) as perspectivalism, has strongly influenced the way in which the canon of European art, from Mediaeval times to the Impressionists, has been interpreted. Bryson has argued that Gombricht sees artists almost as Popperian scientists, developing through a process of trial and error the means to most accurately replicate the world as seen through the human eye.[2] Certainly developments in painting have sometimes been directly influenced by the science of vision and by the technology of recording visual images: the use of the camera obscura in the working practice of artists such as Vermeer is a case in point (see for example Steadman 2001).

Reading the history of art through Gombrich's perspectivalist eye it might be thought that modernism – which can be seen to challenge the presuppositions lying behind illusionistic representation – would have been less concerned with the nature of vision, but thinking thus would be to confuse seeing with what was seen. Richard Brettell, summarizing the viewpoint of the Canadian modernist Emily Carr, writes that

> Art is not so much a mode of representation as it is a mode of seeing, and that in making important representations artists present the viewer not simply with an internally consistent image, but with an entire view of the world... This idea is of course not unique to modernism, but it is so powerful a part of modernist theory that it deserves to be canonized as one of the two principal ways of thinking about art that has prompted modernism. It was thought by many artists that the perspectivalist trajectory had so affected the ways in which people saw the world that there was a need to break away from that heritage of European painting in order to see the world anew. The science of vision had become contaminated by the very methods used to analyse it and the artist's role was to look at the world again through less educated eyes. Picasso reported that he could draw like Raphael when he was twelve, and needed to unlearn that facile skill in order to draw like a child; Mondrian saw the need to erase the history of art through a

supreme effort of mind, and Kandinsky and Klee used the drawings of children to escape
conventional ways of seeing. (Brettell 1999: 83)

The interest in 'primitive' art has often been interpreted as part of this process of breaking
away from European vision and returning to what were considered to be less culturally
determined roots.

These presuppositions of modernism have of course long been challenged. The Impressionists, for example, were just as strongly motivated by a desire to interrogate vision
and free themselves from the past as were those who followed them. Indeed it has been
argued that many of the directions taken by modernism were prefigured in the artworks or
theoretical discourse of the Impressionists. And in the case of primitive art the assumptions
that it was primeval, almost acultural in nature, has long been recognized as a projection of
European assumptions rather than a reflection of that art in terms of its own history, or of an
understanding of the vision that it reflects. On the other hand it seems reasonable to explore
cross-culturally the generally accepted European idea that there is a relationship between
painting and vision. Just because African or Oceanic motifs were borrowed without first
being researched in their cultural context does not mean that such research will not be
highly productive.

The focus of this chapter is on Yolngu art. I will discuss two broad questions: the relationship between how the Yolngu see the world and how they represent it, and the way in
which Yolngu use visual effects to convey meanings and evoke feelings. Here I am separating
out two of the key ways in which the science of vision has entered the history of European
art: one a concern with the representation of the world as it is seen, and the other the more
general concern of the creation of visual images that have an effect on the viewer. At various
times in the history of and discourse over European art, the first concern has been absorbed
into the other. The two are really quite distinct enterprises, which were sometimes united
by an intention or an objective: to create images that reflected 'reality'. The realization that
such a goal was in itself a chimera was one of the factors that motivated modernism's search
for new ways of seeing that were simultaneously new ways of conveying ideas through the
creation of visual forms. And here Yolngu art and modernism converge, although this is not
at first apparent because of surface differences. For Yolngu, rather than using techniques of
visual representation to imitate the reality of the seen, are more concerned with conveying
the reality of the unseen, the underlying forces in the landscape. In this respect, then, Yolngu
art might also be deemed more conceptual than perceptual.

Aboriginal people in Arnhem Land today cannot be seen as representatives of earlier
stages of human society, nor can they be seen as separate from the world of images in which
other Australians partake. Yolngu artists watch television, read magazines and are exposed
to many different representational systems. They visit art galleries, and participation in the
annual pan-Australian Aboriginal and Torres Strait Islander art award is in itself sufficient to
expose them to a huge range of contemporary Australian art. Yet at the same time Yolngu

have continued to practice forms of art that are quite distinct from those of other Australians and indeed see such works as integral to their cultural identity.

Yolngu develop an acuity of vision that seems remarkable to an outsider. My knowledge of this is anecdotal. My experience of hunting with Yolngu is being told to lie flat and not move as people pursue game animals that I never see until after they are shot. I have conducted no scientific tests, though on many occasions people have tested me by pointing out some feature in the distance and then being incredulous that I am unable to identify it. In recent years to save face I have taken to lying. It may be that my vision is particularly inadequate but more likely it is poorly trained. In 2002 Frances Morphy and I spent a week with a group of Yolngu on a boat mapping coastal Arnhem Land and the waters offshore. To me the sea is the sea, rough or smooth, and I have to see a rock breaking the waves to be able to differentiate between features. But to the Yolngu who accompanied us the sea was highly differentiated and they were able to monitor changes in depth, the presence of shoals of fish, currents flowing from different rivers, all from looking over the edge of the boat. Of course it is difficult to separate out knowledge from vision in cases like this. Yolngu live off the sea and are far more knowledgeable than I am about what exists below the surface. They are able to interpret the way that characteristics of the deep are reflected in subtle variations of surface form. They know what is below the surface and are educated to look for its signs. It would be immensely interesting to conduct a study of Yolngu seeing in the environment, as a means to understanding the relationship between knowledge and vision in a hunter-gatherer society. However, this is not my purpose here. My intention is simply to draw attention to the cultural context of viewing and to the possible nature of the relationship between the conceptual and the perceptual in Yolngu art.

The intention of a Yolngu painting is not to create an illusionistic representation of reality. In painting the sea the Yolngu do not concentrate on reproducing that subtle modulation of colour by which they identify the hidden reef and distinguish it from the faint shadow of a cloud on the water. Indeed it may not even be possible to reproduce and communicate such information, however dependent it is on vision, by visual representation alone. It may be abstracted from the sea in motion by interpreting subtle changes in the effect of light on water and the movement and direction of flow on the surface, or the shape of the ripples – it may be much easier to teach someone to see these things than to actually represent them as they are apprehended. Yolngu do represent such features in art, and in music and dance, but they do not represent them as they are <u>seen</u>.

One major way in which Yolngu represent features that lie beneath the surface of the land and water is through mythological maps of landscape. Throughout this discussion, 'land' and 'landscape' can be taken to incorporate sea, since mythological maps of the sea are continuous with those of the land. Yolngu paintings are both maps of land and representations of the ancestral forces that are embodied in the landscape. Particular features in the landscape are thought to be the result of ancestral action: a river marks the route taken by an ancestral being, a sandhill is the transformation of a pile of ancestral string, a

Figure 22   *Yathikpa II, 1997*. Artist Bakulangay
Marawili. Australian National Maritime
Museum, Sydney. Copyright the artist's family.
Reproduced with the permission of Buku-
Larrnggay Mulka Art Centre, Yirrkala.

rock is the body of the ancestor, and so on. Paintings acquire map-like properties through
representing the land in terms of its ancestral presence.[3]

A painting by Maḏarrpa artist Bakulangay Marawili represents the coast off Yathikpa, a
promontory stretching out into the north of Blue Mud Bay (Figure 22). The dugong hunters
at Yathikpa are associated with a complex of ancestral forces centred on fire. Fire connects

most of the clans of the Yirritja moiety and its journey or presence is marked by a diamond design. Each clan has its own version of the diamond design that is readily identifiable. The fire at Yathikpa was created by the crocodile ancestral being *Bäru*. *Bäru* had a fight with his wife *Dhamilingu*, blue-tongued lizard. She set the bark hut in which he lived on fire, and *Bäru* in order to quench the flames on his back rushed into the waters north of Yathikpa.

However, the fire continued to burn beneath the surface of the water and can be seen today in the waving banks of sea grass and in the swirling waters of the wet season that rush into the bay and sometimes form a boiling whirlpool off Yathikpa. Close to this is a group of rocks that can spell disaster for boats caught in a storm. In other versions of the story the crocodile carried the fire on its back to the country of other clans further to the north.

The dugong hunters of Yathikpa hunted their prey offshore, paddling a dugout canoe and using a harpoon. On one occasion when they threw their harpoon at the dugong, the harpoon was caught by the tidal swell and carried away out to sea. On another occasion the dugong dragged the boat beneath the waves and the hunters were immolated in the fire that burnt beneath the surface of the waves. The crocodile and dugong hunters are major themes of Madarrpa clan paintings, some of which consist entirely of geometric elements whereas others represent elements of the myth in figurative form. The mythic episodes are also danced out in mortuary rituals and initiation ceremonies, and form a backdrop to the everyday experiences of the people hunting dugong in small boats, who are always aware of the dangers of the sea. The mythic episodes are also embodied in further features of the land. The place where the hunters set off from the shore is marked by the impression of a giant harpoon in the ground. The place where the crocodile went into the water is manifest in the form of a rocky bar with a serrated edge in the shape of a crocodile's tail, and the burnt 'hand' of the crocodile is there as rocks off the beach. It would be a mistake to reduce the ancestral presence in the land to any one of these stories or manifestations. The ancestral presence is seen in the places scarred by ancestral action, but it is also inherent in the energy of fire as it burns the country in the dry season and in the swirling forces of the wet season floodwaters as they rush into the bay. It is manifest in the form of the crocodiles that breed in the estuary and patrol the waters of the bay, and in the dangers faced by today's dugong hunters and the speed and power of the dugong as it tears the harpoon shaft from their grasp. I will argue that this painting by Bakulangay represents the ancestral forces associated with the dugong hunters in very powerful ways. However, before returning to it I will look at some more specific features of the Yolngu artistic system.

In particular I will focus on some techniques or properties of the representational system: the evocation of ancestral power through the effects of cross-hatching, and what I refer to as emergent iconicity. All of these involve the interaction of semantic and formal/aesthetic dimensions of the art and are as much concerned with understanding and insight as with emotional affect. Underlying them are more general human capacities to discriminate between forms, and the neurophysiological effects that particular forms have on the human mind and body. It is this universal component that allows art to be interpreted cross-culturally and to be used to communicate ideas and emotions across time and space. However these universal properties can also encourage viewers to interpret other people's arts according to their own culturally specific meanings. Context influences perception, and cultural context no less than any other. A stimulus can be painful in some contexts, pleasurable in others. The same effect can evoke feelings of religious awe in some cultures and anxiety and fear in others. This is why I stress the relative autonomy of aesthetic effects from culture rather than their absolute autonomy. People are socialized into aesthetic systems just as they are into other aspects of culture. Relativity lies in the interpretation but also in the emotional affects that are engendered.[4]

## SHIMMERING — BIR'YUN

The first property of Yolngu art that I would like to explore here is captured by the Yolngu verb *bir'yun*, which can be glossed in English as 'to shimmer brilliantly'. I have written about it in detail elsewhere (Morphy 1992), and here shall only summarize the main points of my argument. Yolngu see paintings as transformational. They had their origin in the ancestral past when they arose out of ancestral action. They are ancestral in three senses: their underlying form arose in ancestral times, they encode ancestral events and they were given by ancestral beings to Yolngu as sacred designs. However, what I am concerned with here is the transformation that occurs in the painting process. Yolngu paintings move from a state that is relatively speaking rough, dull and ill defined, to one of shimmering brilliance in which the elements are nonetheless sharply defined. This process of painting is seen as adding ancestral power. The surface to be painted is first covered with red ochre and the basic design elements marked out in yellow and occasionally black. This initial stage of producing a painting is accomplished relatively quickly, usually taking no more than an hour, often much less time. The surface is then covered with a pattern of cross-hatched lines in various combinations of red, yellow, white and black. Finally the basic pattern elements, the geometric designs and the figurative representations are outlined in white. The process of cross-hatching on a large painting takes place over a number of days, the painting on a young initiate's chest three or four hours, during which time the initiate must remain absolutely still. This cross-hatching is done with a brush of human hair, a few long strands of straight hair bound to a stick. The brush is dipped in pigment and then drawn across the surface of the painting.

The optical effect of this technique is to create a painting in which the surface shines (Figure 23). The underlying pattern is clearly defined yet the surface of the painting appears to move; it is difficult to fix the eye on a single segment without interference from others – indeed, in some paintings the image seems unstable, almost threatening to leave the surface of the painting. This effect is clearly demonstrated in Welwi Wanambi's painting of wild honey, which represents places on the journey of the ancestral woman Ganydjalala in search of honey. The effects are analogous to those created by Bridget Riley in her op-art paintings, and have resonance in the work of many other artists in the European tradition. In the

Figure 23   *Wild Honey*, 1973. Artist Welwi
Wanambi. Private collection. Reproduced with the
permission of Buku-Larrnggay Mulka Art Centre,
Yirrkala.

Yolngu case the effect is at a general level interpreted as a manifestation of ancestral power, which in the case of particular paintings is interpreted as an expression of the power of the ancestral being the painting represents. The specific connotations or evocations vary from painting to painting. The surface may evoke the fierce heat of a fire, the shimmering white of the coastal dunes, the glistening of honey or the brilliance of eucalyptus in flower, or non-material properties such as the sharp pain felt by the ancestral shark speared by a harpoon, or the flash of anger in the eye of a trapped animal. The connotations in a single painting may be multiple, varying according to different attributes of the ancestral being concerned, the events in its journey, or the purpose for which the image has been made.

In ritual, meaning is cued by context, with song, dance and ritual action combining to create the particular meaning. Paintings are produced in ceremonies for a purpose, which may be generalized as in associating a boy being circumcized with a particular ancestral journey, which in turn links him to a particular set of kin and area of country; or it may have a more narrow instrumental function, such as helping the soul of a dead person accomplish

Figure 24   Wild-honey design painted by
Bokarra Maymuru, on an initiate's face in a
Djungguwan ceremony at Gurka'wuy, Trial Bay,
1976. Photograph Howard Morphy.

its spiritual journey. Dotting can produce a similar effect. For example the painting shown in (Figure 24) inscribed on a boy's face during a Djungguwan ceremony, represents the same ancestral wild honey collectors as those in Welwi's painting.

The honey-eating ancestral beings cut down trees inland to extract wild honey from the hives in their hollow trunks. One great tree crashed down the hillside, gouging out the course of the Gurka'wuy River. When it reached the sea, the tree created various features in Trial Bay, including a number of small rocks over which the sea breaks in rough weather. During the ceremony the connotation of the face painting shifted from the sheen of the wild honey and the brilliance of the eucalypt flowers to the white foam of the breakers on the rocks offshore. The child's face was being painted at Trial Bay itself and the songs that accompanied the paintings followed the journey of the ancestors from inland to the sea.[5]

At a burial ceremony in 1974 a woman's coffin lid was painted with the design of an ancestral shark, a painting similar in design to the one of Manydjarri's shown in Figure 25. In burial ceremonies each episode of the ritual represents a place connected to the person

Figure 25  *Djambarrpuyngu Märna*, 1996.
Artist Manydjarri Ganambarr. Kluge-Ruhe
Aboriginal Art Collection, University of
Virginia. Copyright the artist. Reproduced
with the permission of Buku-Larrnggay
Mulka Art Centre, Yirrkala.

who has died, and is part of the process of guiding that person's spirit back to the ancestral dimension. Often the burial ceremony takes the form of a symbolic journey: the movement of the body from the place of death to burial in a grave is an analogue for the journey of the spirit from the place where the person died to its incorporation within the spiritual reservoirs of the person's clan estate. The painting on a coffin lid both represents a stage in the journey and enacts a theme of the ceremony. The ancestral shark is associated with a number of clans of the Dhuwa moiety. It began its journey off Buckingham Bay where it was speared by a harpoon. It rushed into the shore, gouging out watercourses and diving beneath the surface of the land to come up further inland. In another episode the shark was caught in a fish trap held back by the stakes that dammed the river mouth. In its anger it smashed the fish trap down and continued on its journey. The shimmering effect of the cross hatching conveys the passion of the shark and its pent up energy and aggression. In the burial ceremony, a set of stakes representing the fish trap were stuck into the ground at the entrance of the shade in which the woman's body lay. After her body had been placed in the coffin a group of men danced it outside, smashing down the fishtrap in the process. The shark had escaped the trap just as the woman's soul was commencing its journey to the ancestral dimension.

## EMERGENT ICONICITY

I will return again later to *bir'yun*. Before doing so I would like to consider the next property of Yolngu paintings, which I refer to as emergent iconicity. When Yolngu view their paintings, they see in them images of ancestral action and transformation. The form – or, as I might better express it, the idea or the essence – of the ancestral beings emerges as much in the geometric forms of the clan designs as in the figurative representations, if not more so. There is a synergy between the process of encoding meaning and the expression of meaning in the formal properties of the painting, both through representational processes and aesthetic effect. What Goodman (1976) might refer to as the notational aspects of Yolngu art interact with its expressive dimensions.

Yolngu paintings form sets on the basis of two main criteria: ancestral journey and place. One set of paintings includes the designs that represent a particular ancestral being as it journeyed across the country from one place to the next. The other set of paintings is centred on each place in turn and elaborates on the events that occurred there. Theoretically it might seem that the first set includes the second set, but in practice they are conceptually quite distinct. The ancestral being's journey connects places belonging to different clan groupings, and in each place the ancestral being is represented by a unique set of paintings. While Yolngu are aware of the wider links along the ancestral track, and indeed may on occasions produce paintings belonging to another clan, the focus of the artists' activity is primarily on the set of paintings belonging to their own clan, or clans to which they are closely related by descent.

Yolngu paintings, as I noted in the previous chapter, are comprised of two main elements: geometric forms and figurative representations. The geometric representations are of two main types: clan designs and a set of geometric shapes that represent the form of sand sculptures or sacred objects. In addition there are structuring elements which divide up the painting into different segments. These are usually in the form of lines cutting across the surface but segment boundaries may simply be marked by the presence of a different pattern in two adjacent segments. Within the set associated with a place, paintings can be imagined to exist in an inside-outside relationship to each other, with the inside paintings being predominantly geometric and the outside ones including more figurative representations. 'Inside' in Yolngu terms has connotations of being underlying, more powerful and generative, whereas 'outside' is more descriptive and fixed.[6] In effect the meanings associated with place are condensed into the forms of the geometric art and represented or enacted separately in other contexts. The elaboration of meaning may indeed be as often through the words of a song or the expressive movements of a dance as through a painting.

I will give two examples of how this process works. The first is centred on the significance of the form of a *yingapungapu* sand sculpture (Figure 26), and for the second I shall return to the ancestral dugong hunters at Yathikpa. The sand sculpture is used in mortuary rituals for two main purposes. It can enclose the place where a body is laid before burial or it can be used to purify the participants after a burial ceremony. In both cases it functions to contain the pollution associated with a dead body. Like all Yolngu forms it has its origins in the ancestral past, and is associated with the journey of the Wuradilagu, two ancestral women who journeyed the shores of Blue Mud Bay in ancestral times. When they had eaten, these women would bury the remains of their fish in an oval scooped out in the sand. The women drew an analogue with the sand crabs on the beach that scuttled around cleaning up the sand and dragging the rotten food remains into their holes. One day their brothers went out to sea, and in a great storm their boat was overwhelmed. Days later, their bodies washed up on the shore. The scooped-out hollow made for fish remains provided the

Figure 26   A Yingapungapu ground sculpture at Yilpara, Blue Mud Bay, 2000. Photograph Howard Morphy.

model for the elliptical sand sculpture that they built for their brothers' mortuary rituals, in the centre of which they laid the bodies for burial. Today, at the conclusion of a burial ceremony, the people who had prepared the body for burial and close relatives of the dead will sit in the centre of the sculpture and be cleansed first by washing and then by smoke from smouldering branches.

Paintings of the *yingapungapu* sand sculpture condense all of the meanings associated with the ritual and the mythology of place. These can then be developed in figurative form in paintings that tease out individual elements. Here I shall illustrate only one such chain of connection, but one that is directly connected to the themes of purification and regeneration that are central to the function of the sculpture.

The exquisite small painting by Narritjin Maymuru shown in Figure 27 appears to reduce the image to that of the hollow scooped up in the sand by the women. The painting shows two parrot fish in an oval depression. The surrounding clan design belongs to the Manggalili clan and represents marks on the beach and the movement of the tide, up and down. The dotted design represents the remains of the fish in the first stages of decay, maggots and the claw marks of the sand crabs as they scuttle up and down the beach making it clean. These meanings are reinforced in mortuary rituals when the mourners, before being brushed

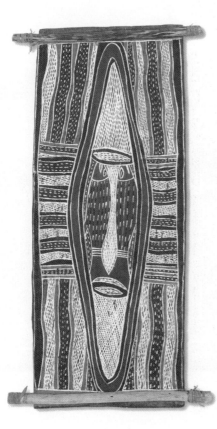

Figure 27   *Fish with Maggots*, 1960. Artist Narritjin Maymuru. Kluge-Ruhe Aboriginal Art Collection, University of Virginia. Copyright the artist's family. Reproduced with the permission of Buku-Larrnggay Mulka Art Centre, Yirrkala.

with smouldering branches, dance on their knees around the fire lit in the centre of the *yingapungapu* and eat imaginary parrot fish. And when they have finished that stage of the ceremony, they dance as maggot, initially crawling along the ground wiping out the walls of the sand sculpture as they go.

Manggalili paintings develop the connections in many different ways. A core image is that of the activity on the beach when the tide is out (Figure 28). Turtle tracks are shown in the centre of the painting accompanied by human footprints. Sand crabs are shown clearing the sand of organic matter, leaving behind a scatter of tiny balls of sand; a *guluwitjpitj* bird hunts along the beach, eating the sand crabs, and finally the tide comes in and washes away the activities of the day. The image expresses key themes of the funeral: the removal of the physical presence of the person who has died, and looking forward to the future.

Figure 28   *Sand Crabs and Turtle Tracks*, 1978. Artist Narritjin Maymuru. Collection unknown. Copyright the artist's family. Reproduced with the permission of Buku-Larrnggay Mulka Art Centre, Yirrkala.

Manggalili paintings show how a density of meanings can be encoded in the background geometric design with a minimum of iconicity, patterning the relationship of form and content. I now consider briefly the clan designs that are a dominant component of Yolngu art, returning once more to Yathikpa. Bakulangay's painting (Figure 22) is made up of two main Madarrpa clan designs, the linked chains of diamonds associated with the crocodile and fire and the wavy parallel lines associated with the deeper waters of the bay (Mungurru) and shared by a number of Yirritja clans. The structure of the painting is complex, in that it contains paintings within paintings. The main part of the painting represents the sea off Yathikpa, stretching from the place where the crocodile caught fire to the place in the middle of the bay where the dugong was speared. The top two segments focus in on the dugongs, shown swimming around the rocks of fire beneath the surface of the bay as they feed on the sea grass, illustrated waving above them. I shall consider here only the diamond design.

The diamond design tracks the route of fire across north-east Arnhem Land and each clan associated with fire has its own version of the design which differs in minor detail from every other. Each design specifies the ancestral actions that took place over a particular area of land or sea. In this case the design indicates the Madarrpa clan and fire, crocodile, and dugong at Yathikpa. In most clan designs there are elements of iconicity, in the relationship between form and content, that can be emphasized or diminished according to context. We have seen that the Manggalili design echoes marks of the tide on the beach, and the maggots and the foot marks of the crab are represented by dashed lines outlining the design. In the diamond pattern, segments are painted in colours that correspond to different aspects of fire: red ochre indicates flames, red and white cross-hatching the sparks, white signifies smoke and ash, and black the charcoal. This iconicity is reinforced for Yolngu by participating in ritual in which fire is either literally or symbolically created. The most powerful manifestation of fire is in the purification rituals which end mortuary ceremonies, in which people's bodies are purified by contact with fire, by dancing around the flames of a fire, or beating one's body with smouldering branches of leaves. The climax of many Madarrpa ceremonies is the ritual firing of the hut in which the dead person's body lay during the ceremony, which in turn represents the crocodile's nest at Garrangali. These events are always associated in song and dance with ancestral fire and its movement across the country, and the link between iconography and physical affect is reinforced in many different ways. The fire may be lit by dancers representing crocodile or quail ancestral beings associated with fire. The power names for fire will be called out as the flames rise high, and the dancers who dance into the heat of the flames may have the fire pattern painted on their chests.

In a recent series of paintings (made in 2003) Djambawa Marawili develops variations on the theme of the Madarrpa diamond design to express the power of the ancestral crocodile (Figure 29).[7] The crosshatched diamonds represent the crocodile as it dives into the waters off Yathikpa carrying the fire that burnt into its back, express the heat of the flames as they leap through the bush, the boiling waters of the sea as the crocodile thrashes about in the water, the waving tresses of sea grass as they flicker beneath the waters. The meanings are

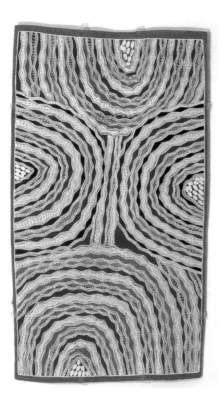

Figure 29    *Little Mapu*, 2002. Artist
Djambawa Marawili. 2002. Private
collection. Copyright the artist.
Reproduced with the permission of
Buku-Larrnggay Mulka Art Centre,
Yirrkala. Photograph courtesy The
Annandale Galleries Sydney.

latent in the designs, and influence how they are seen and felt. The lines of diamonds are powerful expressions of the ancestral crocodile and in context allude to the forces of the sea and the cross-cutting nature of the currents. The curved lines in some of the paintings refer to the rounded crocodile's nests at Garrangali.

Different variants of the diamond designs are associated with different places and different clans. The differences between the forms of designs can be quite subtle and contextual; their reference is clear in the painting as a whole but depends on interpreting the particular configuration of elements. The Yirritja-moiety diamond design connects a whole complex of ancestral beings to the seasonal elements of fire and flood waters. In the previous painting, representing the waters of Grindall Bay, the focus was on the crocodile ancestor *Bäru* as the bearer of fire. Djambawa Marawili's painting *Burruṯ'tji* (Figure 30) represents waters that flow into the adjacent Jalma Bay, and is centred on the river mouth at Baraltja in that

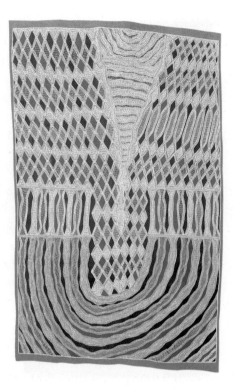

Figure 30    *Burrut'tji*, 2002. Artist
Djambawa Marawili (b. 1953). Queensland
Art Gallery, Brisbane. Copyright the Artist.
Reproduced with the permission of Buku-
Larrnggay Mulka Art Centre, Yirrkala.

bay at the height of the wet season. The region is dominated by a seasonal cycle in which
fresh water and salt water flow across the coastline, mixing together in different places at
different times of the year. In the dry season the salt taste of the water moves far inland as the
creek-beds dry out. In the wet season the cycle is reversed. The inland becomes inundated,
flooding the coastal plains. The rivers become raging torrents bursting through the river
mouths and sending great plumes of fresh water far out into the bay. *Burrut'tji* the Lighting
Snake moves with this cycle of the seasons. In the dry season it occupies the flood plains
hunting small marsupials; in the wet season it is associated with the river mouths. The snake
tastes the fresh water. It stands up high and spits it into the air. The great snake spits into
the sky, its tongue the flickering of lighting and its voice the roar of thunder. It is talking to
ancestral snakes from other places and times.

Djambawa's painting *Burrut'tji* represents the coming together of the flood waters of
three Yirritja-moiety clans. The bar across the centre of the painting represents the coastline

at the head of Jalma Bay. The linear pattern inside it belongs to the salt-water Maḏarrpa and represents the stakes of an ancestral fish trap. The diamond pattern in the left-hand segment represents the flooded waters of the Baykurrtji River to the west, in the country of the fresh-water Maḏarrpa clan. The bars that cut across each intersection characterize the pattern. The chains of diamonds containing elongated ovals in the panel on the right represent the Dhaḻwangu clan waters. The swollen figure that divides them represents flood waters from further inland that are believed to surge through an underground tunnel before joining the surface waters as they flood through the river mouth. The tunnel is the home of *Burruṯtji* as he travels between the inland and the sea. The snake's head can be seen emerging in the waters at the river mouth. As the waters come together, they can be seen moving out into the bay, pushing aside the swirling deep salt waters of Mungurru.[8]

The painting illustrates the ways in which the geometric component of Yolngu art acts as a generative component for the expression of meaning. The clan designs are multi-referential. The diamond design can represent the turbulent flood waters, the ancestral fire, the marks on a crocodile's back, the cells of a bee hive; its colours can represent flames or burnt wood, smoke and sparks, honey or foaming water; and the distinctive variants of the design belonging to different social groups mark their country and are part of the clan's identity. There is a thin line between representation and expression in Yolngu art, and in Djambawa's painting we can see the geometric motifs come to life, the flooding of the country inland, the intense force of the flood waters coming together in the river mouth and thrusting out into the bay, pushing aside the salt water. But we can also see in the painting *Burruṯtji* the lightning snake gaining power from the flood waters, his flickering tongue joining in with the diamond pattern of the painting, creating the explosive force of lightning. And behind the imagery, and of crucial importance to Djambawa, are the relationships between the groups themselves – the Fresh-water Maḏarrpa, the Salt-water Maḏarrpa and the Salt-water and Fresh-water Dhaḻwangu. 'We always come together for burial ceremonies'[9] – and in those ceremonies the flood waters are danced and sung, fire is braved. Baraltja, *Burruṯtji* and the flood waters are created through ceremonial performance, just as their spiritual identity is manifest in the painting.

A painting is not a literal representation of mythological events. Rather, it is a form of meditation on them. It is conceptual, and yet the ideas are firmly located in place. The dugong painting (Figure 22) conveys the idea of the hunt: the dugong is sighted out to sea; the harpoon is prepared; the dugong is speared. It refers to the dangers of the sea: the turbulence of the waters and the strength of the dugong. It refers to the creation of fire by the crocodile and to the ownership of the land and sea country. The straight lines that run along the centre of the painting represent the direction of vision of the hunters, the shaft of the harpoon, the taut line of the rope as the dugong pulls the boat along. Where the line divides in the top central panel it both duplicates the spearing of the dugong and shows the transformation of the harpoon shaft into a log coffin, container of the bodies of the dead hunters, infilled with the diamond designs of the Maḏarrpa clan. In the horizontal plane the changing form of the background design and the cross-cutting segments of design disrupt the symmetry. Here the background design conveys the fierceness of the fire and its analogue in the turbulence of sea. Once initiated, as it were, we can sense the rip of the tide and almost witness (= see) the overwhelming of the boat as it was torn from its straight line by the dugong's dive. The different segments of the background design refer both to different areas of sea and to the different groups who are connected by the story: the ribbons of diamonds belong to the Madarrpa clan, and the wavy lines around the dugong and canoe represent the coming together of the Mungurru waters of the Manggalili, Dhalwangu, and Madarrpa clans. The figures hint at details of the story (the empty canoe connected by rope to the mangrove wood float) or provide a view from the land (the dugong as they move about in the swirling sea). But the meaning of the painting is part of a wider understanding of the relationship between people and place that lies in its interconnection with the songs, sacred names and the sacred geography of the landscape at Yathikpa.

In Djambawa's painting of *Burrut'tji*, figurative representations are almost absent – one has to look hard before seeing the snakes' heads rising through and leading on the turbulent waters. And indeed in many paintings of the same theme the snake's presence may be invisible – in a figurative sense.

We have now reached the point where I can provide examples of what I refer to as emergent iconicity. I hope that you are convinced, in theory, of the system by which latent meanings are encoded in the painting. Indeed, in knowing the range of meanings encoded in the painting it should be possible to see how elements of the geometric art have been structured, painted, to represent aspects of the ancestral creativity and environmental forces associated with place. It is possible to read into the way the diamond patterns weave and cut across each other the movements of the waters, the power of the dugong as its body bends beneath the boat, and the movement of the sea grass as it burns beneath the surface of the waves.

In some paintings Yolngu make the meanings more explicit in a number of different ways. Occasionally they modify the forms of clan designs to point in the direction of one or other interpretation – the diamond design may turn into a flowing strand of sea grass or it may be marked in the body of a crocodile or another animal associated with the fire. But frequently, the opposite process occurs. The relationship between figure and ground is disturbed by the reproduction of the same clan designs within the body of the figure and as the background outside. In such cases the figure almost disappears into the background patterns of clan designs and cross-hatching. In other cases the figurative representation may be produced in more and more abstract ways until eventually it disappears.

Manydjarri's painting of the shark at Buckingham bay (Figure 25) can be read either as emergent or disappearing iconicity. The figurative representation of the shark in the upper panel almost dissolves into geometric elements, evoking the force of the ancestral shark as it crashes into the land and becomes in its death agony an angry explosion of power. The shark rushed headlong inland, transforming into features of the landscape as it went. The painting shows its transformation from the physical to the spiritual – a process that ultimately frees it from the constraints of its bodily form. A minor modification in the head of the shark, and its body would disappear altogether.

The immanence of figuration, which has always been a feature of Yolngu art, has recently been developed in interesting ways in a series of paintings produced by artists associated with Yilpara – Galuma Maymuru, Djambawa Marawili and Wanyubi Marika. Wanyubi has described this visual and conceptual effect as *buwayak* – the property of faintness, or transparency.[10] The derived verb *buwayakthin* means to fade, become indistinct, dissolve, and disappear. The technique may involve the simple outlining of the figurative representations across the background pattern of clan designs.

In Djambawa's painting (Figure 31) of the dugong hunters, that reproduces an area of the sea represented in Bakulangay's painting (Figure 22), many of the figures are represented only by a thin white outline that cuts across the background pattern of clan designs. Indeed,

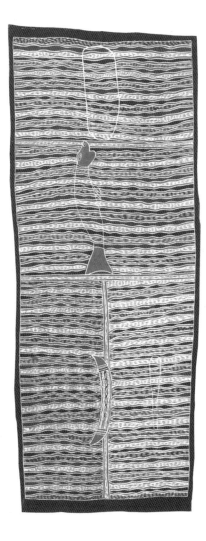

Figure 31   *Yathikpa*, 1997. Artist Djambawa Marawili (b. 1953). Australian National Maritime Museum, Sydney. Copyright the artist. Reproduced with the permission of Buku-Larrnggay Mulka Art Centre, Yirrkala.

one has to look hard to find the paddle from the boat turned over by the dugong. The figures almost function as a pictographic title for the painting, taking up one element of the story.

In Wanyubi's own paintings, *buwayak* sometimes takes a similar form, with figures being outlined in white against a background of cross-hatching. In *Daymirri* (Figure 32), the delicately outlined image of the whale is drawn over a background pattern that represents the sea in Rirratjingu clan country surrounding Bremmer Island (Dhambaliya). The image represents the whale as it appears from the depths off the island. Rarely seen, it is manifest in the form of a sacred rock, exposed at low tide, that glistens white in the sun. Both the whale and the rock literally appear and disappear beneath the surface of the water.

Figure 32   *Daymirri*, 2002. Artist, Wanyubi Marika. Copyright the artist. Reproduced with the permission of Buku-Larrnggay Mulka Art Centre, Yirrkala. Photograph courtesy The Annandale Galleries, Sydney.

We have seen that the technique of Yolngu painting involves the building up of the final surface image as the result of a series of layers of painting beginning with the ground cover, followed by the rough marking out of the figurative and geometric motifs and finishing with layers of cross-hatching. Quite frequently figures are redefined as the process continues and patterns overlie patterns. The technique lends itself to the creation of complex and multi-dimensional images. Djambawa frequently uses this technique to create images that appear simultaneously above and below the surface, by redefining them at different stages of the process (Figure 33). The photograph shows the final stages of the painting of a hollow-log coffin. The painting in this case is again off the seas of Yathikpa. The dugong hunters' boat has been overwhelmed and their bodies tossed into the water. The drowning body of one of them can be seen being tossed around in the turbulent waters.

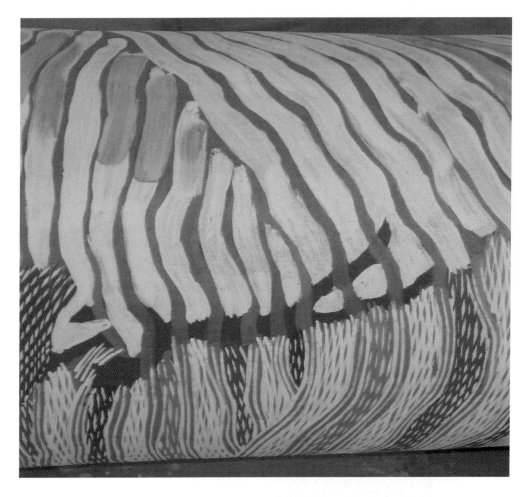

Figure 33   Drowning man (detail of an unfinished painting by Djambawa Marawili). Photograph Howard Morphy 2006.

This imminence of iconicity, the emergence and then masking of figurative form, the disruption between figure and ground, represents the natural world as it is apprehended. It is deeply connected to the semantics and symbolism of Yolngu ontology. For a concluding example, we can look at the way in which Galuma Maymuru employs this technique of *buwayak* to express symbolic ideas associated with the *yingapungapu* (Figure 34). One theme of her paintings of her clan's estate at Djarrakpi is of the ancestral women burying the remains of *yambirrku* (parrotfish) on the beach. The *yambirrku* is eaten by maggots, scavenged by crabs, picked at by *guluwitpitj* birds and eventually all evidence of it is washed away by the tide. We have seen that the fate of the *yambirrku* is a metaphor for what happens

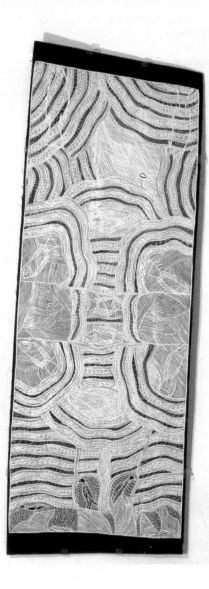

Figure 34    *Monuk*, 2002. Artist Galuma Maymuru. Private collection. Copyright the artist. Reproduced with the permission of Buku-Larrnggay Mulka Art Centre, Yirrkala. Photograph courtesy The Annandale Galleries, Sydney.

to the human body after death. The imagery is connected with ideas of cleansing, of hope, of coming to terms with death, of reconnecting with life, of ancestral forces in harmony with nature. The sand crab and parrotfish sometimes stand out boldly; on other occasions, they are present as footprints in the sand or as skeletal forms faintly discerned, merging in with the background pattern to the point where they disappear. In her painting *Monuk* (salt water) we can see the parrotfish as they come in with the tide as the waters swirl around the rocks offshore. The painting hints at the movement of the fish beneath the waters, just visible to the hunter's eye. Yet the near disappearance of the fish also conveys symbolic meaning: the immanence of birth, the inevitability of death, themes that are acted out in the *yingapungapu* ceremonies which enact the fishermen bringing their catch back to the shore where it is shared and eaten and where the remains are buried in the sand, returning them to a natural cycle of decay and regeneration.

## CONCLUSION

The relationship between the visible and the invisible is a central trope of Yolngu art. In part this reflects the fact that paintings are connected to a revelatory system of knowledge about the world in which people learn deeper meanings as they pass through life. While some elements of meaning are secret, it is more the case that, as with any system of knowledge, people need to acquire information over time in order to develop a fuller understanding. In harmony with this is the belief that the surface forms of things derive from underlying structures and relationships. Yolngu art condenses and expresses extremely complex relationships between things – between social groups, and in the seasonal cycle between fresh water and salt water, fire and water, between life and death, and male and female – and underlying all is the template of the ancestral past. Ancestral design is revealed in action – in the continuing relationships between people, in the fertility of the land, and in the renewing and cleansing power of the wet season. But it is also demonstrated in the paintings which can express the unity of the clans that come together at ceremonies or in marriage as readily as they can allude to the presence of the fish hidden in ancestral waters, or the drowning figure of an ancestral human. Events that happened in the ancestral past are made part of the present, simultaneously reflecting and creating an ancestral presence in the world. Just as the powers that bring about the transformation of the landscape are both seen and unseen, so too is much of the imagery of Yolngu art. The relationship between abstraction and representation provides the continuing dynamic of Yolngu art and gives it the power to continually explore new forms of expression.

Through the diversity of their representational techniques, in which semantic and aesthetic factors combine to express meaning and affect, Yolngu artists are able to convey the nature of the world as they see it or, more accurately, experience it. It is a world in which ancestral presence is clear and marked, yet dynamic and transforming. Their paintings allude to the fact that the landscape itself is active, animated by the presence of ancestral beings. The ancestral beings transformed themselves into features of the landscape – into rocks, sand-dunes and lakes – but they are not thereby frozen immutably in time and space. They are a continuing presence, moving on in space and time, remaining active in the present.

In talking about their paintings Yolngu artists stress continuity with the ancestral past. Paintings are based on inherited designs that belong to clans. Certain components of paintings, such as the particular form of the diamond design associated with the Madarrpa crocodile, are considered the sacred property of the clan and can only be used with permission and on paintings associated with particular places. However, the paintings are no more slavish reproductions of an inherited design form than they are mimetic of what is seen by the eye. Yolngu paintings are dialogic. Yolngu use the potentialities of their visual system to create images that reveal and sometimes reproduce an aspect of nature – the flash of light, the movement of fish beneath the surface of the water – images that are simultaneously conceptual and perceptual. They also see paintings as a means of conveying knowledge about the world, communicating the mythological significance of place and representing the particularities of ancestral beings. They exploit the potential of visual effects to create a sense of the sacred. In doing so they enable people to experience ancestral power when they see paintings, or have them painted on their body. Vision is an internal phenomenon, in that it is processed by the brain and mind. But it is also external – reflecting that which is and acting as a vehicle for communication between people. Perhaps this dual aspect of vision is the reason why, when Yolngu talk about painting, they emphasize the role of the mind. Narritjin Maymuru attributed wisdom to the thin brush used in cross-hatching to create *bir'yun* or 'brilliance'. The brush is made of human hair. This is in turn linked to the fontanelle, which is seen as a focal point for both spirituality and knowledge. Yolngu paintings are *thought* as much as they are *seen*.[11]

# 6 STYLE AND MEANING: ABELAM ART THROUGH YOLNGU EYES

## PROLOGUE

This chapter is both part of the argument of the book and also to an extent part of the history that the book engages with. It is also a very personal chapter since its main characters are people who have been very influential in my life – Narritjin Maymuru, a great Yolngu artist and teacher, and Anthony Forge, supervisor of my doctoral thesis. During my second period of fieldwork in 1976, the Yirrkala mission store was unable to purchase artwork. I persuaded the Aboriginal Arts Board to lend me the money to purchase works to sell at an exhibition on my return to Canberra. Narritjin came down to open the exhibition.

Following the success of the exhibition, Anthony Forge and I put forward a proposal to the Creative Arts Committee of the Australian National University that they award a three-month fellowship to Narritjin. Creative Arts Fellowships were awarded to artists to enable them to spend time working in the University and contribute to its artistic life. Fellows were paid a modest stipend, provided with studio space, given some help with accommodation and encouraged to organize an exhibition at the end of their stint. No equivalent position had been awarded at the time to an Aborigine anywhere in Australia, and our expectation was that such a proposal would prove attractive.[1]

The proposal was rejected on the grounds that Aboriginal art was the work of clans, that there was no individual creativity involved and that there would be problems with accommodation. I return to some of those issues in the next chapter. Anthony Forge was away when the decision was made and it was left to John Mulvaney, the Professor of Prehistory and myself to formulate a reply. While we were still working one out, something happened that was to make our case much stronger. I was telephoned by a person who said that she had been appointed a Creative Arts Fellow and that she had been told that I might be able to help in getting her project off the ground. The person concerned was Penny Tweedie, an internationally renowned photographer who gained her reputation in part from photographing Third World themes. Together with a colleague, she had the project of photographing and videotaping aspects of the life of a well-known Aboriginal artist, and she was thinking that Narritjin Maymuru might be a good subject.

In appointing a photographer, the committee quite rightly thought it was making an innovative decision. The University saw that some people might see the decisions made by the Fellowship committee as being inconsistent, and shortly afterward two additional Fellowships of status equivalent to that of Creative Arts Fellowships were awarded, to Narritjin

Maymuru and his son Banapana. The Fellowships were generously supplemented by grants from the Aboriginal Arts Board, which enabled the artists and their families to spend the last three months of 1978 in Canberra. At the conclusion of their stay an exhibition of their work was held.

Narritjin and Banapana also took part in teaching students in the anthropology of art, conducting tutorials jointly with me and on one occasion with myself and Anthony (see Dunlop 1981b). Anthony took the opportunity of their visit to show them his collection of Abelam paintings and to record their commentary on them. I am not sure what Anthony expected. I knew Narritjin was very interested in other cultures and other ways of life. I don't think that either of us expected that they would engage in quite the way they did, in adopting a very analytical approach, eliciting information from Anthony about Abelam society in order to try to make sense of their art. Perhaps despite ourselves we shared those presuppositions of modernism, of the unreflective primitive artist locked into his own world of conservative tradition. That may be the reason why there have been so few attempts to engage Indigenous artists in cross-cultural discourse about art – it is another example of how Western artworlds maintain their distance.

Although I transcribed the tapes, Anthony and I never found the time to write the article we intended to, though we both sensed it was an important encounter. And when I was asked to give the first Anthony Forge memorial lecture it was the obvious topic for me to address. This Chapter is a slightly reworked version of that lecture.[2]

## STYLE AND MEANING

It is significant that the concepts of style and meaning figured prominently in Anthony Forge's anthropology of art. In the 1960s, style was a concept strongly associated with art history. Although it had its brief life in the grand theoretical schemes of Kroeberian anthropology in the United States it had hardly entered British anthropological discourse.[3] But style was a key term in the study of non-European art, linking it to the fields of art history, archaeology, cultural history and equally to connoisseurship. Style enabled the anthropology of art to engage with art history. Meaning, on the other hand, was what allowed art to be seen as relevant to anthropology itself at a time when the structural functionalist paradigm as a whole was under challenge from many different directions. By focusing on style and meaning, Forge brought together the concerns of the two disciplines – anthropology and art history – and pointed the way to a more challenging and interdisciplinary anthropology of art.

Although style and meaning are key concepts in Forge's anthropology of art, nowhere are they rigorously defined. Forge uses style in two different senses, both of which are familiar uses in art history, without clearly differentiating between them. Style is used for the formal description and categorization of objects, which enables them to be allocated a place in space and time, and style is used in the more metaphysical sense of reflecting a coherent element in the production of objects. In the second sense, Forge is concerned with the reason behind the particularities of form: with the idea that style is the product of a specific way of conveying meaning, expressing ideas, or marking status. It is this concept of style, as the result of a process for producing meaningful forms, on which I focus here and apply to two geographically distinct artistic systems, that of the Abelam of the Sepik River Province of Papua New Guinea, which was studied by Forge, and that of the Yolngu of eastern Arnhem Land in Northern Australia, which was the subject of my own research. The choice is not an entirely arbitrary one. On the surface at least there appear to be some similarities of form between Abelam flat painting and Yolngu bark painting. Indeed, Forge himself thought that there were similarities in the underlying structure of the systems. While formal similarities do not necessarily mean that the systems which produce them have anything in common, they provide a focal point for comparative analysis. Moreover, an additional motivation for the comparison was the visit of the two Yolngu artists, Narritjin and Banapana Maymuru, to the Australian National University and their willingness to take part in a discussion with Anthony Forge and me over Abelam art.[4]

To understand Forge's analysis of Abelam art and recognize its originality, it is necessary to see it in the context of its times. It was influenced both by the problematics of Western art history and by recent analyses of non-European art, including Australian Aboriginal art.[5] These provided comparative perspectives on the Abelam and influenced the terms in which Forge was to present his analysis of their art. He was concerned in both cases with the difference of Abelam art as well as the similarities. As an anthropologist, Forge approached Abelam art with a number of questions in mind: what the art represented, what its meaning might be and how the Abelam interpreted it. In comparison with Yolngu art, as analysed by Charles Mountford (1956), Abelam art seemed to lack external referents (Forge 1966: 23). In eastern Arnhem Land and Australia in general, art appeared to be closely integrated within the Dreamtime and the myths of world creation. Art could be interpreted, at least in part, as the representation or illustration of myth. For every painting there appeared to be a 'story' that was part of its meaning. Among the Abelam, Forge had found few myths, and the meaning of the art appeared at first to be elusive. The Abelam had names for individual elements of a painting and often had a gloss in English – 'flying fox', 'eye', 'breast', or 'leg of pork' – but this did not seem to get him very far. The meanings were not organized syntactically to illustrate myths or stories, but seemed almost arbitrary. Moreover, the same element could have a variety of meanings, which again did not appear to vary systematically with context. The same element could represent a leg of pork, immature fern fronds, black palm cockatoo and swirls in a river. In some cases, he notes that the artist refused to say in advance what he was painting, and sometimes changed his mind halfway through; and if there were two people collaborating they might disagree.

From Western art theory Forge drew on the distinction between abstract and representational forms. Forge defined as 'abstract' cases where there was no clear relationship between form and meaning. Representational paintings were ones in which the parts were organized to represent a more encompassing whole, which at one level might be a face, or a person, and at another level might be a mythic episode. Representational art covered similar ground as terms such as figurative or iconic. He was able to apply the distinction to contrasting Abelam images, some of which were more representational than others. He drew a contrast between two paintings of the same ancestral figure '[Figure 35] is clearly anthropomorphic albeit highly stylized. The other [Figure 36] is a pattern and little else to non-Abelam eyes. Yet both are called *ndu*, both comprise the same elements and both are equally effective in ritual terms' (Forge 1973b: 183). Forge notes that the important thing is not what the paintings represent but that they are comprised of the same set of elements. To Forge the fact that they share an identity despite apparently being structured on different organizational principles challenged the opposition that was often drawn between representational and abstract art. The point he is making, that in Abelam art 'there is no line to be drawn between representational and abstract' (ibid.), is a fundamentally important one. However, Forge somewhat overstates the case because the distinction between more representational and less representational forms is central to his argument. Forge's analysis at times lacks

Figure 35   *Ndu* 'man' by Nyagere. Photograph Anthony Forge. From the Anthony Forge Papers, Mandeville Special Collections Library, University of California, San Diego.

clarity because he uses a very generalized concept of meaning. As a consequence, he fails to do justice to the brilliance of his ideas about the meaning-creation process in Abelam art, in which the meanings of the individual elements play a significant part in producing meaning in the system as a whole.

The paintings use a restricted range of elements that can be combined in many different ways. Forge implies that there is a basic set of designs that make up the repertoire of a particular community, but elsewhere suggests that the designs themselves are subject to individual variation. The design elements often have names and meanings associated with them, but since Forge does not list many of the names or provide an inventory of meanings, it is impossible to analyse them in detail.[6] However, from the examples he gives, it is possible to say that the relationship between form and meaning is patterned by iconicity at least as much as is the case with Central Australian graphic signs.[7] In Abelam art, circles have ranges of meanings – from eyes to stars – that are consistent with a circular form. Even in the case of more specific designs, such as the leg of pork, other meanings such as fern

13 *Ndu*, 'man', by
Tsirətsitban

Figure 36 *Ndu* 'man' by Tsiretsitban.
Photograph Anthony Forge. From the Anthony
Forge Papers, Mandeville Special Collections
Library, University of California, San Diego.

fronds and swirls in the river's course seem motivated by formal considerations. That does not of course suggest that every meaning is attached on the basis of iconicity, in particular abstract meanings such as male power or ancestors. Even in such cases, however, iconicity may be one factor in complex metaphorical and semantic processes. Eyes are represented by circles and have close associations with stars (*kwun*) and by way of fireflies (also *kwun*) with ancestors (Forge 1973b: 190).

The paintings as a whole are associated with certain spiritual entities, and express Abelam ideas and values. In many cases they represent *nggwalndu*, clan ancestral spirits. These are present in the cult houses in the form of figurative wooden carvings, and are the most powerful spirit known to exist. Some *nggwalndu* can combine human and non-human features and some paintings represent animal forms, but Forge does not elaborate on the cosmology of the Abelam. Each painting of a *nggwalndu* has a series of elements associated with it. At one point Forge draws an analogy between the elements of a *nggwalndu* and the letters of a word: 'they form a code built out of a finite number of stylistic elements: various arrangements of those elements signify *nggwalndu*, butterfly or flying fox' (Forge 1970: 282). He then qualifies this by continuing, 'the flat painting code has an essential ambiguity in that varying interpretations of elements are possible and equally legitimate' (ibid.). However, here he is in danger of opening up the interpretability of the system too much.

There is no question that Abelam representations are ambiguous at all levels of the system, and that Abelam designs are highly productive semantically. It is quite wrong to look for a single representational meaning for each design and every design element. Nonetheless the range of meanings associated with particular design elements is limited and the range of meanings is often unique to that element. Certain design forms such as that for flying fox have a referential meaning at their core, even though it contributes only partially to the overall meaning of the design. It is unlikely, then, that the flying fox design will be used if the design as a whole has no reference to flying foxes. The meaning of Abelam designs is both the product of the system of design generation, of the meanings it is possible to encode within it, and the product of interpretative processes that extend far beyond the design system itself. Forge attempted to deal with the properties of the design system by labelling it as a closed system, emphasizing its independence from any external system of referential meanings. However, this merely creates a logical problem of where the meanings associated with the closed system come from and how the meanings conveyed by this closed system articulate with those associated with language or ritual. Abelam flat painting as a system has properties that, he argued, are independent of verbal language or ritual action and cannot be reduced to those other systems. Nonetheless one might argue that its semantics could only be understood in the context of more general social and cultural processes. Anthropologists seem to have had tremendous difficulty with the fact that meaning is relatively independent of form but that form is necessary to convey meaning. Once the nature of this relationship is grasped then all systems of encoding meanings can be seen to be both relatively restricted and relatively open-ended, depending on the nature of the system and the way it is used. Abelam flat painting is more ambiguous than verbal language used in a certain way, and some Abelam images are more ambiguous than others.

So far I have been focusing primarily on the elements out of which Abelam paintings are composed. As Forge noted, the elements can be combined together to produce representations that are, on the surface, figurative or abstract. Abelam flat painting involves a number of complementary principles of selection and organization of elements. A picture of an ancestral figure has to contain a certain set of elements associated with that figure, and once those elements are selected then they can be organized into a whole in a number of different ways. In some cases the picture as a whole represents an image of the animal or ancestor concerned, in other cases it is impossible to discern any such relationship. Forge calls paintings of the first type representational and of the second type abstract (Forge 1973b: 174). However, quite rightly he does not wish to imply that these are discrete alternatives, that the painting is either one or the other.[8] The ordering of elements in the case of those that appear abstract is clearly related to the way elements are ordered in other paintings, including the representational ones, and vice-versa. Likewise the meaning of the paintings is not determined by the representational order since the other relationships between the elements may also be significant. In contemporary jargon there is no one-way of reading an Abelam painting.

Abelam paintings are frequently organised to represent a human face or human body, usually the face and body of a *nggwalndu* ancestor. In representing a face appropriate elements will be chosen to represent the eyes, nose, mouth, body and limbs. A characteristic W- or M-shaped design is used to represent the arms and legs, and the body itself is frequently represented by a pointed oval. The designs for limbs produce triangular shapes, which express meaning independent of the M- shaped outline itself, and can indeed be part of other figures within the painting as a whole. The interplay between different bases of ordering the elements gives a great deal of freedom to the Abelam artist, and artists create multiple representations of the human body by exploiting the ambiguity inherent in the representational system.

My account so far suggests that Abelam paintings consist of elements that can be combined on a number of different bases. The elements have a set of meanings that are intrinsic to them but which can also be defined, specified or extended in context. In combination with certain other elements they are part of *nggwalndu*, or a butterfly, or a flying fox; in the context of certain representations they are an eye, a vulva, a body, or a leg. The meanings are cumulative and more than one can apply in a particular case. Multivalency acts as a channel of connection within a painting and between paintings and contexts of interpretation: 'to identify a representation, is not to find out what the painting means, it is merely one element in a complex web of meaning which is to be found in the relationships of the parts that compose them' (Forge 1973b: 187). This much is clear from Forge's analysis of the system, which at all points is supported by some limited exegesis from the Abelam.[9]

The next stage of Forge's analysis involved following these pathways of connection, and it is here that he seems to find a systematic pattern of meaning for the first time in Abelam art. It is this level of meaning that excites Forge, and it is the hardest level to confirm from exegesis. It might be termed the symbolic meaning of Abelam art, in opposition to its referential meaning. Forge gives relatively few examples of what these symbolic meanings might be, but one theme that he considers important is the nature of the relationships between men and women, in particular with reference to spiritual power and fertility. He argues that art uses images of sexuality and female creativity to produce images of ancestral power, and provides a context for expressing the ambivalent nature of the relationship between men and women.

He gives as an example the relationship between two sets of designs on a house façade (Forge 1973b: 187–9). The top line consists of a frieze of women. The representations clearly indicating breasts and vulva make an emphatic statement of the femaleness of the pointed oval (Figure 37). Underneath is a frieze of *nggwalndu* heads. Initially there is no reason to suppose that these heads are constructed on the same basis, but on further inspection Forge realizes that the overall head design is contained within a pointed oval (Figure 38). The *nggwalndu* heads express the primacy of female creativity. Forge then links this association between female figures and *nggwalndu* heads to a tradition in which women are said to have

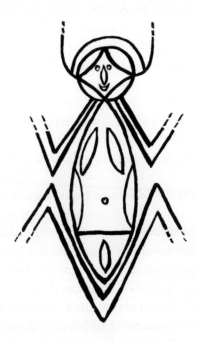

Figure 37   Female figure from a façade in Yanuko Village, north Abelam (Forge 1973b: 188).

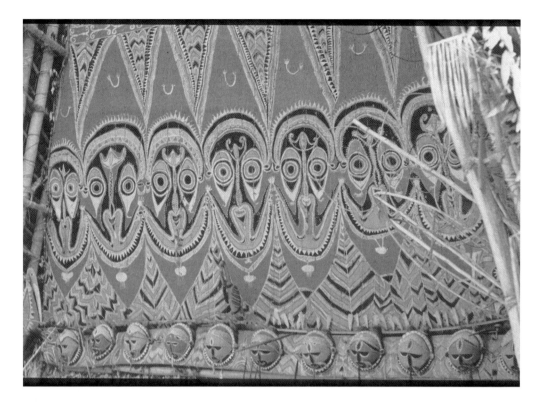

Figure 38   Bottom of ceremonial house façade, *nggwalndu* faces.
Bugiaura ceremonial ground, Yanuko village. Photograph Anthony Forge.
From the Anthony Forge Papers, Mandeville Special Collections Library,
University of California, San Diego.

discovered the original *nggwalndu* ancestors and became their lovers. When jealous men discovered this the *nggwalndu* turned into wooden form. We can see why Forge regrets the relative absence of myth among the Abelam, since in this case myth appears to confirm his insights.

Indeed, this has been a recurrent problem in the anthropological analysis of symbolism in societies which have limited traditions of exegesis and in which there are no parallel systems of song or oral tradition that add weight to the interpretations derived from the analysis of art and ritual action. Analyses such as Forge's have often been criticized precisely because there is no verbal confirmation of the conclusions drawn.[10] This was another reason why Forge emphasized the closed nature of Abelam art, arguing that the ideas may not have been expressible in other ways. 'Such themes are not talked about openly by the Abelam, they may even be denied ... [the forms] communicate directly to the Abelam not as an illustration of some spoken text' (ibid.: 190).

There are striking formal similarities between the art of the Abelam and that of the Yolngu of eastern Arnhem Land. Both use the same range of colours, and both employ a similar technique of cross-hatching. While the distribution of colours and infill varies overall, it is possible to find paintings in the two cases that look remarkably similar. Some Yolngu artworks also consist of a limited number of geometric elements that can be combined together in an almost infinite number of ways.

However, rather than simply presenting my own analysis of the relationships between the two bodies of art, I can take the opportunity afforded by the presence of Narritjin and Banapana in Canberra to present a more dialogic analysis. Narritjin and Banapana spent the day with Anthony Forge and me going through Anthony's collection of Abelam paintings and commenting on them.[11] It was a mediated discussion between two anthropologists about the art of societies in which they had worked, with the questioning being partly directed by artists from one of those societies. It is what Diane Losche perceptively refers to as a hybrid moment, 'particular moments of question and answer, which sometimes occur randomly, [in which] differences and difficulties of comprehension become clearest and most tangible often signalled by responses of puzzlement, irritation and unease. It is at these points that one faces knowledge of difficult, perhaps intractable, questions that won't go away. These same moments also point towards a path of further research which may lead to some important understanding only barely glimpsed amidst the feelings at the moment of encounter' (Losche 1997: 37).[12]

The interpretative process that Narritjin and Banapana engaged in was interesting for a number of reasons. We might have expected them to interpret the art according to the properties of their own artistic system, as if it were Yolngu art, and to interpret only those paintings that were formally similar. I think it is fair to say that this was Anthony's expectation. Instead, they entered into an ethnographic and analytical process, interrogating Anthony about the structure of Abelam society and the ways in which art was incorporated within social process. Toward the end they were beginning to interpret Abelam art as a system very different to their own, along lines that showed remarkable similarities to Forge's analysis. However, their view of Abelam art was not quite as distanced as his and they were able to incorporate Abelam paintings within their own social universe.[13]

If Anthony's analysis of Abelam paintings was influenced by his own historical position and by the questions and categories of his culture, so too was Narritjin's and Banapana's analysis. In both cases the analysts reveal much about their own culture through the act of interpreting that of another people. The very questions that Anthony posed about the relationship between representation and abstraction lay at the heart of modernist discourse. The questions Narritjin and Banapana posed were closely related to the place of art in their own society. Interestingly, both parties found some of the same aspects of Abelam art puzzling.

Anthony, as we have seen, was puzzled by the fact that Abelam paintings had no myths associated with them – a concern that came up several times in Narritjin's questioning.

Narritjin's first comment to Anthony was 'did you get a story about this?' About halfway through he commented, 'they have got names but they have got no stories. They have got no myths.' And at one point he asked almost incredulously 'Couldn't the artist understand what they are meaning?' This line of questioning thus produced precisely the conclusion that Anthony had made, and affirmed the contrast he drew between Yolngu and Abelam art.[14]

The next topic that Narritjin took up was the relationship between art and social organization. In Yolngu art there is a very precise relationship between designs and group organization. Yolngu society is divided into two patrimoieties, Dhuwa and Yirritja. The moieties are exogamous and patrilineal so that Dhuwa people marry Yirritja people and vice versa. People's primary attachment is to smaller groups within the moiety, which I call patrilineal clans. The clans are landowning groups. They play a role in structuring marriage relationships and they have rights in the sacra associated with their clan lands.[15]

North-east Arnhem Land, as we have noted in the previous chapter, is criss-crossed with the tracks of ancestral beings. In the ancestral past they stopped at particular places on their journeys, they created features of the landscape, and left behind the people who were to succeed them. Each area of land is associated with a distinct set of paintings, songs, and dances and objects that represent the clan's sacred inheritance and derive from the actions of the ancestral beings who created the landscape. Designs may mark the relationship between groups along an ancestral track. For example, the fire/wild-honey complex of the Yirritja moiety is associated with variations of the diamond design (see chapter 5). The Djan'kawu designs of the Dhuwa moiety are associated with different combinations of circle-line motifs. Each clan has its own particular version of the design that unambiguously marks it as the property of a particular group. The system of clan designs as a whole enables a precise mapping of the relationship between land, ancestral beings and social groups (Morphy 1988).

The Yirritja-moiety diamond designs are associated with a number of clans linked by the fire/wild honey ancestral complex (Figure 39), and each clan has its own variant of the design. Starting geographically in the west, the Dhalwangu design is associated with fresh water inland (Figure 40). The diamonds are small and equilateral, incorporating within their sequence pointed ovals representing billabongs. Manatja diamonds are similar but larger and infilled differently (Figure 41). The Madarrpa diamonds are more elongated and often end in a shield-shaped figure. They are associated with the coastal region of Yathikpa in the east where the crocodile ancestor was caught in the conflagration and dived into the sea to escape the flames, carrying the fire with him (see Figure 9). North along the coast at Caledon Bay the Gumatj design is associated with a crocodile who carried the fire inland.

This sociological level of interpretation is only one component of the meaning of the design. In each case the design has other meanings that relate to the actions of the ancestral beings, and therefore has enormous interpretative potential. I shall briefly consider the Manatja design to show the directions in which interpretation might go (see Figure 41). The

| Clan Design | Owning Clan | Description |
| --- | --- | --- |
|  | Dhalwangu | Equilateral diamond, smaller than the Munyuku one. |
|  | Munyuku | Equilateral diamond, larger than the Dhalwangu one. |
|  | Gumatj | Elongated diamond. |
|  | Madarrpa | Separate strings of elongated diamonds, ending in  ⋀⋀ |

Figure 39   Variants of the diamond design type
(see Morphy 1991: 172).

design represents wild honey and fire; it originated in ancestral action when the diamond pattern was burnt into the surface of a ceremonial object. The designs encode many elements of the wild-honey complex. Yirritja-moiety wild honey is associated with paperbark trees in the swamps. From this perspective the diamonds represent the wet season floodwaters. The white cross-hatching is the foam on the raging waters, the cross pieces are logs being tossed around in the current, and the red and black cross-hatching represents weeds being dragged along in the water. The honey is ready in the mid-dry season when the land has dried out and the country is burnt by fires lit by hunters. The diamonds now represent the passage of the fire. The red diamonds represent flames, the white ones smoke rising, the red

Figure 40   *Long-necked Freshwater Tortoises at Gänganbuy*, 1976. Artist Yanggarriny Wunungmurra. The background pattern represents wet-season floodwaters surging down the river. The zigzag lines represent streamers of weed caught in the turtles' feet. Copyright the artist's family. Reproduced courtesy of Buku-Larrnggay Mulka Art Centre.

Figure 41   *Wild Honey*, 1976. Artist, Dula Ngurruwutthun. The diamond design represents the Wild Honey Ancestral forces at Mandjawuy. Copyright the artist's family. Reproduced courtesy of Buku-Larrnggay Mulka Art Centre.

and black ones sparks flying, and the cross bar represents a log left behind by the fire edged with ash. The honey is now accessible and the diamond pattern represents the beehive itself. The white diamonds represent grubs, the red ones cells filled with honey and the crosspieces sticks inside the hive. In the case of each clan's diamond pattern, the interpretations of the diamonds will vary slightly according to the mythological events that took place in the country concerned. In the case of the crocodile, for example, some of the meanings refer to the pattern burnt into its skin by the fire.

On the surface, Abelam art could represent a very similar system, consisting as it does of geometric elements that look remarkably similar to north-east Arnhem Land designs. This apparent similarity provided an initial basis for Narritjin's interpretations (Figure 42). Geometric clan designs are present in all Yolngu sacred paintings. Sometimes the painting is comprised only of the clan design. The design may simply be outlined, the segments may be painted in red, yellow, white or black pigment, or each segment may be infilled with elaborate cross-hatching. The design signifies the clan and ancestral being associated with the painting, and acts as a constraint on the interpretation of other elements. Both Narritjin and Banapana initially drew analogies between the geometric patterns in Abelam art and

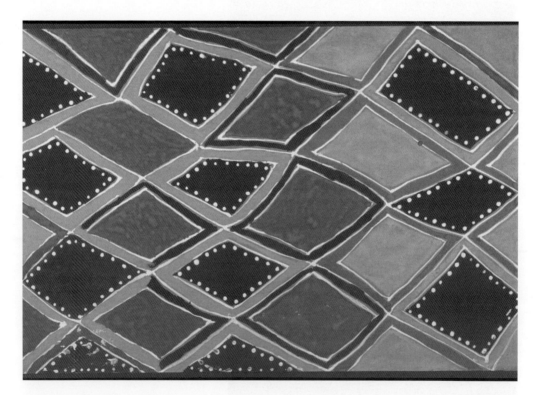

Figure 42   A diamond pattern in Abelam art. Photograph Anthony Forge. From the Anthony Forge Papers, Mandeville Special Collections Library, University of California, San Diego.

Yolngu clan designs. Narritjin unsurprisingly interpreted an Abelam diamond design as a wild-honey/fire design similar to those associated with the Munyuku and Dhaḻwangu clans. Indeed, designs looking almost identical to this occur as Yolngu body paintings.[16] Another painting (Figure 43) characterized by zigzag patterns was interpreted as a design for salt and fresh water coming together that his own clan, the Manggalili, shares with the Munyuku.

The most frequently occurring design element in the paintings Anthony collected were pointed ovals and sequences of triangles. The pointed oval is a central element in many of Narritjin's own paintings. It is not strictly speaking a clan design but the shape of the *yingapungapu* sand sculpture used in mortuary rituals, which we have come across earlier (and see Chapter 5 and Morphy 1991, chapter 11). The sand sculpture represents one that was made in the ancestral past (*wangarr*) by female ancestral women called Nyapililngu. The sand sculpture can be used to represent the bodies or parts of the bodies of the ancestral women in an analogous way to that of the Abelam tradition.

Triangular patterns are closely associated with a group of Yirritja-moiety clans that include the Yarrwiḏi Gumatj clan of Narritjin's maternal grandmother and a set of clans associated with the mythology of a race of ancestral hunters who came from overseas to visit the

Figure 43   Zigzag patterns in Abelam art. Photograph Anthony Forge.
From the Anthony Forge Papers, Mandeville Special Collections Library,
University of California, San Diego.

Figure 44    Pointed oval and triangular
designs in Abelam art. Photograph Anthony
Forge. From the Anthony Forge Papers,
Mandeville Special Collections Library,
University of California, San Diego.

Arnhem Land coast. They can also occur as a design element in Manggalili clan paintings. One of the first paintings that Anthony Forge showed to Narritjin and Banapana contained both a pointed oval and a complex of triangular designs (Figure 44). The painting was initially interpreted by Banapana as looking like a butterfly. Narritjin, on the other hand, associated it with the lake at Djarrakpi made by the ancestral Nyapililngu, with sand dunes on either side. He identified the (yellow) semicircles and the triangular patterns as sand dunes and the central feature as a *yingapungapu* sand sculpture, which in turn represents the lake. He thought that they might also represent the clouds that rise up above the lake and are associated with the symbolism of mortuary rituals. The bottom two figures were seen as triangles within triangles and, from a Yolngu perspective, were appropriately interpreted as clouds and sand hills associated with a Yirritja-moiety clan. The central feature was said to represent a string girdle that the women wore around their breasts. Narritjin and Banapana had both entered into the spirit of things. It might be argued that Banapana, in interpreting the figure as a butterfly, was responding simply to its formal properties, whereas Narritjin began by looking at it in terms of his own iconographical tradition. The dialogue between butterfly and Yolngu clan design continued as a theme for the next set of paintings.

Narritjin began to emphasize the possible connection with the whale hunters, 'to us it means sand dunes but to them from New Guinea, they are putting out cloud like the spout from the whale – connected to Balanda dreaming.'[17] In Narritjin's iconography the diamond design as cloud represents the distant horizon at the beginning of the wet season, the time when the mythical whale hunters would visit the Yolngu country. Narritjin interpreted a later painting as the home of the Balanda people, picking up on a structural detail of Yolngu painting in which a central feature surrounded by clan designs is seen as a representation of the *djalkirri* or foundation place of a clan. Once again, however, Banapana thought that it 'might be a butterfly'. At this point, Anthony intervened, saying that this was precisely the meaning given by the Abelam and that indeed they interpreted the whole painting as butterfly. Banapana then said that the triangular pattern must represent the colours and pattern on the surface of the wings. The presence of the butterfly, however, contradicted the interpretation as clan design. Butterflies are Dhuwa and the triangular design is Yirritja. Yolngu paintings almost never combine Dhuwa and Yirritja elements together. So Narritjin concluded in this case that the painting as a whole might be representing Dhuwa and Yirritja people living together.

A critical difference between Yolngu and Abelam paintings was beginning to emerge. They could not be interpreted on the same basis. Realizing this, Banapana asked Anthony: 'Do they have anything like Dreaming tracks?' Anthony replied: 'They are not really about places, they are about spirits. But they don't think the spirits are ancestors, they are different.' At which point I intervened: 'So you are not connected to them', and Anthony continued: 'So there is no clan ownership. They have moieties and one moiety paints the other and then they reverse this next time. But they paint the same pictures.' Narritjin laughed and said 'Yes I can see that.' While Anthony was out of the room Narritjin expressed concern about Abelam marriage practices 'Very good paintings, but no story. How are they born? Into the same group of people like a clan? How do they manage themselves?' I repeated that they did have two moieties, which Narritjin interpreted to be exogamous (as in the Yolngu case), continuing: 'As long as they do that then they are good for marriages, if they were married according to their own blood then that would not be good for them.' When Anthony returned, I said: 'we were talking about if they were exogamous', and Anthony replied 'Well yes at the level of clan not moiety, but they don't marry into the same blood.' 'That is good', said Narritjin.

Narritjin had thus identified fundamental differences between the Yolngu and Abelam systems which influenced the ways in which paintings were interpreted and the ways in which art articulated with social organization. Yolngu art is integral to the dynamics of moiety and clan organization, and the identification of clan designs is part of the interpretive process. Much of the content of paintings is determined by the mythology of the place represented.

Yirritja-moiety paintings will only have Yirritja-moiety animals and vice versa.[18] The correct identification of the clan design thus provides guidance to interpreting other elements in the painting, whether they are represented by figurative or geometric representations. Crocodiles, for example, are only associated with Yirritja-moiety clans while certain kinds of shark are associated with Dhuwa-moiety clans. While Abelam paintings look as though they might be organized on such a basis, it does not take long to discover that they are not.

When Narritjin and Banapana began looking for representational meaning in Abelam designs, their interpretations were often quite close to Anthony's and reflected principles used by Abelam in producing them (though from a Yolngu perspective). Many Abelam paintings include within them paintings of human figures and faces, often distorted and reorganized. Banapana, in Anthony's words, became expert at identifying Abelam figures. Figure 45 was the first image identified by Narritjin and Banapana as a face. They initially identified the mouth, teeth, and eye but also thought it might have the features of a butterfly.

Figure 45    Abelam face motif with lizard-skin pattern. Photograph Anthony Forge. From the Anthony Forge Papers, Mandeville Special Collections Library, University of California, San Diego.

Anthony then said that the pattern around the outside was said to represent a lizard skin, and Narritjin said that he could use a similar pattern to represent a Yirritja goanna. Narritjin then turned the image upside down and pointed out that it also looked like a head the other way up.

The next image we looked at represents a whole body rather than a face (Figure 46). I tried to interpret it in Yolngu terms as a representation of landscape, suggesting that the central feature was a waterhole. 'No', said Narritjin, 'they think it is a body and those are the

Figure 46    Body motif. Photograph Anthony Forge.
From the Anthony Forge Papers, Mandeville Special
Collections Library, University of California, San Diego.

arms and legs. And we can see that they are hunting for fish.' 'And', said Banapana, 'those are eyes up there.' This interpretation greatly pleased Anthony: 'But if you ask the Abelam they say they are stars, but according to Forge they are eyes and you can see Banapana picked it in one.' Narritjin then noticed that the motif seemed to repeat itself at the bottom and continued: 'They say they're eyes here but what is in the bottom looks like eyes too! But which way up is it? – very tricky.'

Narritjin quickly grasped the idea that many Abelam paintings could be interpreted as faces and tended to identify the elements at one level with similar meanings to those Forge recorded from the Abelam. As we looked at another painting (Figure 47) Anthony said to Narritjin: 'You are the expert on finding things – you pick out bits of faces which are true.' Narritjin identified the painting initially as a face with two eyes and a nose in the centre. When Anthony confirmed this identification, Narritjin continued to develop further interpretations. He switched his reference point and suggested that the figures on the outside represented the person when he was alive and the central figures a whole lot of bones. The white circle that had previously been identified as the mouth became the skull and the white lines bones. He also said that the outside figures represented two faces looking

Figure 47   Abelam face motif. Photograph Anthony Forge. From the Anthony Forge Papers, Mandeville Special Collections Library, University of California, San Diego.

in toward each other. Perhaps he saw the figures as combined eyes and mouths looking inward. In Narritjin's own paintings, dead animal and human figures are painted in white – in contrast to living ones – and the transformation from life to death is a major theme.

The next painting that Anthony presented (Figure 48) again provoked an interesting discussion. Narritjin identified it as a human figure. Anthony suggested a face with three eyes and Narritjin qualified it as really three people with three eyes. He thought that the pointed oval was probably a ceremonial ground and the semi-circles on either side were sand dunes. He went on to suggest that the painting was deliberately designed to obscure meaning and to confuse the interpreter: 'What they are giving you is a trick, they are putting a person but on the inside they are putting little bits of people [cut up] so you can't decide.'

A number of interesting points arise out of this process of interpretation. Narritjin and Banapana find the principles of Abelam bodily deconstruction easy to grasp. They interpret the ambiguous and multiple images partly according to the underlying principles of their own artistic system. The figures are transformational human figures which can have the characteristics of animal forms. But the interpretations came equally out of the structure

Figure 48   Human figure. Photograph
Anthony Forge. From the Anthony Forge
Papers, Mandeville Special Collections Library,
University of California, San Diego.

of the paintings, the information they elicited from Anthony Forge about their meanings, and reflections on what significance the paintings might have in the context of Yolngu culture. They saw the paintings as comprising elements of animals and humans cut up and reassembled to contain elements of both. They used Anthony as an informant to identify meanings of elements when he knew them. And they reflected on what the significance of the particular combinations might be. One conclusion that they came to was that the paintings represented spirit beings and that many alluded to transformations between animal forms, in particular butterflies and human beings. The idea of transformational spirit beings is salient to Yolngu artists, since their own system of representation is centrally concerned with representations of transformational ancestral beings (see Morphy 1989). The connection with butterflies suggested a particular association with the Dhuwa-moiety land of the dead, Buralku, since butterflies abound there and have resonance with human spirits.

The dissected human or animal body is a familiar theme of Yolngu culture. The bodies of Ancestral beings are distributed throughout the landscape where they have been transformed into features of the environment. In mortuary rituals and initiation ceremonies across Arnhem Land, images of the divided body abound. It is also significant that Narritjin in this context and on other occasions suggested a way in which Abelam art might function as a system of restricted revelatory knowledge. The three eyes might be there to suggest three people but maybe this was deliberately misleading. Certainly Narritjin's view of Abelam art would be consistent with Forge's that 'there is no line to be drawn between representational and abstract art.'

I suggested at the beginning of the chapter that Narritjin's and Banapana's interpretations of Abelam art were never as distanced as Anthony's, never as much an 'outsider's' view.[19] Although they were able to identify key differences between the structure of Yolngu and Abelam art, their interpretative process nonetheless attempted to incorporate Abelam art within their own system of meaning. Art is one of the ways in which Yolngu have incorporated outsiders in their world: they use their own structures to transform outsiders into insiders. I have shown elsewhere how the Macassan traders became incorporated within the Yolngu universe by being projected into the ancestral past as ancestral beings of the Yirritja moiety (Morphy 1991: 140–1). People from New Guinea are linked with the same mythology, and the ancestral world from whence they come is said to be the Yirritja-moiety land of the dead.[20] To Narritjin and Banapana it was no coincidence that designs from coastal clans of the Yirritja moiety figured prominently in Abelam art. This mythology became a reference point for interpreting many of the paintings. And Narritjin used the term *Balanda* to refer to the New Guineans (Abelam).

This came out clearly in the interpretation of one painting (Figure 49) where Narritjin and Banapana refused to adopt Anthony's interpretation as the most relevant one. The painting is another representation of two human figures, on this occasion headless. Discussion of the painting began a little embarrassingly. Narritjin reasonably thought that the representations were of two flying foxes. Anthony said: 'No it is not flying foxes.' I then said 'I couldn't even

Figure 49   Two human figures. Photograph Anthony
Forge. From the Anthony Forge Papers, Mandeville
Special Collections Library, University of California,
San Diego.

guess,' which elicited the cutting response: 'You haven't been to any of my lectures, have
you? – No it is the human body again and this is the big ornament made out of baler shell.'
And then Narritjin took over: 'They are looking for whale, that is the sea grass and this is the
fire place here and here for cooking up the whale.' In later paintings Narritjin identified the
baler shell ornament as a representation of the knife used to cut up the whale, the coloured
segments as pieces of whale, or the spout of the whale. On another painting he identified the

diamond designs as representing one of its other meanings: the flags put up by the Balanda people and which Yolngu use today in mortuary rituals.

The mythology of the Balanda is associated with whale hunting. Yolngu paintings focus on the cutting up of the whale into various parts for division among relatives. The paintings represent the skin, flesh and blubber and often include the knife used to cut it up. The whales are connected with the wet season. The spout of the ancestral whale is thought to create rain clouds represented by the anvil shape of the tail. In Yolngu paintings the triangular patterns represent the wet-season clouds lined up on the horizon and the effect of light reflected through them. The whale is rarely represented figuratively and the paintings usually comprise geometric elements. Figure 50 is an example of a Lamamirri-clan painting

Figure 50   *Lamamirri-clan Painting of the Whale*, 1997. Artist Deturru Yunupingu. Copyright the artist. Australian National Maritime Museum. Reproduced courtesy of Buku-Larrnggay Mulka Art Centre.

of the whale by Deturru Yunupingu. In Deturru's painting the triangular patterns in red, yellow, black and white represent the wet-season clouds on the horizon. The knives represent ones used to cut up the whale; the central zigzag pattern is rough water covering a rock that is a transformation of the body of the whale. The tail of the whale is shown floating in calm water at the bottom and at the top the figure alludes to the tail, the spume of the whale and storm clouds. In other paintings of the whale, bands of colour are interpreted as cut-up pieces of the whale.

Neither Narritjin nor Banapana thought that they were interpreting the paintings as Abelam themselves would have. Rather, they entered into a process of interpretation and comparison that moved them toward an interpretation of Abelam art and its relationship to their own. In interpreting paintings as representations of human faces and bodies, they adopted Forge's 'Abelam' perspective. They attempted to see the paintings as Abelam saw them. They de-emphasized the placedness of Yolngu art, its reference to landscape and its close association with a system of clanship.

In other cases, such as in the case of the whale hunters, they developed avenues of interpretation that on the surface moved some of the paintings well away from Abelam experience. The association of a number of the paintings with the mythology of Balanda whale hunters, that belongs to a set of Yirritja-moiety clans, came more out of the form of art rather than from any information that they could elicit from Anthony. They knew that the Abelam did not hunt whales and had established that the designs were not directly linked with patrilineal clan organization. Yet a number of things about the paintings persuaded them of the salience of their interpretations. The whale hunters who visited Yolngu country in the past were associated with New Guinea and eastern Indonesia. The whale hunters were associated with spirits of the dead as they understood the Abelam paintings to be. In Yolngu myth the whale hunters themselves were transformed eventually by fire into flying foxes (the form in which they return to Yolngu country to this day), and flying fox was given by Anthony as a meaning to elements on the same set of paintings. But more than anything else it was the formal elements of the paintings that kept bringing them back to the whale hunters – the triangular patterns of the wet-season clouds, the knives that were used to cut up the bodies of the whale. The strips of whale that they saw in the paintings, the cross-hatching that referred to whale fat and flesh, and the black curved forms that hinted at the whale's tail and cloud, made the interpretations hard to resist. In the paintings Narritjin saw whale. But it was a mythical whale that is characterized as much by its absence as by its presence. Of the Abelam paintings Narritjin said: 'You never put out the picture of the whale. But every time you show me one of these paintings I know it is still on the whale side.' He was referring to the whale in Abelam art, but he could equally have been referring to the whale in Yolngu art. Deturru's painting of the whale is as literal a representation of a whale as one ever gets in Yolngu paintings and it is usually much more hidden than this.

The Balanda mythology as a whole is concerned with transformation and passage across the seas, positioning Yolngu cosmology in relation to the wider world outside. The mythology provides a basis for the symbolism of Yirritja-moiety mortuary rituals in which different elements are associated with different stages of the ceremony. The cutting up of the whale meat, for example, is associated with the division of responsibilities of kin in the ceremony, and is also a metaphor for the process of bodily decay and disintegration following death. The process of interpretation Narritjin and Banapana were engaged in here runs parallel to the more analytic approach they adopted to other aspects of Abelam art, and is part of the process of incorporating outsiders on the edge of their known social universe within an existing though changing framework of understanding.

## CONCLUSION

What have we learnt about the relationship between Abelam and Yolngu art? Perhaps as important, what have we learnt about the properties of each system from adopting a comparative perspective? Anthropologists have always been aware of the implicitly comparative nature of their discipline, of the fact that the concepts and concerns of the anthropologist's own culture have influenced the questions posed and the way they are answered. Gradually, over time, the questions and methods change as part of the process and become more sensitive to the cultures studied. In this chapter, I have described a mediated discussion in which Abelam art was analysed in relation to Yolngu art. Anthony Forge approached Abelam art with two key questions in mind. One, derived from the history of Western art, concerned the significance of form in art, in particular the relationship between representation and abstraction. The other came out of the symbolic anthropology of the 1960s and concerned what the art 'meant'. Forge concluded that the distinction between abstract and representational art was unhelpful in analysing Abelam art. As far as meaning was concerned, Abelam art was a closed system in which meaning was generated internally by the relationship between formal elements. He came to this conclusion partly because the Abelam did not provide the kind of answers to the question of meaning that he anticipated. While they gave meanings for individual elements and sometimes a name for a whole painting, they did not come out with detailed exegesis of their art – they appeared to have no stories.

Narritjin's and Banapana's interventions in Anthony Forge's analysis of Abelam art are of interest partly because they challenge the assumption that questions about meaning in art are in themselves somehow Eurocentric. Forge's question, 'what does it mean?' was an entirely reasonable one to Narritjin and Banapana, and they found the absence of myth or story just as puzzling as he did. And like Forge they drew conclusions that moved interpretation in a different direction, toward transformation, toward restricted knowledge, directions in which Diane Losche's analyses of Abelam art also turned. They responded to the 'aesthetics' of Abelam art, seeing the brilliant surface forms reflected in the designs, the colours of the butterfly's wings and the lizard's skin. And they also began to learn Abelam conventions of figurative representation. While Narritjin and Banapana had been exposed to my own line of questioning about meaning, I believe that the questions they posed about Abelam art were very much their own and reflected in turn differences between Yolngu and Abelam art. They also suggest that the puzzles of the anthropology of art are not solely a Western concern.

The simple answer to the difference between Yolngu and Abelam art might be that the Yolngu do have stories. However, this is misleading since Yolngu stories are not what the painting represents but a parallel genre which articulates with art. Yolngu paintings are also a product of the fact that Yolngu use art as a general system of communication and have a tradition of exegesis. Yolngu art, in comparison with Abelam flat painting, is a highly differentiated system. In Yolngu art many different kinds of meaning can be encoded and art can be used for different purposes in different contexts. Narritjin and Banapana's interrogation of Abelam art revealed some of the key features of Yolngu art. Yolngu art contains within it a system of clan designs which precisely identify the relationship between people, place and ancestral being. The system is a flexible one that can accommodate changing relationships and is integral to the ongoing politics of Yolngu society. However, it is important to stress that in the system of clan designs it is possible to encode complex messages with a minimum of ambiguity. This level of specificity is absent from the Abelam system.

In other areas, however, Yolngu art is every bit as open-ended and ambiguous as Abelam art. Yolngu geometric art is multivalent, and many different meanings can be condensed in the same form, as in the case of the wild honey/fire design. This multivalency is exploited to make connections between things and to create metaphors in the Yolngu case, as it is in the Abelam case. In both artistic systems, however, it is necessary to recognize that there are different ways in which the same meaning can be encoded, and that different ways of encoding influence the way the meanings are understood and interpreted. In the Yolngu case there is, in addition, a tradition of figurative representation that can encode many of the meanings of the geometric art. In both the Abelam and Yolngu case, though, meaning is conveyed by the relationships between representations as well as by the representations in themselves. The fact that a *nggwalndu* ancestor can be represented in human figure form or deconstructed into various component parts is an integral feature of the Abelam system. In Yolngu art this type of deconstruction is exploited in many ways. The capacity to represent ancestral beings in different forms, ranging from figurative representations to particular combinations of geometric forms, enables the transformative nature of ancestral beings to be conveyed (Morphy 1989). It also enables them to be understood as abstractions that are only partially manifest in any one representation.

Yolngu art is also concerned with those fundamental themes of human existence that Forge identifies as the real 'meaning' of Abelam art. The issue which he comes back to again and again is that of the relationship between men and women and the fact that 'women are generally considered the inferiors of men throughout Australia and New Guinea, but analyses of the ritual system in both areas … [reveal] women to be truly creative and naturally powerful' (Forge 1979: 286). Forge argues that art and ritual exploit and articulate such fundamental contradictions, 'giving fundamental comprehension of the culture at an

Figure 51   *Yingapungapu and Digging Stick*, 1978. Artist Narritjin Maymuru. The painting represents two ancestral women, the Nyapililngu, on either side of a figure that represents both a digging stick and the elliptical shape of a sand sculpture, the *yingapungapu*. Collection unknown. Copyright the artist's family. Reproduced courtesy of Buku-Larrnggay Mulka Art Centre.

emotional as well as an intellectual level'. But he also goes on to say that such meanings are unlikely to be articulated verbally, perhaps precisely because they are not fully worked-out or fully expressible in a simple sentence, and hence the absence of stories in Abelam art. While I do not entirely agree with Forge's conclusions, there are many areas of Yolngu art too where meanings remain implicit, and often they are concerned with the nature of things, with relationships between things, and of course with relationships between men and women. I shall conclude with a painting by Narritjin (Figure 51) which delighted Anthony when he saw it, and which would have communicated well to an Abelam interpreter.[21] It shares a key iconographic element with Abelam art: a pointed oval. We may remember that the pointed oval on the frieze of women in the house façade became, lower down, the contour that outlined the face of the male *nggwalndu* figures. The implicit meaning was the male face incorporated within the ancestral vulva. In Narritjin's painting we have an analogous set of incorporations. In the centre is a sacred object, a digging stick, representing an ancestral being. It is acknowledged to have a phallic reference. The figure is repeated within two human figures on either side. The figures are ancestral women and the digging stick is included within an outer ellipse which represents their pregnant stomachs. Narritjin said the digging stick is her baby. What could the meaning be of a woman being pregnant with a penis? Ask Freud or Forge, an Abelam or a Yolngu. But don't expect a straight answer.

# 7 ART THEORY AND ART DISCOURSE ACROSS CULTURES

## INTRODUCTION

At the beginning of Chapter 6 I mentioned an exhibition of art from Yirrkala in 1976 at the Australian National University. I remember having a long conversation with an Australian art-historian as to whether the works in the exhibition were artworks or something else – ethnography or perhaps craft. His argument was that the works were the product of clans, corporate groups, rather than the work of individual creative artists. Moreover they were replicas – copies of designs that had been previously produced by members of the clan, and hence they failed to fulfil some of the main criteria for belonging to the Western category 'art'. Perhaps mistakenly I tried to take up the argument in his terms, by referring to the diversity of styles of painting produced within each clan, pointing out the formal characteristics that differentiated one artist's work from another's, and how it was possible to show the development of formal sequences over time in Yolngu art. 'But do they recognize these distinctions?' he enquired. And I had to admit that I did not know, but that more often than not they would deny that there was any difference. To me this was an interesting contradiction to be explored in Yolngu art practice – the contradiction between an ideology of continuity in the production of collective forms and my perception of a rich and innovative practice in which individual artists continually produced new forms. Maybe this innovation was an unrecognized and unconsciously produced epiphenomenon of something else; perhaps change was produced by the process of reproduction in a non-literate tradition, where the record of the past was continually being reproduced through its representations in the present.[1] Changes occurred but they were either unperceived, or not emphasized because they were unimportant. Whatever the explanation, to the art historian the conclusion was obvious: these were not works of art as he understood the category.

The issue is important because it has significance for the ways in which Aboriginal artworks are accepted in the Euro-Australian artworld, how they are classified, and how they are catalogued; it has consequences for the recognition of Aboriginal individuals as artists. In this case the issue under debate was whether Aboriginal art should be included in its own right within the Australian National Gallery, or only exhibited in its supposed relationship to European art, side by side with a Fairweather or a Preston. But it could as easily have involved a debate about whether, in cataloguing the works, priority should be given to the clan or group associated with the work or to the individual artist, or whether, in exhibiting works, indigenous categories should be used as the basis for hanging the exhibition.[2] The issues thus range from whether Aboriginal works can be accepted as art, to whether they should be curated as art in a different way from that used for European paintings.

Too often anthropologists and art historians have made assumptions about the differences between Western and non-Western conceptions of 'art' objects. These tend to make the non-Western objects more distant than they prove to be after more rigorous investigation. (See Van Damme 1997 for a relevant discussion.) To understand the significance of the perspectives adopted by an Indigenous as opposed to a European artist, it is necessary first of all to place the objects they produce in their respective cultural contexts and examine those contexts more fully. On the surface, the differences between two cultures' concept of an art object may seem quite profound when measured according to singular criteria. Further investigation into the discourse that surrounds the objects in the each case, and an analysis of the ways in which they are conceived and how they are used, may problematize the degree of difference.[3] Differences that at first sight appear categorical may be revealed as differences of emphasis or different interpretations of similar phenomena. In some cases Indigenous Australian artists may appear to prioritize group affiliation over individual agency in attributing works of art to people, but this should not in itself be a criterion for defining works as ethnography rather than art. If that were the case then many works of European art should be removed from the gallery, since they were produced at a time when individual authorship was a less significant factor in Western art practice and when the concept of art differed markedly from that associated, for example, with modernism.[4]

The works that art historians deal with come from very different cultural contexts and times. It must be presumed that the intention of art history is to understand those works initially in the contexts of their time and of the societies that produced them before relating them to historical processes that link objects across place and time. As I suggested in Chapter 1, it is possible to imagine an art history that is only concerned with the history of art objects once they have been included as part of the Western canon or accepted as objects worthy of inclusion in a fine art gallery or museum. However, this would be a particularly narrow form of art history and would be of little help in explaining many aspects of the form of the objects being studied. Of course, those aspects could be part of a separate study – 'research into the cultural background of objects subsequently included in the Western category of art object'. However, to create this as a separate area of study would be to accept a priori that the place of objects in the original context of their production is irrelevant to understanding how they work as art objects. It would also have the effect of separating the producing cultures from world art history.

Certainly, in many cases, the ways in which non-European artworks have been incorporated in the history of European art or influenced the practice of European artists had nothing to do with their original significance in the societies of origin. However, it does not follow that in their original context they were not art objects – that is to say objects that can be accommodated by a cross-cultural and cross-temporal definition of art. It is necessary to investigate the sense in which these are the same kind of object as European artworks and the senses in which they differ. Otherwise they have the status of found or adopted objects, or, to use Maquet's apposite phrase, they are art by metamorphosis (Maquet 1986) – objects that are appreciated by the Western artworld without reference to their significance to members of the producing cultures. They are part of the history of Western art as objects incorporated within Western art but not part of the history of the objects as art in their own historical and cultural context, a point well made by Susan Vogel (1988).[5]

It is true that some of the objects from other cultures that have metamorphosed into works of art in a European context – that have become examples of primitive fine art – may not be art in the context of the societies that produced them. In that case they are not in themselves the subject of art history in their indigenous context but of the history of the kinds of object that they are – a Zande net, for example, may or may not be an art object to the Zande even if it can be considered from certain Western perspectives to be a work of art.[6] They may of course be relevant to the study of Zande art in that they are part of its contextual background, just as the history of technology is relevant to studying Western artforms and the forms of baskets and spears are relevant to studying Yolngu art (see Chapter 2) – art is a subset of the material culture produced by a society. A similar case might be made for a Dogon ladder or a Tikopean headrest.[7] And that critical approach needs to be applied to all objects encompassed in the Western category of fine art whether they be Mediaeval, Classical, African, Egyptian or Indigenous Australian. There can only be an African or Australian Aboriginal art history if it is acknowledged that some objects are in some sense art objects in the context of the societies that produced them; and that requires the development of a definition or conception of art which is capable of encompassing the diversity of cultures concerned. But the study of non-Western arts will inevitably encompass a different set of objects from those that have been adopted into the Western category of fine art. It will not be restricted to works that have been placed historically in the art gallery as opposed to the ethnographic museum.

Many of the issues that are raised by the curation and marketing of Aboriginal art – the artist as author, the institutional context of art, the role of individual creativity, the autonomy of form – are central to Western art history and art theory, and in turn influence the production of art. The relationship between art theory, art history and art practice can be seen to be problematic. Art historians not only write about art but also have had a role in defining art and in 'discovering' art. There is of course no simple deterministic relationship between art history and art practice. Art history is not a unitary hegemonic discourse but consists of many discourses, which change over time, and which may reflect quite different views of what art is and artists are. The struggle over the recognition of Aboriginal art has been in part an argument in Western art history and theory about what 'art' is – with questions of ontology.[8]

If Western art history has an important role in Western art practice, is there an equivalent area of Aboriginal discourse about their art objects that could play an important role in the exhibition and interpretation of Aboriginal art, even if that art is apparently being exhibited in a non-Aboriginal context? Are Aboriginal views about art and creativity best framed as they conventionally have been, as ethnography, cultural background or cultural context? If this premise is accepted, there is a danger that Aboriginal views will be used to position the works in Western art discourse rather than contributing to the discourse itself. Aboriginal art will be included in a particular way, with essentialized assumptions about its difference from European art – such as that 'Aboriginal artists are members of groups, the rights in Aboriginal paintings are corporately held, and the designs have been handed on unchanged from the Dreamtime'. Unless due attention is paid to Indigenous ideas about what kinds of things art works are – ideas which in turn influence artistic practice – all of the changes that occur in Aboriginal art will be perceived as having occurred in the European frame, or as a consequence of the movement of that art into Western contexts, rather than as being influenced Aboriginal discourses about art. Aboriginal art history will only begin when the works are incorporated within the Western frame. Before that moment all of their life is viewed as an ethnographic artefact, and the existence of an Aboriginal/indigenous frame for discussing art is denied. In the Yolngu case I argue that, at least from the perspective of the artists themselves, both frames exist, and there is a relatively smooth transition between them.[9]

The ways in which Aboriginal people conceptualize art objects, the ways in which they talk about them and the kind of knowledge that they bring to bear on them has to be the basis of art history's writing about Aboriginal art. And if that information is included within the framework of Aboriginal art history or the approach of Western art historians to Aboriginal art then not only will it open up different possibilities of discourse about the relationships between Aboriginal art and the art of other cultures, including the diverse history of cultures encompassed within the rubric of European art, but it will also reveal synergies that are otherwise obscured by the kind of art history that is overly constrained by a narrow conception of what art is.

My reason for pursuing the idea of an art history/art theory that is synergistic with the Aboriginal discourse about art is partly a pragmatic one. If in European art there is a relationship between art, art criticism and art theory, when introducing Aboriginal art to Western contexts one should be attuned to the possibility that an analogous body of discourse exists within Aboriginal society. Aboriginal art discourse is likely to produce a different understanding of the relationships in space and time among art objects than does conventional European art history, but both would nonetheless be encompassed within the rubric of a more cross-cultural art history.

While I do not intend to argue that art history is a cross-cultural concept, there is a greater overlap between indigenous and Western discourse over art than most theorists allow for. If there is a relationship between the two then it may be possible to see Aboriginal art discourses entering into a dialogue with European art discourses and each being influenced by the other. If there is compatibility between discourses then this may be shown to have influenced the ways in which Aboriginal art has developed in a post-colonial context. In simple terms, it changes the premise of the debate from 'this [piece of information] does not fit, or challenges, the Western definition of art' to 'under an Aboriginal theory of art, or from the perspective of Aboriginal art history, the following is the case'. It presents the European artworld with information that it has to come to terms with and accommodate to rather than simply presenting information that can be used to adjust the space the art occupies in European classifications of objects.

My aim in the next section is not so much to produce a cross-cultural definition of art history, as to develop an art history that is sensitive to the different ontologies of art cross-culturally – to different ways in which people talk about and conceive of artworks. I am not convinced that art history as an academic discipline is the kind of thing that is likely to prove to be a cross-cultural category, but I believe that, as an institution of Western society, it should become more cross-culturally sensitive; it is important that it articulates with relevant fields of discourse in the societies whose art history is being researched. Art history is in part concerned with dates and sequences, and with relationships between objects in time and space, but it concerns equally the ideas associated with those objects that in part produce them and influence the trajectories of form over time (see Kubler 1962). Art history is part of Western art discourse and as such it has inevitably at times influenced art practice. It is thus all the more important that when it approaches the history of non-Western art it is cognizant of local art discourse and of the ontology of art in the particular case, to ensure that it is not unduly influenced in analysing other art histories in terms of Western presuppositions about the kind of thing art is. In order to understand the trajectory of Indigenous Australian art, it is important to consider the kind of thing art is to the producing societies and how that influences the relationships that Indigenous Australians see between artworks and the conclusions that they draw from those relationships. By making Indigenous art discourse part of the data of art history and critically examining the ontological concepts and their relationship to practice, we should become aware of conceptual similarities and differences between different traditions. And in the case of different art traditions that occupy the same temporal space we should be able to better understand how they articulate with one another – in the case of Aboriginal art, how Indigenous artists embrace contemporary Australian art worlds.

## TOWARD A MORE CROSS-CULTURAL ART HISTORY

There have recently been signs of a rapprochement between anthropology and art history (for example Volkenandt 2005 and the essays in Westermann 2005). The time when anthropologists of art neglected form and avoided concepts such as 'style' and when art historians paid too little attention to social context is over, certainly in individual cases, if not right across the disciplines. The exchange has been an unequal one. The neglect of art by anthropologists has continued to be a negative factor, limiting the opportunities for an art-historical anthropology to emerge. In Africa in particular it has been the art historians who have shown the way, adding the methods of anthropology in the form of long-term fieldwork to the objectives of art history in elucidating the distribution and significance of forms in art (see Boone 1986, McNaughton 1988 and Blier 1987, among others). But in Australia and the Pacific the situation has if anything been reversed, with anthropologists playing a leading role in analysing the forms of art and analysing historical relations (for example Kaeppler 1978, Thomas 1991 and 1995, and Morphy 1998).

However, this chapter is less concerned with the respective contributions of the two disciplines to some joint enterprise than with the metatheoretical questions that the combining of art history with anthropology provokes. In other areas of anthropology these kinds of question have proved productive at the interstices between disciplines: examples are questions about the nature of belief and rationality at the boundaries with philosophy, and about the nature of culture at the boundary with biology, as are the productive debates over ideology, memory and the imagination, among others, at the boundaries with history. Anthropology challenges the assumptions of other disciplines through cross-cultural analysis and is in turn challenged to account for phenomena in other than cultural terms by the general propositions of other disciplines.

In the past, anthropology and art history have often been opposed as disciplines. I would argue that they should be complementary. Art history was and is still often cast as a discipline which approaches art in relation to one set of questions, and anthropology as a discipline that approaches art according to another set of questions. There then can occur a series of slippages. The two sets of questions become associated with different kinds of society – art history is an approach to objects as they are exhibited in an art gallery, and anthropology or ethnography is associated with works as they are exhibited in an ethnographic museum. Inasmuch as art history maintains these distinctions, it is in fact part of the process of reproducing the categorical distinctions between Western fine art and ethnographic artefact, since it has defined its field according to the Western category of fine art in its institutional mode – art history deals with art as it is encompassed by Western art worlds (cf. Danto 1964).[10] The opposition that is thus created makes art history blind to evidence that contradicts the categorical distinctions between Western and non-Western art.[11] A similar critique can be made from the perspective of anthropology, which in the past tended to over-emphasize the differences between human societies, create over-defined boundaries around them and essentialize the Western other.

This association of anthropology with one set of questions and art history with another has set them apart when they attempt to approach the same subject matter. And I shall argue that it fundamentally miscast the relationship between the two from the outset. Anthropology is primarily concerned with issues of cross-cultural translation – recording and analysing the world from the perspective of a particular society and reproducing the data in such a way that it can be understood, in its own terms, by members of another. The product of anthropological analysis, the data that anthropologists provide can be subject to the analysis from other disciplinary frameworks – in this case by art historians. Such cross-disciplinary interaction of course requires that the anthropologist records the kind of data relevant to the other discipline – data relating to categories of thought in the case of philosophy, relevant Indigenous knowledge in the case of science, data relevant to explaining the form of the object in the case of art history,[12] The net result of a more collaborative approach should be to reveal, where they exist, perspectives from the societies in question that are relevant to the subject of the particular discipline.

It is not so much that Aboriginal Australia will be revealed to have its own discipline of art history, rather that the processes and discourses on which art history is centred will be found to exist more generally cross-culturally. Inasmuch as art history is concerned with the explanation of form, then it must be concerned with theories of art in the societies it encompasses, since their theories about art and the ontology of art, including the theories of the art practitioners, are likely to be relevant to explaining the relationship between objects in space and time. In the case of Western art the relationship between art history, art theory and art practice is subtle since there is an overlap between the discourses – art history and art theory are both concerned with the relationships between objects in time and space, and both at different times have influenced Western art practice.

Most academic disciplines are grounded in the common-sense knowledge and experience of members of the societies in which they develop. Art history is no exception and has evolved as part of Western systems of knowledge with an inevitable bias toward the common-sense understanding of the societies concerned. If we include overlapping fields of discourse and knowledge systems from other cultures, then we enter that process of adjusting the parameters of the discipline to enable it to take part in cross-cultural dialogue in a way that responds to the common-sense knowledge and understandings of other cultures.[13] It is possible that the art historians may find themselves extending the boundaries too far. Disciplines are always concerned with maintaining their distinctive boundaries. In the case of art history, I would argue that in looking at Aboriginal society from the perspective of providing data relevant to art historians, we do find synergies between Aboriginal discourses about art and art history, just as we shall find synergies between Aboriginal knowledge about the seasonal cycle in Arnhem Land and Western science. And if one reflects back on Western art history, it becomes apparent that within its own domain it has always been encompassing of other cultures and times, stretching out for information to make sense of the historical record, from the moment that Winckelmann engaged with the trajectories and contexts of Classical antiquity (Irwin 1972).

I shall begin by outlining the field of discourse in Aboriginal society which overlaps with topics approached by Western art historians when analysing Aboriginal art. The discourse centres on the formal relations between paintings in space and time and the attribution of works to individuals or groups, but will stray into the more specific areas of individual creativity and artistic influence. While these may not be considered as core components of the definition of some contemporary schools of art history, they do reflect a concept of art history associated with museum collections and art galleries. I would be interested to know if they were indeed entirely absent from any Western version of art history.

## ABORIGINAL PERSPECTIVES ON THEIR ART

The history of Western art has to contend with different conceptions, even ontologies, of art in space and time; an Aboriginal art history has to accommodate differences between different Aboriginal societies. One benefit of adopting the perspective of Indigenous artists is that it gives us a means to identify regional differences in the way art objects are categorized and related to one another. This may in turn influence the trajectory of art practice and the way in which works are influenced by exposure to other arts. For example, some Aboriginal theories about what art is may encourage greater degrees of conservatism to others. My main focus will be on the art of the Yolngu people from the Yirrkala region of north-east Arnhem Land. But I will make a brief comparison with neighbouring Kuninjku to the west.

### A YOLNGU PERSPECTIVE

On the surface, as we have shown in earlier chapters, Yolngu theory about art represents an archetypal Aboriginal view of the world in which the forms of the present are viewed as a reproduction of the forms of the past.[14] Paintings are creations of the *wangarr* ancestral beings and have been handed on in unchanged form to the present. The designs arose as a result of ancestral action and have been handed on to the social groups who occupied the land. They are the title deeds to the land, and rights in them are both shared and closely guarded. Sets of people hold equal rights in the designs and the designs can only be reproduced with permission from senior members of the owning clan. The contexts of production are closely specified and the form of the designs was set in the past. The only skill involved is that required to replicate the design. The designs are a form of knowledge rather than the product of individual creativity. Over the years I have recorded many statements in which people denied their creativity and emphasized the unchanging nature of their art.

The topic I set off to study in 1974 was art and social change; in particular I wanted to look at the impact of commercialization on the form of Yolngu bark paintings. Before going into the field, I took photographs of most of the bark paintings from the region that were then housed in Australian collections. These photographs included the paintings collected by Donald Thomson in the 1930s and 1940s in eastern Arnhem Land close to the beginning of intensive European contact in the region. On almost my first night in the field I was slowly leafing through my sets of photographs in front of a well-known Yolngu artist Narritjin Maymuru. After I had shown him several photographs from different points in time, he appeared to see right through my project. 'I know what you are trying to do; you are trying to show us that our art has changed. We will show you that it hasn't.'

On another occasion Narritjin emphasized the dangers of innovation in art when he said: 'We can't follow a new way – the new way I cannot do that – I go backwards in order to work. I cannot do any new things because otherwise I might be making up a story – my own thoughts you see – and people over there, wise people, would look at my work and say, Ah! that's only been made up by him.'

This view reflects a socio-cosmic perspective on Yolngu art, which is directly reflected in aspects of its form.[15] Paintings are comprised of components which make them readily identifiable as the property of particular clans associated with particular places. This relationship between ancestral beings, social group and land is often said to be immutable – set in the ancestral past and reproduced in the present. Paintings can be ordered into a number of different sets according to different criteria, the two most common being the set associated with an ancestral track and the set associated with a clan or segment of a clan. There is a multidimensionality to Yolngu paintings, which reflects the articulation between the actions of the *wangarr* ancestral beings and the formation of social groups who inherited the earth from them. Paintings form a complex framework of interlocking genealogies to which people can relate on the basis of kinship and mythical connection.

The Yolngu 'art historian' is able to place paintings on the basis of their form in relation to this grid of connectivity and to state precisely who the painting belongs to, what his or her own relationship to it is, which country it belongs to and which ancestral track. This grid is integral to the interpretation of Yolngu art, and one of the consequences is that the body of interpreters, of 'wise people', is regionally quite extensive. Thus most adult Yolngu artists of the Djalkirripuyngu clans and beyond will be able to look at Bakulangay's or Djambawa's paintings (Figures 22 and 31) and state that they are Madarrpa clan paintings of Yathikpa in Blue Mud Bay, and provide some account of their mythological significance and topographic reference. There is great interest in paintings, both in ensuring that rights in paintings are not being abused or usurped and in monitoring the extent to which people have maintained knowledge over their paintings. The political significance of this knowledge is considerable, since the reality is that land changes hands over time as groups expand and contract, and art is part of the currency of change. In a system where others may hold a group's knowledge for them until the new generation of leaders are sufficiently mature and authoritative to hold it themselves, groups are kept under control by denying them access to knowledge of the religious law associated with their land. Knowledge of religious law is useful in making a claim of inheritance and succession.[16] The political significance of art means that people will look with interest, though often with the appearance of disinterest, at the paintings that are being produced by other clans either in ritual contexts or for sale at the craft store.[17]

The importance of the ancestral grid and of maintaining the formal distinctions upon which it is based have strongly influenced Yolngu interpretation, attribution and, perhaps, perception of earlier paintings. It has been common practice for Euro-Australian museum curators to do what I did and take photographs of art in museums back to the field or invite Yolngu into the storerooms to interpret or re-document paintings. While this is certainly a valid exercise, it may not produce the anticipated result if the goal is to identify the individual artist. Although there will often be consistency in the attribution of paintings to particular clans, there is likely to be considerable variation as to artist. Indeed the first point of identity is that of the clan, and individual artists' names will only be given if asked for or if that is known in advance to be what is wanted. Usually if the age of the painting is known it will be attributed to one of the senior right-holders of the time who is known to have painted. There is likely to be a bias toward those who have painted more frequently or whose reputation in the European art world is established, or who are close relatives of the person asked. If the age of the painting is unknown, then it is likely to be attributed to a senior right holder who is still alive or who belongs to the recent past. In cases where I had independent information about the artist's hand from contemporary documentation, people would frequently attribute the painting to a different artist. People would even 'mis-attribute' paintings recently produced by themselves to other artists, especially when the date of production was uncertain.

Even in the case of works of that were produced for me during my fieldwork, the identity of the individual artist was seldom a topic of interest. The emphasis was on what paintings shared in common rather than what differentiated them. In teaching younger people to paint, senior people would emphasize a process of copying, of reproducing things in the correct way, even at the level of detail of precise sequences of cross-hatching. Personal style was very rarely referred to and then usually with reference to the figurative component of the paintings and not the choice of colours, detail of the infill, overall structure or form of clan designs. People would sometimes comment on the ant-like nature of Mithinari's human figures and on rare occasions one younger artist claimed to paint animals more 'realistically' than his father. But these cases were exceptions. And yet within a clan different artists produced the same painting in what to me were strikingly different ways. Indeed the same artist often produced very different versions of the same painting each time he produced it. The differences were such that I could readily distinguish between the 'styles' of different individual members of the same clan.

In the 1970s the Manggalili clan was a clan of painters. The four senior artists were Narritjin Maymuru, his sons Mändjilnga and Banapana and his brother Bokarra. It is possible to differentiate between their paintings on a number of different bases.

There were differences in the frequency of certain figurative representations in different artists' versions of the 'same painting'. Narritjin produced far more human figures than any of the others and created detailed action sequences that are absent in the others' paintings. Indeed Narritjin developed, with two other senior artists, a genre of paintings in which myths were represented in episodic form in different segments of the same painting (see Figure 55). Moreover there were considerable differences in the ways in which figurative representation of particular species were produced by different artists. Narritjin's figures were more rectangular and less flowing than those of his sons. However, what I want to focus on here is differences in the technique and colour of infill and the overall effect achieved.

Manggalili paintings display forms of infill that are rare in other Yirrkala barks: for example, dotted and dashed infill which occur frequently in Manggalili art are rare in the art of other clans. Narritjin was a past master at this elaborated infill. His art is characterized by the great variety of cross-hatching employed in the same painting and by the fact that different parts of the same painting were often elaborated in different ways. The overall

Figure 52  Narritjin Maymuru's cross-hatching. Detail of a painting *The Marawili Tree at Djarrakpi*, 1976. This segment of the cross-hatching represents the body of the lake at Djarrakpi and is particularly intricate even for Narritjin. The lake at Djarrakpi is the source of Manggalili conception spirits. At the time the artist was troubled by the behaviour of some of his sons and by the disruption caused by the mining town of Nhulunbuy. Reflecting on spirit conception he remarked with a sense of irony, 'you never know how the spirits will turn out'. Photograph Howard Morphy.

colour balance of Narritjin's paintings was very even, with no one colour predominating, and he tended to combine red, black, yellow and white more frequently in the same segment than other artists (Figure 52). In contrast Bokarra's paintings were more uniform with a particular pattern of infill predominating in each painting (Figure 53). His paintings seemed darker than those of other Manggalili artists, with a greater emphasis on red yellow and black and much less use of white. Banapana's paintings in contrast appear light and bright. He used a predominance of white with yellow and red but very little black (Figure 54). The composition of his paintings meant that very often large areas of bark were covered with fine long cross-hatched lines. Sometimes he used contrasting shades of ochre to create graded contours of colour that had an almost tapestry-like effect. His older brother Mändjilnga, whose paintings shared many of the same characteristics, used less varied infill but characteristically included more black in his cross-hatching.

It would be wrong to overemphasize these individual differences. On many occasions members of the family worked together, and in the case of Banapana's paintings the quality of the cross-hatching was often a joint product with his wife Maymirrirr. Small barks in particular were the product of two or three people working together, with one marking out the basic design while others worked on the cross-hatching. Nonetheless, in most cases

Figure 53    Bokarra Maymuru's cross-hatching. The cross-hatching surrounding the figure of a possum illustrates the characteristic density and uniformity of Bokarra's work. Photograph Howard Morphy.

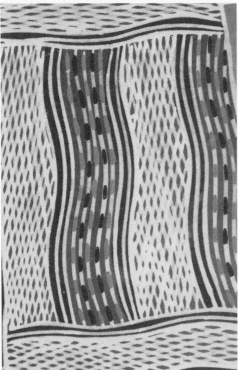

Figure 54    Banapana Maymuru's cross-hatching. Banapana's cross-hatching is characterized both by the sureness of the line and by the overall brightness of the effect, covering large areas with a higher proportion of yellow and white than the other two artists. Photograph Howard Morphy.

– adopting a Western art-historical approach – I was readily able to differentiate between paintings produced by the four leading artists, and using micro-stylistic analysis was able to identify the hand of most paintings produced while I was at Yirrkala. Yet I was not taught by Yolngu to do this, and from my observation of Narritjin teaching his sons he stressed the importance of copying the order in which he infilled the paintings and emphasized that this was to ensure continuity with the past. It would be wrong to conclude, however, that he did not recognize the individuality of different people's techniques of infilling and that he did not himself delight in creating particular aesthetic effects. Maymirrirr would sometimes comment on the beautiful effect of the cross-hatched lines achieved in one of her and Banapana's paintings. However, in public discourse – in official Yolngu art history – such things were not emphasized.

To an extent, I think that the issue is a matter of emphasis and of misinterpreting the objectives of a pedagogical technique. As well as being ancestrally set designs, Yolngu paintings are semantically dense and aesthetically powerful objects. The form of the paintings, their meaning and their aesthetic force all derive from the same source – that is, the ancestral dimension. What Yolngu see and value as ancestral forms are also forms that they know are reproduced by themselves, and they believe that in reproducing them they are moving closer to the ancestral dimension. The ancestral form, however, is an idea that only exists through its replication, and the criterion by which the success of a replication is judged is that it is a recognizable token of its type: for example that it has the correct clan designs, that it is an effective encoder of ancestral meanings and that it conveys the power of the ancestral past through the aesthetic effect of its infill.

Infill on Yolngu paintings is thus simultaneously an ancestral form, a semantic component of the painting and the producer of an aesthetic effect. It is possible to produce infill that contradicts the ancestral specifications or fails to evoke the required response, through the use of a wrong colour, or the wrong sign, or an appearance of dullness. However, there are considerable areas of flexibility and freedom in the reproduction of ancestral forms and indeed some of those freedoms may make the painting a more successful token of its type than others. Cross-hatching is precisely one of those areas in which the individual aesthetic success of the painting is in harmony with ancestral design. The more effective the cross-hatching in producing a sensation of shimmering brilliance, then, the more it evokes a sense of ancestral power (see Morphy 1992).

As a pedagogical technique, the emphasis on faithfulness to pre-existing form nonetheless allows for the development of variations in individual styles of cross-hatching over time. Although people are instructed to produce paintings by following their elders, what they learn is a technique and the boundaries of what is permissible in a particular painting. Individual variation is thus de-emphasized in the learning process and in the interpretation of paintings, but within certain constraints it is allowed and even desirable.

On the basis of the information given so far, it can be argued as the art historian stated at the exhibition opening that the emphasis in Yolngu art history is not on the individual autographic aspects of paintings but on the clan sets to which they belong. At the same time, it would be wrong to deduce that artistic practice is conservative or that new forms are not consciously being produced. Infill is one example where variation continually occurs. But change also occurs in other aspects of paintings, although there are also remarkable continuities. Most dramatically, certain types of painting are claimed as inventions by the artists themselves.

There are some categories of Yolngu paintings that are produced specifically for the outside market and which have no set form. In 1973 these were referred to as 'anyhow paintings', as that was what the missionary Chaseling was supposed to have asked people to paint on the first barks that were produced for sale after the founding of the mission station of Yirrkala in 1935. Today they are more commonly referred to as 'hunting stories', or *wakinngu*,[18] making reference to their secular nature. Paintings of this type are today usually produced on small barks, though larger representations of secular scenes can be produced for sale or on commission to illustrate a particular theme.[19]

Another category of invented paintings is associated with a set of public myths that take the form of moral tales for amusing children or instructing them in appropriate behaviour. The Bamabama story, directed against incest, is one and the Djet story, directed against greed and selfishness, is another. Although these stories are associated with songs and particular locations, they are semi-sacred forms and are not represented in the clan's sacra. Nonetheless they are more closely associated with some clans than with others. Djet and Bamabama, for example, are both associated with a limited set of Yirritja-moiety clans. According to Narritjin the form of the Djet paintings was invented by him in the 1950s (Figure 55). Djet is a boy who lost his temper when reproached for his greed. Jumping up and down in a state of hysteria he gradually began to take on the form of a sea eagle, and ended up flying into the sky. The painting is innovative in a number of ways, the most obvious being that it shows the process of transformation from human to animal form.

In this case Narritjin would emphasize with some degree of pride that he had invented the painting. It was a new category of painting, not a *wakinngu* painting, but not a *likanpuy* painting, a sacred clan painting. Indeed in the case of sacred clan paintings there is a degree of freedom as to how the overall painting is composed and which figurative elements are included as long as it is recognizable as an example of its type. In inventing the new Djet paintings he was involved almost in the reverse process, creating a painting that became an example of a type. The Djet paintings include generalized geometric designs that are associated with the Yirritja moiety and often include the outline of a *yingapungapu* sand sculpture, the sculpture for burying fish remains. Also, the figurative content of the paintings are limited to the creatures mentioned in the myth and the features of the place where the events took place, and the painting once invented became subjected to precisely the same constraints on production and ownership as ancestrally-created forms. The right to produce the painting has spread to a number of closely related Yirritja-moiety clans, and people can only produce it if they are linked to those clans by descent or marriage.[20]

Figure 55    *Djet Story*, 1967. Artist
Narritjin Maymuru. The painting
illustrates in rich detail the story
of Djet, and his transformation into
a sea eagle. National Museum of
Australia, Canberra. Copyright the
artist's family. Reproduced courtesy
Buku-Larrnggay Mulka Art Centre.

It is quite possible that we are seeing here a process by which new paintings have always been added to the inventory of ancestral forms, since all memory of their connection with an individual innovator would rapidly have been lost. Indeed, Yolngu paintings show considerable evidence of having been influenced by other traditions well before European colonization and quite independent of any craft industry. Paintings of both moieties include elements from the time when Macassan traders visited the shores of Arnhem Land to trade and gather trepang. Such paintings include representations of Macassan boats, cloth designs, knives, axes; and sacred objects include Macassan anchors, gin bottles, ships' masts and many other things. The issue of Macassan influence on Yolngu art has hardly been explored, but the evidence exists in song, dance and ritual form of close observation by Yolngu of the Macassan way of life and material culture, which was almost certainly part of a two-way process of cultural exchange. Interestingly, however, Yolngu are as likely to deny that their art has been influenced by the Macassans as to acknowledge their influence. Myth incorporates the Macassans as part of Yolngu ancestral history and distances them from actual historical events.

A sand sculpture in the form of a Macassan prau is sometimes constructed in Yolngu mortuary rituals, which may be evidence of influence from Eastern Indonesian beliefs about the ship of the dead. The sculpture is certainly modelled on the form of Macassan boats. On one occasion, sitting beside such a sculpture watching the dancers, I asked Jack Marrkarakara, a Marakulu man, if Yolngu had learnt to do such a sand sculpture from the Macassans. 'Oh no,' he replied. The sand sculpture came from the Dreaming: it represented Dreaming (*wangarr*) Macassans. Yolngu had produced the sculpture long before the actual Macassans began their trading visits. I must have looked a little sceptical, for he continued: 'Maybe we did not know that the boat was made of wood and the sails were made of cloth until the Macassans came but we always had the design'.[21]

## MAINTAINING A DIFFERENT TRAJECTORY

A historical view of Yolngu art suggests that it has changed over time in response to influences from outside and to changing internal circumstances. Yolngu are undoubtedly interested in the forms of art; other people's as well as their own.[22] Having developed designs based on Macassan elements, more recently they have invented paintings and sculptures to satisfy new markets for their art. They pay great attention to aspects of the form of paintings and train their children in the skills of its production. Paintings are objects of great value in Yolngu society and, following European colonization, Yolngu have actively used art in their attempts to persuade Europeans of the value of their culture. They have seen an analogy between their paintings and carvings and what Europeans produce and classify as art, and have pushed for their paintings to be treated with the same respect and housed in the same institutions as European art.

The form of their art has been influenced by exposure to other arts and to the stimulus of the art market. They have accommodated to European requirements that artists should be known by name and works should be associated with individual artists. At the same time, they have held to a view of the relationships among paintings, which radically contradicts the way in which they are classified, documented and ordered by the European art market. And this internally focused view has influenced the formal trajectory of Yolngu art much more than the new frames in which it has been included. This Yolngu view of the nature of their art and the principles underlying their art practice can also contradict or challenge the very categories into which Europeans try to place it.

Yolngu 'art history', like all art histories, is in part an ideology intimately connected to value creation processes. The ideology underlying Yolngu conceptualization of agency in paintings prioritizes group rights over individual authorship, emphasizes the relationship between paintings, social groups and ancestral beings, and emphasizes continuity over change even to the point of denying change. It is moreover a public ideology, an official ideology of the relationship between art and society operating in the context of a system of restricted knowledge in which contradictions disappear with time.[23] At a public level of knowledge, paintings belong to clans as part of their ancestral inheritance. Thus, when paintings are produced in ritual or made for sale, the identity of the artist is much less important than the fact that the production is the instantiation of the use-rights of the group to which the paintings belong. It also means that collaboration between artists in producing a work is considered unremarkable.

Yolngu conceptions of the kind of object that a work of art is have had consequences on the form of art, on the ways in which art is used and on the ways in which it has changed over time in response to new circumstances. The continued importance of clan designs in Yolngu art is the most obvious consequence. Clan designs show great continuity, and the specifications of difference between one group and the next remain relatively constant over time.[24] However, almost as significant is the effect of clanship and kin relations on the themes an artist can use and the direction of influence and inspiration. The introduction of new themes such as Djet, Bamabama, and Morning Star occur in the context of clanship. The paintings are innovated within the context of pre-existing clan forms using appropriate clan designs and centring on the myths and practices associated with particular places. Once invented, the paintings spread along kinship lines as rights to produce them are extended to mother's and mother's mother's groups, or to groups sharing the same mythology. By no means all changes occur under such constraints – new forms of figurative representations, techniques of cross-hatching, and general themes such as mortuary rituals cross-cut clanship even though the particular form they take will be influenced by more localized mythology.

Although a particular view of the historical relations between paintings thus acts as a constraint on production, it would be wrong to conclude that Yolngu art is conservative, or that people do not consciously innovate new forms, or that the skill of individual artists goes unrecognized. From the perspective of European art history, these conclusions would seem to be the logical correlates of Yolngu ideology, and are precisely the assumptions that were made about Aboriginal art – and indeed much non-European art – until quite recently.

However, as I have shown, innovation occurs routinely in Yolngu art and, although it is not stressed ideologically as it has been in the recent history of European art, it is neither unconscious nor undesired. It is, however, subject to constraints which shift the emphasis away from the creative individual toward art as the property of groups and integral to the rights that extend throughout networks of kin.

Yolngu artists produce art in a number of different frames: in Yolngu ceremonial contexts, for the wider Australian art market and for special commissions for museums or international exhibitions. As Yolngu have become increasingly engaged with the art market and increasingly involved in discourse with non-Yolngu artists, some have become more conscious of the innovative processes in their artistic practice and have entered into the kind of dialogue with audiences and potential purchasers of their art that the Western contemporary-art market encourages and values. Recent paintings by artists from Yilpara, a remote settlement on Blue Mud Bay, have consciously emphasized components of Yolngu art that resonate with the art market. In the previous chapter we introduced the concept of *buwuyak* which I have referred to elsewhere as 'emergent figuration' (Morphy 2005b). The artists employing this technique include Narritjin's daughter Galuma Maymuru and his sister's daughter's child (*gutharra*) Djambawa Marawili.

Yolngu art has always had a strong geometric component, which in the case of sacred forms–both paintings and objects – has often dominated the surface. The paintings made today for sale by the Blue Mud Bay (Djalkiripuyngu) artists emphasize this geometric component. Djambawa, for example, covers much of the surface of the bark canvas with swirling and intersecting patterns of interconnected diamonds (see Figures 29 and 30). The geometric motifs enable the technique of cross-hatching to be applied to maximum effect, creating a dynamic surface of shimmering brilliance which in turn is characteristic of the most sacred Yolngu art.

*Buwuyak* is a technique or a number of techniques that enable figurative representations to emerge from the background pattern of the clan designs, to become visible when the viewer focuses on a particular area of a painting or sees a motif in a particular way. *Buwuyak* harmonizes well with the emphasis in European terms on abstraction.[25] The immanent figurative component allows the representational meaning to be simultaneously both present and absent. The paintings produced can be seen to respond to an external audience whose aesthetic has been influenced by the modernist abstraction of the Western tradition. But though the synergy is exploited, the process of abstraction comes from the relatively autonomous history of Yolngu art. The techniques – the emphasis on the geometric and the play on visibility – come out of the history of Yolngu art, and the ability to employ them comes out of the training the artists have received from the previous generation. The effects are ones that Yolngu have always exploited to give insight into the ancestral dimension of existence – to convey the idea of *wangarr*. The particular geometric patterns that are used depend on the clan of the artist and the rights in paintings that he or she has inherited, and the figures that emerge on the surface refer to the mythology of their clan. But today artists will point out that they are doing something that is new, that is the result in part of their own creativity (see Keller and Coleman 2006).

## COMPARING THE KUNINJKU

So far I have been looking at an Aboriginal art history from the perspective of the Yolngu people of eastern Arnhem Land. It would be quite wrong, however, to assume that an identical perspective holds sway across Australia. While some features are widely shared, such as the belief in the ancestral origin of certain categories of design, and the dispersed nature of rights in objects and designs, there is also great regional variation. If we compare the Kuninjku with the Yolngu case very different factors can be seen to influence the perceived relationship between paintings. Among the Kuninjku variations in infill style have a central role in differentiating between schools of artists, and clanship as such plays a much reduced role in structuring the system.

Luke Taylor (1996, in Chapter 4) has identified a number of contemporary schools of Kuninjku art, identifiable in terms of their style and content. These schools centre on co-residential groups of kin oriented toward a particular region. One of these he labels the Kuninjku/Dangbon School, reflecting the fact that the artists all belong to Kuninjku clans with strong links to Dangbon country to the south. The artists are all associated with Oenpelli and with the outstation of Manmoyi which is near their own clan lands. The artists in this group included Dick Nguleingulei, Nabarrayal, Kalareya and Nabarlambarl. The most striking feature of their work is the use of a cross-hatching technique employing very thin parallel lines, which on close inspection show a characteristic quiver (Figure 56). It is almost as if they had been painted with a shaky hand, and yet the consistency and fine definition of each line contradicts such an interpretation. The artists tend to use a single colour, in contrast to many other contemporary painters, and claim that the style is the one that used to characterize the rock art. They often work together and share each other's pigments, adding to the similarity across their paintings. Although the line work is in some respects austere, the outlines of the animal species produces forms of extraordinary elegance and naturalism, the high point of realism in Kuninjku art.

The second school is that of the Mumeka/Marrkolidban artists and centred around Marralwanga (Figure 57). Other recent members of the school include his son Namirrki and his sons-in-law Njimirnjima and Mawurndjul. The artists belong to the Kardbam and Kuralk clans and have reciprocal responsibilities for each others' paintings. Marralwanga in turn derived much of his inspiration from Yirrawala. Yirrawala was originally part of a school of artists based on Croker Island in the 1950s and early 1960s, and many of his early paintings are difficult to distinguish from those of Namatbara, Nangunyari-Namiridali and Midjaw Midjaw. The paintings associated with the Croker Island School consist of extraordinarily elaborated and contoured multi-limbed figurative representations of spirit beings as well as finely drawn X-ray figures. Later Yirrawala developed a style of complex infill within geometric segments loosely based on the form of *marrayin* designs. This resulted

Figure 56    *Ngalyod, the Rainbow Serpent*, 1991. Artist Lofty Bardayal
Nadjamerrek. The Kluge Ruhe Collection of Australian Aboriginal Art,
Virginia. Copyright the artist. Reproduced courtesy Injalak Art Centre.

in the tapestry style of painting in which the figures occupy a large expanse of the bark
canvas, allowing room for the development of intricate cross-hatched segments that are so
characteristic of the later Mumeka/Marrkolidban works.

Yirrawala's paintings tended to be brighter than those of other members of the school,
with strong yellow and red ochred lines being emphasized by the white background that he
often used. The later Mumega/Marrkolidban paintings are dense and deep in their effect
and tend to draw the viewer into the bark, whereas Yirrawala's figures tend to leap out of
the surface of the painting. The aesthetic impact of the paintings owes much to the dense,
heavy but often flowing nature of the forms lightened by the tapestry of fine cross-hatched
lines that seem to lightly scratch the surface of the painting. The cross-hatching is a constant
source of variation, with each segment often differing from the rest and setting off at obverse
angles to the others. Yet at the same time the effect can be one of extraordinary unity with
the segments blending together as a whole.

Although the composition of the membership of two schools considered so far reflects
both place and kinship networks, it is partly based on historical contingency and individual

Figure 57   *Two Rock Wallabies*, 1979. Peter
Marralwanga. The black wallaroos are shown
dancing together in a representation of a dance
sequence of the Wubarr ceremony. They wear
the feather headdresses of creator beings called
Nadulmi, the 'leaders' of the Wubarr ceremony.
Museums and Art Galleries of the Northern
Territory. Copyright the artist's family and
DACS 2007.

relations. Marralwanga deliberately set out to differentiate his paintings from those of Yirrawala, his original teacher. One of Marralwanga's sons, Birriya Birriya, belongs in turn to a different school from the Mumeka/Marrkolidban school of his father. The Marrkolidban II school followed the style of Mandanjku who, until his death in 1981, was joint leader of the outstation with Marralwanga and Milaybuma. The paintings of this third school are again based on figurative paintings with infilled geometric segments. However, in contrast to Marralwanga these artists produce broad bands of cross-hatching in regular colour sequences which create an overall pattern of striped bands across the surface of the figures (Figure 58). Birriya Birriya explicitly says that he follows Milaybuma's style, 'otherwise people will say I copy my father'; thus presenting an interesting reversal of what is officially considered desirable in north-east Arnhem Land.

A final school of Kuninjku artists is based to the west of the region at Oenpelli, centred on members of the Nganjmira family. The paintings show some similarities with the Marrkolidban artists in that the figures are infilled with alternating bands of single-coloured

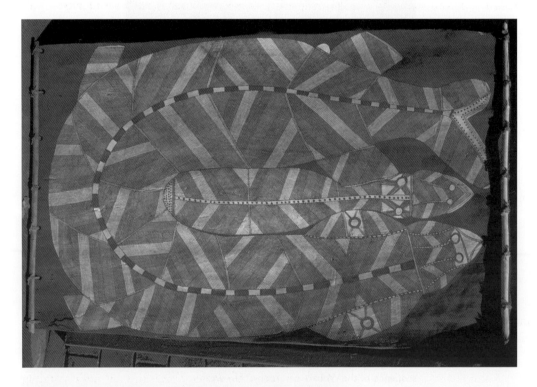

Figure 58   *Yingarna*, 1983. Artist David Milaybuma. Yingarna giving birth to the Ancestral Frog at Kudjidme in his Nadangkorlo-clan lands. The frogs are present as large boulders at this site. Yingarna is said to give birth through a hole cut in her side. Copyright the artist's family. Reproduced with permission of Maningrida Arts and Culture.

cross-hatching. However, whereas Marrkolidban artists paint mainly single figures, the Nganjmira family, and in particular the youngest member of the family Robin Nganjmira, paint complex compositions in which Mimi hunters are combined with animal representations in energetic scenes.

Although the Kuninjku schools identified by Taylor reflect relations of kinship and clanship, and although the ancestral beings depicted have associations with particular sites, it would be wrong to argue that Kuninjku bark paintings are clan-based in either their form or their content. Certain themes of the art can be produced by people belonging to clans from across the region. Paintings of food animals such as kangaroo and barramundi, for example, are produced by most Kuninjku artists, and major regional themes such as that of the Rainbow Serpent or Luma Luma can be treated by senior artists of any of the schools.

Taylor (1996: 95ff.) shows that it is possible to discern patterns in the adoption of particular themes that reflect both clan membership and authority within the regional ceremonial system. Young artists tend to produce themes associated with their father's clan first, then those connected to their mother or mother's mother, before moving further afield. As people gain in age and status, so too the range of themes represented in their art increases. This pattern results in part because rights to paint certain general themes are easily acquired; however, it is also the case that learning to paint is a long process in which the skill is gained only slowly. Initial attempts to produce figurative forms are often clumsy and the young artist needs detailed instruction. Younger artists produce a limited number of new forms because of the need to perfect the ones they have already acquired. Not only do they have to learn the way to represent the features that distinguish particular animals or fish, but they must learn the elaborate techniques of cross-hatching which enhance the aesthetic effect of the painting. Some aspects of form, such as the divisions made in the body of a kangaroo, may be part of ancestral law. Others, such as the production of particular effects through cross-hatching, are much more subject to individual variation. In both cases, however, the technique must be learnt.

An old man of ritual authority such as Yirrawala or Marralwanga produced paintings on themes drawn from right across the Kuninjku region. In such cases, however, there are limits to the set of paintings that an individual produces, but these seem to be set by personal life history and rights gained during the artist's lifetime rather than by clan affiliation. Marralwanga produced paintings of places that he became associated with through residence, kinship and ceremonial participation, and because such factors vary from individual to individual the set of paintings he produced differed from the sets produced by other artists of his generation.

Kuninjku and Yolngu artists thus have very different emphases in their understanding of the relationships between paintings, and between the artist and the work of art. On the surface, Kuninjku art history shares features in common with certain perspectives in European art history. Kuninjku artists, for example, relate their paintings to earlier generations of paintings preserved on rock surfaces. In some cases they are able to identify the individual hand of artists of the previous generation and to assist archaeologists to identify their corpora of works (Haskovec and Sullivan 1989). They emphasise change and originality both within their own corpus and as a basis for differentiating the works produced at one place and time from those of another. They recognize differences between paintings on the basis of micro-stylistic features, and adopt different styles from their relatives as a means of asserting personal identity. These characteristics of Kuninjku art practice and art history may in part explain why an artist such as Yirrawala was able to produce a huge corpus, characterized both by its individualistic nature and by its stylistic variability over time (see for example Holmes 1992).

Just as it is necessary, however, not to overemphasize the extent to which Yolngu were constrained by their ideology of conformity to clanship, so it is also necessary to emphasize that Kuninjku artists also operate under some constraints. Although the structure of rights in paintings may appear less clear-cut than those in eastern Arnhem Land, it is nonetheless publicly acknowledged and enforced. People who produce paintings without authority or who stray into areas of ambiguity are likely to be reproached, fined or punished in some other way for their transgression. Kuninjku artists are incorporated within a master-apprentice structure that simultaneously receives the sanction of ancestral law and is integrated with the system of ritual authority.

The contrast between Kuninjku art history and Yolngu art history cautions us against positing any essentialized, uniform and continent-wide Aboriginal art history. Of the two, the Kuninjku variant could sit more happily within a framework of an art history that emphasizes individuality, innovation, formalism and cross-cutting ties of identity. It could be argued that Kuninjku art practice would have to change less than that of the Yolngu in order to be incorporated in the individualistic autographic framework of a particular kind of Western art world. It might be postulated that the ready acceptance of Yirrawala's work had something to do with its pre-adaptation to the requirements of a particular kind of Western art market. However, such a conclusion would be highly problematic. In the Kuninjku and Yolngu cases, art is integrated in a similar way within social process and equally subject to a dispersed system of inherited and constructed rights in designs. Moreover, Yolngu art practice also allows for the development of innovative artists, such as Narritjin (Morphy et al. 2005), Mithinari, Malangi (Jenkins 2005) and contemporary artists such as Djambawa, Galuma and Wanyubi.

Both Yolngu artists and Kuninjku artists have in recent years been able to respond to, engage with and influence contemporary Australian art by emphasizing features of their art that resonate with a modernist aesthetic. The emphasis on geometric art and the masking of the figurative component that we have seen occurring in the recent paintings of the Yolngu artists from Yilpara is paralleled in the work of the Kuninjku artist Mawurndjul. However, the 'abstraction' in Mawurndjul's case comes out of the trajectory of Kuninjku art and characterizes its particular difference (Taylor 2005). While Mawurndjul's paintings are similarly located in landscape, they are not comprised of clan-owned geometric elements

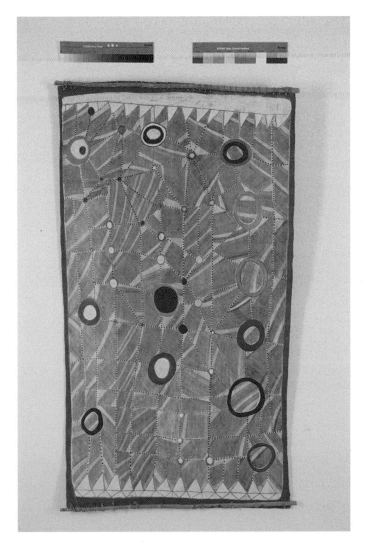

Figure 59   *Mardayin Ceremony*, 1999. John Mawurndjul.
Laverty Collection, Sydney, ID 2047. Copyright the
artist and DACS 2007.

(Figure 59). His paintings have evolved out of the deconstruction and reconstruction of the figurative component of Kuninjku art almost to the point of its disappearance. The geometric structure created by this process then becomes the framework for an exquisite layering of cross-hatching covering much broader expanses of bark than is the case in contemporary Yolngu art, where the geometry of the clan designs creates the dominant pattern. Coming from their own different but related traditions, contemporary Yolngu and Kuninjku artists respond to the encompassing Australian art market in complementary ways.

However, it would be quite wrong to see the artistic production as parallel responses to the market's desire for a particular appearance of abstraction. In both Mawurndjul's and Djambawa's cases, the particular paintings are the outcome of a trajectory of artistic practice that is relatively autonomous from national and global market forces. Mawurndjul's abstraction is patterned by the ancestral landscapes that he represents, and the structure of the paintings is motivated by landforms. In Djambawa's case, after several years of working through the idea of *buwuyak* and developing techniques that move figurative form beneath the surface for the painting, he invented a new medium which enabled figurative form to rise above the surface of the bark or hollow-log coffin. His most recent paintings, produced in 2006 for the Asia Pacific Triennale in Brisbane, include moulded figures of mythic subjects – crocodiles on their nest, dugong rising above the surface of the water, overturned canoes. The figures are moulded onto the surface of the bark using his own medium of stringy bark fibre ground into a fine sawdust mixed with wood glue and pigment. An innovation, and yet as in the case of most artistic innovation one that can be placed in a historical context. The figures gain their power because the work as a whole combines different techniques of representation that carry the eye from above to below the surface of the bark, connecting with the Yolngu metaphysics of inside and outside, inner and surface form. Moreover, the previous generation of Yolngu artists used beeswax to mould figures that were subsequently painted. Mountford collected several of them on his 1948 expedition.

## CONCLUSION

This chapter is based on the premise that it might be useful to look at the idea of art history from a cross-cultural perspective that articulates with non-Western discourses about art. I have focused on issues relevant to a particular area of discourse in Western art history, which has influenced the way in which Aboriginal art has been approached both by curators and by the art market. I have been concerned with the process of putting artworks into sets on the basis of historical and formal relationships and the attribution of works to individuals. There are many art histories and not all would favour this particular methodological orientation. It has been argued that the particular Western discourse I have outlined is associated with the ideological process that has resulted in the formation of the modern capitalist state, and which is linked to the development of modernism, individualism and beliefs about the value of 'progress'. A form of art history which defines works according to progressive sequences of formal development and emphasizes individual creativity and the identity of the individual artist is clearly not going to approach paintings in the same way as Yolngu artists do. What it shares in common with Yolngu art discourse or perhaps art theory is that it provides a framework for relating paintings to one another and in turn relating them to their human producers in a spatiotemporal context. A cross-cultural art history which attempts to take into account different ways of conceiving of the relationships between artworks over time is going to be set at this level of generality. It must enable paintings to be placed at least initially in the context of the producer's own art discourse rather than re-inventing them as a component of someone else's art world – neither should works of Aboriginal art be defined as non-art because they do not fit into a particular Western art historical framework. A cross-cultural art history that embraces Kuninjku art because its art theory shares some features in common with European art theory, but rejects Yolngu art, would clearly be absurd.

Aboriginal 'art histories' are as interconnected with ideological and social processes as European ones. The entry of Aboriginal art into predominantly Western arenas makes it subject to Western art discourse, and this in turn has inevitable consequences for the way in which the art is conceptualized in its Indigenous context. Conforming to the demands of other art discourses can produce values contradictory to those that are central to the place of art in Aboriginal societies. However, the relationship between art histories, ideologies and other aspects of social process is a loose one, so art histories themselves are always in the process of change, and change can involve fundamental shifts of perspective. Aboriginal theories about the kind of thing that an artwork is can insert themselves in this process of changing Western art discourse and also be subject to change themselves. Art objects can simultaneously be the product of groups and subject to multiple right-holders, and the recognizable product of individuals or a definable set of collaborators. The juxtaposition of art histories brought about by the movement of Aboriginal art into the Western frame, while it simultaneously remains a part of Aboriginal society, brings to the fore new ways of seeing the relationships between objects and people (see Thomas 1999).

Yolngu 'art history' and art theory, the ways in which Yolngu conceptualize the relationships among paintings in terms of their own cultural categories, has affected the response of Yolngu artists to the changed circumstances brought about by European colonization. It has influenced Yolngu ideas about how their art should be incorporated in the Euro-Australian and global art frames. Yolngu have accepted their identification as individual artists, but they have also argued for a particular kind of individuality. And recently they have begun to influence in significant ways the discourse that surrounds their work in the Euro-Australian arena. The Yolngu conception of the relationships between paintings, and the constraints on individual artists, are having an impact on curatorship and on the Euro-Australian artworld, partly because they happen to engage with current debates in European art history/theory. But Aboriginal people have also been influencing more directly the ways in which their paintings are incorporated within the wider Australian frame. Most Australian institutions now consult Aboriginal people before organizing exhibitions of their works, and rights in cultural property and indigenous knowledge have entered the legal arena. Exhibition practice now takes account of Aboriginal concerns in matters such as the propriety of exhibiting certain categories of objects to unrestricted audiences, the suppression of dead people's names, consciousness of the extended body of right holders in the case of some works, and Aboriginal categorizations of artworks.

# SECTION III

# YOLNGU ART AND THE CHIMERA OF FINE ART

We have now almost reached the end of our journey connecting Yolngu art to more general discourses about art. In Section I, a short history of Yolngu art was developed, intended to demonstrate a family relationship between Yolngu art and other art cross-culturally. It is in the nature of fuzzy categories like art – that encompass a diverse range of practices under a single rubric – that the recognition of likeness within the category is going to be partly intuitive. That process of intuitive recognition is what enables people to employ a concept of art and categorize certain things as examples of art practice where they find it – it is the reason why, despite differing definitions of art, most writers about world art find themselves including broadly similar examples. Not everyone's sets are going to be the same – at the margins the category is highly contested, and in particular social and cultural contexts great energy is invested into including or excluding objects and actions from the category of art. It is often in these arenas of contest that particular institutional definitions and substantive definitions of art come into conflict. Understanding the issues involved requires that both dimensions be taken into account – the analyst needs to investigate the sociological and phenomenological dimensions of art from a broad and historically grounded perspective.

My short history of Yolngu art was written from the perspective of the ways in which Yolngu art was used in different contexts for different purposes; and how the formal structure of the art – reflecting its properties as an expressive and aesthetically powerful medium – enabled it to have its particular affect and potential for action. The history of Yolngu art revealed a society connected to worlds outside, at the local level through the ever-extending system of clan relations, with visiting traders from South East Asia and more recently, but perhaps no more intensively, with the European society that encapsulated them and incorporated them within a modern nation state. In recent years Yolngu have extended their agency through art into new arenas as part of a value creation process that has had internal as well as external consequences.

Section II provided examples of areas in which Yolngu art has entered into cross-cultural discourse on art, and how it can contribute to discussion about the nature of representational systems, the utility of the concept of style, and the nature of aesthetic experience. If we avoid the somewhat sterile question of 'is it art in the sense of Western fine art?', and instead focus on the kinds of thing Yolngu art is under a broader cross-cultural conception of art practice, then we create the possibilities for seeing why art has been for so long part of human society.

Section III now presents an argument for the place of Yolngu art in the art gallery, but not on the grounds that it fits the particular definitional criteria of the Western fine art category. Indeed, here I argue that in anthropological, sociological and art historical terms, fine art is a chimera, revealing more about the social and institutional context that supports the category than it does about the objects it includes. The art gallery should be the context for an informed and reflexive viewing of artworks, disentangled from overly narrow definitions of art and from an ideology of segregation. I argue that the art galleries need to be freed from the constraining and exclusionary clauses associated with the Western definition of fine art and reconfigured as contexts for viewing. Connected to this argument is a questioning of any opposition between seeing objects as art and as sources of information about the worlds in which the producers lived or live. Anthropology and art history, ethnography and art, museum and art gallery are not opposed but complementary categories, concepts and institutions which enable the same objects to be appreciated, understood and experienced in different ways.

# 8 PLACING INDIGENOUS ART IN THE GALLERY[1]

## INTRODUCTION

Writing in 1904, Otis T. Mason begins his compendious work on American Indian basketry with a reflection (or perhaps more truly a lack of reflection!) on the newly awakened interest of that ubiquitous follower of ethnographic fashion, the private collector.

> In the past few years a sympathetic spirit has been awakened in the United States to keep alive this charming Aboriginal art and to preserve its precious relics. In every State in the Union will be found rich collections, both in public and private museums. People vie with one another in owning them. It is almost a disease, which might be called 'canastromania'. They resemble the 'merchantman seeking goodly pearls, who, when he had found one pearl of great price, went and sold all he had and bought it.' The genuine enthusiasm kindled in the search, the pride of success in acquisition, the care bestowed on them, witness that the basket is a worthy object of study. The story is told of a distinguished collector who walked many a weary mile to the shelter of a celebrated old weaver. He spent the day admiring her work, but still asking for something better. He knew she had made finer pieces. At last flattery and gold won. She tore out the back of her hut and there, hid from mortal eyes, was the basket that was to be burned at her death. Nothing could be more beautiful and it will be her monument. (Mason 1988 [1904]: ix)

The paragraph would provide an excellent text for a critical sermon on ethnographic museums, the presuppositions of early twentieth-century collectors of ethnography and primitive art, the post-colonial context of production, the inequalities in the relationship between Native Americans and the colonial admirers of their artefacts, and any number of other themes. The text is so redolent with the assumptions of the time that it is hard to resist littering the quotation with parenthetical exclamation marks. One cannot help hoping that as soon as the collector left, the basket-maker replaced the missing basket with the next one in line for burning. However, as with any text that presents so clearly the presuppositions of its times, it is too easy to treat it unfairly and ahistorically as if it were written today.

The themes that I want to take up in this chapter are as controversial today as they were at the time that Mason was writing. They concern whether objects of other cultures should be presented as aesthetic forms – as fine art, and the extent to which presentation as fine art involves a distortion or appropriation of value. Underlying these themes is the question of the relationship between the aesthetic qualities of an object as viewed by its Western public and its aesthetic qualities as viewed by its producer, which question in turn has embedded within it the general issue of the usefulness, and even the validity, of the notion of aesthetics for cross-cultural analysis.[2]

James Clifford (1991: 241) has written that 'one of the best ways to give cross cultural value (moral, commercial) to a cultural production is to treat it as art'. Mason's writing is clearly a part of this process and illustrates particularly well the linkage between what Clifford refers to as the moral and commercial dimension of value. The value (as 'a worthy object of study') is proved by the interest of the collector, who is prepared to invest large sums in acquiring an object of beauty or aesthetic value. The basket on the pedestal in the museum becomes the ultimate monument to its creator. On the other hand, in his radically titled 'Toward an anti-catalogue of woodsplint basketry', Russell Handsman (1987: 147) notes: 'When seen as art, artefacts [are] separated from their human, historical and political relations'.

As they stand, the two perspectives are not necessarily incompatible, depending on the particular concept of art applied. Certainly it could be argued, as Handsman does, that the exhibition of ethnographic objects as 'art' often involves the imposition of a nineteenth-century Western European concept, whose application incorporates the objects of other cultures within the framework of Western European values and blocks understanding of their indigenous meaning and cultural context. Moreover, the concept of 'art' can mask the process by which the object was acquired: 'basket diverted by flattery and gold from funeral pyre' is unlikely to be part of the label.

These dangers are certainly there in the aestheticization of the works of other cultures. However, I would argue that the fault lies not just in the overall context of exhibitions, but perhaps more in the particular concept of aesthetics employed. An exhibition may simultaneously use the concept of art as a means of focusing attention on a set of objects in a way that asserts the value of the products of another culture, and yet simultaneously draw attention to the wider context of the objects in their indigenous frame. Used reflexively, the exhibition of ethnography as 'art' may involve a repositioning of the concept of art itself that moves it away from its nineteenth- and twentieth-century meanings toward one that is more relevant to the particular cross-cultural discourse concerned.

The problem has arisen because the more general substantive concept of art has become incorporated within and subordinated to the comparatively recent Western concept of fine art. The incorporation of things within a unitary category of objects that are defined as 'art objects', which are to be viewed together as an exclusive set specifically for their aesthetic effect, is what appropriates their cultural value and history and subordinates them to Western values. If, rather than seeing aesthetics as referring to this unitary category of objects, we see it as a dimension that any object can potentially possess, then the danger of imposing one set of values over others can be avoided. Instead, we may be able to enter into a cross-cultural discourse about the aesthetic potential of objects. And the art gallery and the museum may be equally appropriate contexts for that.

Handsman is certainly right to say that such a discourse requires more than the display of objects on a pedestal in a particular light, and indeed more than the simple presentation of the objects. Such an impoverished and narrow conception of the way in which the aesthetic dimension of an object can be appreciated is indeed an imposition of taste that narrows, rather than opening up, the possibilities of cross cultural appreciation. Handsman and McMullen (1987: 34) go so far as to suggest that 'when presented and interpreted as art, splint baskets were not and cannot be "read" as artefacts of specific societies'. However, by identifying aesthetics and art with nineteenth-century values they may be falling into a trap: by defining art and aesthetics ethnocentrically, they deny the possibility of their existence in other cultures. By creating the category 'art' in relation to a particular kind of non-functional aesthetic display valuable, associated with what Brook (1986) refers to as the 'gemstone' model of art, our predecessors appropriated not simply the objects that were put into that category but also the concept of art itself. For a while, 'art' became limited to a certain category of objects.

## ART ACROSS CULTURES

The anthropology of art seems at times to have been squeezed between – and distorted by – two myths: the myth adhered to by the art market, and by some art curators, that somehow an anthropological approach to indigenous art created its otherness and separated it from Western artworks; and the anthropological myth that classifying works as 'art' imposed a Western categorization upon them. These myths have a number of continuing echoes in practice: for example the emphasis in art galleries on displaying works as art, with the minimum of information lest it provide a distraction to the viewer, in contrast to the greater concern with information in ethnographic museums. This opposition has been reinforced at times by disciplinary battles over public spaces, by indigenous and ethnic politics, and by the desire to be on the right side of the colonial/post-colonial divide. In part it has been maintained by the desire of the disciplines involved to emphasize their distinctiveness in order to maintain their separate identities and sources of funding. This motivation to maintain a structural division provides a clue to the ahistorical nature of the debate and the ever-present desire to lay blame for an unacceptable history on a rival: the art gallery can feel threatened by the ethnographic museum, the anthropologist by the art historian.

In the myth concerning the role of the anthropologist in the creation of the otherness of primitive art, that role has been greatly exaggerated, often attributing to anthropologists the presuppositions of other members of their own societies that they have both at times shared and at other times challenged (Strang 2006). Indeed in the Australian case anthropologists have played a major role in the process of including Aboriginal art within the same generic category as other people's art, and there is evidence that anthropologists have played a similar role elsewhere. This is not to argue that all anthropologists were participants in the process. For much of the twentieth century, anthropology neglected art. Non-Western art and material culture were associated with ethnographic museums, and some museum curators were indeed unsympathetic to the categorization of objects in their collections as art objects. I would argue, however, that their position was often motivated by a desire to increase the understanding of the significance to the original producers of the objects in their collections. Many museum curators and anthropologists viewed the inclusion of non-European objects in the art category as a licence for misinterpretation, through the imposition of universalistic aesthetic concepts and in the creation of difference at the level of meaning and significance.

'Primitive art' was viewed by modernist critics and connoisseurs as formally dynamic, expressive, challenging and incorporable within the Western canon; as to its meaning, it explored the primeval depths of human spirituality and sexuality. It was this demeaning and ill-informed categorization of objects as 'primitive art' that alienated anthropologists from the art connoisseurs and signified the gulf between their discourses.[3] It is ironic, yet inevitable, that for many years anthropologists and connoisseurs of indigenous art found themselves on opposite sides of the art/artefact divide. Viewed historically, 'primitive art' was an important stepping-stone toward the recognition of the art of non-Western societies. However, it has long since outlived its usefulness. The recent challenge mounted to the category of primitive art by anthropologists and art historians, such as Coote and Shelton 1992, Errington 1998, Philips 1998, Marcus and Myers 1995, Price 1989 and Vogel 1988 has allowed museum anthropologists to reincorporate the concept of art within their theoretical discourse and may foreshadow a bridging of the divide between the anthropological and art worlds.

Part of the process of incorporating art within the theoretical discourse of anthropology is the development of definitions which are cross-cultural and distance the concept from its Western historical baggage. An example of such a definition is one I introduced earlier: 'objects having semantic and/or aesthetic properties that are used for presentational or representational purposes' (Morphy 1994b: 655).[4] I am not concerned at this stage to defend this particular definition. Any cross-cultural definition of art, just as in the case of a cross-cultural definition of religion, magic, gender or kinship, is part of a discourse that shifts the term in the direction of broad applicability while still maintaining connections to its previous place in academic discourse. As I noted in chapter 1, the recent history of the world biases epistemology toward Western definitions, but the challenge of anthropology is in part to separate concepts from a particular past, as for example in anthropological definitions of religion which have moved away from Christianity without excluding it. Cross-cultural definitions are as much concerned with time as with space: hence a cross-cultural conceptualization of art must allow the analyst to encompass the fact that conceptions of art have changed in the last 400 years of Western art practice and history as much as they differ cross-culturally. As a consequence, the sets of objects that get included under the rubric of art change continually over time.

However, in relegating Western-based definitions of art to their place in a typology of possible definitions, it would clearly be naive to neglect the impact that Western cultures

– and their definitions – have had on global processes in recent centuries. The material culture of indigenous societies has been changed as they have been incorporated within wider global processes.[5] However, those processes of articulation and transformation are highly complex – both the incorporated and the incorporators are changed thereby (see Thomas 1991 for a relevant discussion). Changing definitions of art are a microcosm of these larger processes. The increased understanding of the role of the commoditization and trade of material culture, including art, has been a partner to the critique of the 'primitive art' paradigm in bringing art back into anthropology (see essays in Marcus and Myers 1995). Graburn puts this succinctly when he writes 'We now realise that practically all the objects in our ethnographic collections were acquired in politically complex multicultural colonial situations. Furthermore we can state unequivocally that unless we include the socio-political context of production and exchange in our analyses we will have failed in our interpretation and understanding' (1999: 345). To this I would only add a corollary: that material culture – however it enters the discourse of art – is an important source of evidence, for anthropologists, to better understand the social conditions and historical interactions of the time of their production.

## EXHIBITING ART

When trying to persuade a Western public of the aesthetic dimension of other peoples' material culture, anthropologists present their arguments not only through their writings but also by organizing exhibitions of other peoples' work as art. And as we have seen, it is in the context of the art gallery that the Western definition of art and the anthropological metaconcept of art have the opportunity to get almost inextricably muddled. As Luke Taylor (1988: 93) has written: 'why is it that we find objects from other cultures so beautiful, even though we know at some level, the aesthetic values objectified in the works must be culture specific?' Clearly an emphasis on the culture-specific qualities of aesthetic values is not sufficient to describe the complexities of the situation. In exhibiting non-Western art in the art galleries, we are interrogating the dialogic nature of the relationships between the universal and the particular.

There are two reasons why the exhibition of objects as art became an almost inevitable part of anthropologists' presentation of their case. First, part of the metadefinition of art involves aesthetics, and one of the Western ways of communicating the aesthetic properties of an object is through exhibition. Much of the art that is collected by Western art in-stitutions is likely to be included within a cross-cultural category of art, and hence the art gallery provides a relevant context for discourse over art and experiencing art objects as aesthetic forms. A cross-cultural definition of art brings different art practices within the same broad rubric and facilitates the appreciation of the artworks of other places and times. Secondly, part of the cultural-relativist agenda is to acknowledge both the differences and the similarities between world cultures by employing a metaphysical criterion of equal cultural value. The cultural relativist demonstrates the equivalence of this difference by explicating the values of the particular culture in terms of its own processes of reproduction and drawing attention to analogous processes operating in other cultural contexts, and/or by using rhetorical devices that assert that objects or processes of similar value exist in different cultures, and that it is possible for a member of one culture to appreciate value as it exists to a member of another through a process of cultural translation. In the case of art the qualities of the object, including such questions as to whether it is good or bad art, are defined from a relativistic perspective within the culture of production – and on a priori grounds all cultures are equally valuable.

The inclusion of the works from different cultures within the same frame is an assertion that the family resemblance between the works is such that they can be seen as objects of equivalent value without being the same. A corollary of such an assertion is that galleries which include artworks from different cultures should include them on their own terms, but on an equal basis to each other, rather than incorporating them within hierarchical structures that make some objects more art than others.

The cultural relativist agenda grew out of opposition to nineteenth-century evolutionary schemas that created out of the world's cultures a graded series in which those at the top had art, science and civilization and those at the bottom did not. This imposition of a particularly culture-bound definition of art, in association with a colonialist ideology, denied art to many cultures and, since art was one of the signs of civilization, devalued the things they produced. George Kubler (1991: 84) has written about the distaste for America in European thought and literature:

> The distaste was and remains a negative aesthetic expression about America and Americans during the Enlightenment, and it survives in Europe and elsewhere to this day. – The dominant belief in enlightened Europe, from 1750 to 1900, was that America was inferior as to its natural and racial endowment. Buffon as a naturalist in 1759 deprecated the animal species as inferior and the humans in ancient America as 'impotent and savage'. Kant's verdict as a philosopher in 1778 – that Amerindians were 'incapable of any culture, still far behind the negroes'– was followed by Hegel's 'immature and impotent continent'.

It is against this background that we should see the work of such early museum ethnographers as Otis Mason and W. H. Holmes, and the even more fundamental contribution of Franz Boas (1927). They were concerned to communicate the aesthetic features of Native American material culture through the development of collections and the organization of exhibitions as well as through their writings. In doing so they were involved in a process of asserting the value of Native American culture and way of life, making Native Americans visible again as people and showing them in a positive light. Similar motivations can be seen operating in Australia. Margaret Preston found it necessary to write as late as 1940 that 'the Aborigines of Australia have always been regarded as in the lowest branches of civilisation. That this is not the case is shown by studying their native art' (cited in Edwards 2005: 193). In this she echoed the words of the anthropologist A. P. Elkin who, in 1938, introduced

Fred McCarthy's booklet on Australian Aboriginal Decorative Art with 'Those who would otherwise ignore or despise the Aborigines ... realise that a people possessing an art which is full of traditional meaning as well as expressive of many interesting motifs, is much higher in the human scale than previously thought' (McCarthy 1938).

The initial division between ethnographic museums (often natural history museums), where Native American, African or Oceanic arts were shown, and art galleries, where art that was part of the European canon was exhibited, made a double statement about art and society. In general the ethnographic museum contained works of material culture from societies that were low down on an imagined evolutionary hierarchy. The art gallery exhibited a restricted category of art objects that could be connected to Western civilization. The existence of the art gallery was in a sense the de facto criterion for the division of global societies in two distinct halves – those which produced works that could be divided on the basis of whether or not they were excluded from or included within the category of fine art, and those in which material culture could not be divided on that basis. Put that way, it seems to be quite an absurd proposition and it can easily be seen why people whose works were excluded from the art gallery could be offended by that exclusion, and why there was pressure to have their works exhibited in an art gallery as opposed to the museum. The category 'fine art' is indeed very closely entangled with the prestige structure of Western society and the concept of the West as the high point of civilization.

There is of course no problem with a society making a division between objects, and categorizing some of them as worthy of inclusion as special kinds of object in an art gallery as opposed to another institution. The problem comes when that division becomes an implicit part of the definition of an art object. The difficulty is then in determining the dividing line and its substantive basis. Any number of criteria could be proposed to justify such a division, but they are all likely to have problems associated with them; the art produced by human societies is too diverse to fit neatly into two categories. Some might argue that the division is between modern and pre-modern societies or pre-industrial or post-industrial, or preliterate and literate, but demonstrating the relationship between those divisions and the type of art produced is not going to be easy. Other criteria might be ones that we have considered already, art by intention and art by metamorphosis, art from societies which have a word for art and those which do not, or art produced primarily for aesthetic contemplation and art that has additional purposes, whether primary or secondary.

Recognition of the essentially arbitrary intervention of the art gallery as an institution for housing fine art in fact solves the problem of the apparent incommensurability between institutional definitions of art (Danto 1964; Becker 1982) and substantive definitions of art (Anderson 1990; Morphy1994b; Westermann 2005). They are really about two quite different kinds of thing. Unsurprisingly, the former apply more to art as it has been encapsulated within the institutional structure and particular history of Western society, and as it has become entangled with structures of power and processes of distinction; and the latter are more concerned with art making as a human practice. It also explains why critical sociologies of art such as Bourdieu's *Distinction* hardly concern themselves with the analysis of the form of art objects, since they are concerned fundamentally with the structures that provide the foundations for the institutional definition of art and the secret language of taste that helps support it.

However, the conclusion to be drawn from this is not that the objects contained within the institutional category of art are irrelevant to a substantive cross-cultural definition of art or that the whole category of art is a chimera. The works of art included in the institutional category are predominantly ones that would fit into a cross-cultural and cross-temporal definition of art – they are the product of artists' agency and bodies of knowledge, and the form and the ideas and emotions expressed are indeed an important part of what it is to be human.[6] The hegemony of the institutional category of art that captured and imposed a particularly narrow conception of Kantian aesthetics is of relatively recent origin and has long been subject to challenge. There is a fundamental disjunction in recent European history between art as a particular kind of action – which includes all the multiplicity of purposes that art has been used for, including self-reflexive aesthetic contemplation – and the institutionalization of art. The discourse over art and ethnography lies firmly in the middle of that disjunction.

On the other hand, the history of dividing art between ethnographic museums and art galleries does cause a logical problem. In the ethnographic museums the objects were not divided on an art and non-art basis but ordered according to place-time or functional type. The deliberate exclusion of the concept art from ethnographic analysis was, as we have argued, the complement of the Western fine art-making process – ethnographic objects were subject to democratic classifications and Western ones subject to hierarchical orderings. How then, and on what basis, can artworks move from the museum into the art gallery? If only certain works are selected for inclusion within the art gallery, being chosen either on arbitrary aesthetic grounds or by analogy with Western categories of art objects – for example, objects with painted designs – then that continues the process of appropriation; the objects are reclassified without reference to indigenous values. It is here that exhibiting ethnographic objects as art becomes part of a radical critique of art galleries: it provides a challenge to narrowly constructed definitions of art and to the separation of art from artefact that was the product of a particular period of European history. And though it can be argued that this strategy also incorporates artefacts within global processes that are essentially part of a Western agenda, it has the advantage of doing so by making people reflect on their own and other peoples' categories and constructions of the world.

## ART OR ETHNOGRAPHY? A FALSE OPPOSITION

Aboriginal art is included today in the collections of every major art gallery and art museum in Australia, and is one of the world's most visible art forms. Its inclusion within the category of fine art is no longer challenged in Australia, though elsewhere in the world this can still be the subject of controversy.[7] It is easy to forget how recently this process of inclusion happened. Aboriginal art was barely recognized as a significant art form until the 1950s and it was not until the 1980s that it began to enter the collections of most Australian galleries, or gain widespread recognition as a significant dimension of Australian art (see e.g. *Australian Perspecta* 1981). However, it is also important not to overstate the lateness of its arrival on the world stage. In 1964 Ronald Berndt was able to write:

> Australian Aboriginal art is becoming better known these days, or at least more widely known, than ever before. Once it was relegated to the ethnological section of a museum, and treated along with the artefacts and material culture of other non-literate peoples. Now it is not unusual to find such things as Aboriginal bark paintings taking place alongside European and other examples of aesthetic expression. And because they rub shoulders with all forms of art, irrespective of cultural origin, the inference is that they are being evaluated in more general terms: that there is not only wider appreciation of Aboriginal endeavour in this respect, but that it is, almost imperceptibly, taking its place in the world of art… Fifteen years ago few of us would have envisaged this meteoric rise in popularity, within Australia and overseas. (1964b: 1)

It is often said that Aboriginal art first entered an Australian gallery of fine art in 1959, with the acquisition by the Art Gallery of New South Wales (AGNSW) of major works from the Tiwi artists of Melville and Bathurst Islands and the Yolngu artists of Yirrkala in north east Arnhem Land. While this is an oversimplified account, nevertheless this gift remains a significant and perhaps, in hindsight, even transforming event. The works were acquired by Tony Tuckson, Deputy Director at the AGNSW in association with Stuart Scougall, an orthopaedic surgeon with a passion for Aboriginal art (see Figure 13).[8] This event has been interpreted as shattering the anthropological paradigm. For example, the curator Terence Maloon puts this position clearly when he states of Tony Tuckson: 'In the role of Aboriginal art expert he had to take an opposing position to the anthropologists who, to put it crudely, generally argued for the radical dissimilarity of all things traditionally Aboriginal to all things traditionally European' (2000). According to Maloon, this enabled Tuckson to lay the foundation 'for the earliest public collection to be acquired for aesthetic rather than ethnographic reasons' (2000: 14). Maloon here echoes Tuckson, who wrote: 'Appreciation of Aboriginal art has widened immeasurably because the general public and the artist have been given a greater opportunity to see it *as art*, not as part of an ethnological collection' (1964: 63). However, in phrasing it 'crudely', arguing in effect that anthropologists have failed to recognize the cross-cultural nature of art, Maloon oversimplifies the issues involved.

It could of course be argued that certain Western definitions of art themselves are inherently cross-cultural since they posit universals in human aesthetic appreciation. Clearly such a view lies behind Tuckson's position as summarized by Maloon,[9] who argues that

> [Aboriginal] artists make their paintings with pleasure and imagination and intuition. They put their feeling into what they do. They exercise skill and ingenuity in their use of materials; they are considerate of the ways their works are organised and elaborated

and are sensitive to the resulting aesthetic effect. Bark paintings and other Aboriginal artefacts are not ethnographic curiosities, but genuine works of art. Furthermore, when non-Aboriginal people respond to bark paintings as art, they are prone to recognise 'the underlying spirit of the imagery' (in Tuckson's [1964: 63] revealing phrase). (2000: 14)

In countering the Maloon/Tuckson thesis, it is necessary to isolate two strands of argument that are only loosely interconnected.[10] The first is an essentialist view that associates art with individual creativity, technical facility and aesthetic sensibility. The second is masked by the phrase that bark paintings 'are not ethnographic curiosities'. I shall address these issues by first stepping back in time to the debate between Tuckson and Ronald Berndt that is the initial reference point of Maloon's argument. The debate occurs in the pages of Berndt's edited book *Australian Aboriginal Art*, which was published to accompany an exhibition of the same name curated by Tuckson. A 'reading between the lines' reveals that the book reflects a heated exchange between the two over how Aboriginal art should be exhibited, appreciated and understood.[11]

Tuckson certainly believed that there is something universal about the character of art objects that makes it possible to evaluate them in isolation from their cultural and social background. He wrote:

> [there is] an underlying unifying quality in art that resides in a visual sense of balance and proportion, but also an underlying spirit of their imagery ... [that makes it possible] for *us* to appreciate visual art without any knowledge of its meaning and original purpose. (1964: 63, emphasis in the original)

In a weak sense there is nothing unremarkable about this position. It is undeniably the case that 'Western art appreciators' can make aesthetic judgments about works they know nothing about, but the question remains about who is included in the '*us*'; and are there differences in the bases of 'our' evaluations? Berndt, writing in the same book, acknowledged that Tuckson was at least partially right, i.e. that the appreciation of the aesthetics of Aboriginal art did attract the attention of the viewer:

> however, we have attempted to go a little farther – to cross over the limits of our own cultural frontiers, and to see something of the broader significance of Aboriginal art. (1964b: 71–2)

But Berndt thought that Tuckson pushed the argument just a little too far:

> Tuckson's contention is based on the universality of *all* art, irrespective of provenance. It is important for us to know here exactly what this means. The cultural background is not, here, seriously taken into account; the function or use of the object or painting, even the identity of the artist, may be completely unknown... Its decorative qualities, its design, its treatment its overall appeal, are what matters; we like its lines, its curves, its sense of boldness, its balance and so forth. We are evaluating it in our own idiom, within a climate of our own aesthetic traditions. (ibid.: 71, my emphasis)

While Berndt probably assesses the core of Tuckson's position accurately, Tuckson (ibid.: 68) acknowledged the importance of what he referred to as the 'work of the ethnologist, archaeologist, and anthropologist', and in the examples that he analyses does indeed use ethnographic data.

In essence, Berndt is arguing that although it is possible to appreciate works purely on the basis of form, this appreciation is only partial, and is biased toward the values of the viewing culture. Following from this, I would argue that while people can thus obviously appreciate any work of art through the lens of their own culture's aesthetics, just as they can appreciate the aesthetic properties of found objects, they must realize that this is precisely what they are doing. They must not be under the illusion that they are experiencing the work as a member of the producing culture would. The failure to provide the background knowledge necessary to interpret the object in relation to the producer's culture can then be challenged both on moral grounds – that the agency of the producer is being denied – and on the grounds that it impoverishes the interpretation.

The counter-argument to this challenge is covered by Maloon's statement that bark paintings 'are not ethnographic curiosities'. While he provides no explanation of what he means, his underlying premise is that, as works of art, they should not be positioned solely or even primarily as sources of information about the way of life of another culture. From this perspective, art is a celebration of common humanity, and too much context distracts the viewer. Indeed he suggests that the 'spirituality' that lies behind Aboriginal art is best revealed when it is viewed as art. This second suggestion poses the greatest challenge to an anthropological perspective on art, since it deems irrelevant the particular cultural meanings associated with objects. The anthropological perspective would not deny that the search for human universals and for categories that can be applied cross-culturally is perfectly compatible with a recognition of cultural difference.[12] But the recognition of cultural difference requires that those categories be distanced from particular Western cultural assumptions. Maloon/Tuckson's universals are in fact not universals at all but the expression of values of a particular (and indeed today unrepresentative) European art world. The debates that raged over Rubin's *Primitivism* exhibition generated similar debates in which it was argued that key assumptions of the ideology underlying European modernism alienated the art from the societies that produced it (Rubin 1985). Bernhard Lüthi, for example, wrote

> Rubin's love of modernism is based on the fact that it took Western art beyond the mere level of illustration. When Rubin notes that African, Oceanic or Indian artisans are not illustrating but conceptualising, he evidently feels he is praising them for their modernity. In doing so he altogether undercuts their reality system. By denying that tribal canons of representation actually represent anything, he is in effect denying that their view of the world is real. (1993: 23)[13]

Interestingly, if we adopt a universalistic aesthetic perspective it is difficult to understand why the art world was so tardy in recognizing the value of Aboriginal art – a value which appears to lie in its formal appearance unmediated by cultural knowledge. Indeed it was art institutionally defined that kept Aboriginal art out of the gallery, not any universalistic perspective. That is why Tuckson's inclusion of the Tiwi *pukumani* poles in the Art Gallery's exhibition space was indeed a radical gesture, and why he received so much criticism from the contemporary art world of the time (Venbrux 2006). Nonetheless, it seems unjust to attribute to anthropologists a significant role in the failure to recognize art's universal attributes unless of course their attention to meaning was too much of a distraction. It was Australian artists and curators who so singularly failed to draw attention (to paraphrase Maloon) to the '[exercise of] skill and ingenuity in their use of materials; [or the fact that] they are considerate of the ways their works are organised and elaborated and are sensitive to the resulting aesthetic effect'. Indeed, Margaret Preston (1930a), one of the few Euro-Australian artists who showed an interest in Aboriginal art until the 1950s, wrote at times as if the simple asymmetric geometry that she found so vital is almost the accidental product of a simple mind and faulty technique! (She later modified her view.) By way of contrast, praise that issued from the pen of the anthropologist Baldwin Spencer foreshadowed Tuckson's own (a fact that Tuckson clearly acknowledges): 'Today I found a native who, apparently, had nothing better to do than to sit quietly in the camp evidently enjoying himself ... he held [his brush] like a civilised artist ... he did the line work, often very fine and regular, with much the same freedom and precision as a Japanese or Chinese artist doing his most beautiful wash-work with his brush.' (Spencer 1928: 793)

Yet from Tuckson's point of view, Spencer's involvement with Aboriginal art may have symbolized the very problem that he was trying to address. While Spencer was able to see the aesthetic dimension of Aboriginal art and responded to it in terms of universal characteristics of form, the paintings in his charge remained in the National Museum, and absent from the walls of the National Gallery of Victoria. The paintings were part of a comprehensive ethnographic collection which included material culture objects in general, and thus the art was lost in the ethnography. It was not seen by others as art because of where it was housed and how it was exhibited.

## CONCLUSION: CONTEXTS OF VIEWING

The theory of a universal aesthetic is intertwined with a theory of viewing that opposes the art gallery to the museum. In this theory, works of art should be allowed to speak for themselves. Thus they need their own space for contemplation and, though their meaning and impact will be affected by their relationship to adjacent works, and to the hang as a whole, it is desirable that the act of viewing should take place in space as uncluttered as possible by supplementary information. While the density of hangs varies, as does the amount of information provided, these broad principles apply in art galleries around the world. Museums, on the other hand, are often defined in opposition to art galleries as places where objects are contextualized by information, by accompanying interpretative materials, by dioramas and by being seen in association with other objects. I think that it is desirable to distinguish the Western concept of 'seeing things' as art from the presumption of a universalistic aesthetic, and indeed to separate 'seeing things' as isolated or decontextualized objects from 'seeing things' as art.

The real problem with the Maloon/Tuckson position, apart from its circularity, is that Western viewers come to an art gallery already laden with information and experience that can be applied to already familiar works of European art.[14] Indeed, in the art galleries this information is generally present in the ordering of rooms on the basis of period, medium and geography. However, it will also have been acquired from seeing works in quite different contexts: not only on the gallery walls, but also in publications, in films, as reproductions, and so on. It is a conceit of a particularly narrow band of Western art theory and practice that the appreciation and production of art has nothing to do with knowledge of its particular art history. For indigenous art to be seen on equal terms with Western art it requires more than the right to an isolated space. The viewer must also have some access to its history and significance. Nigel Lendon has shown that, in viewing eastern Arnhem Land bark paintings, knowledge of the social and cultural background of the works enhances the viewer's appreciation of them:

> The interpretation of these paintings may be compared to how the viewer might under-
> stand Western religious or political art, or the world of allegory. In that case we expect
> both the viewer and the artist to bring to the exchange a prior knowledge of the social
> and mythic space of the narrative, or at least a recognition of the wider reality to which
> the image refers. (1995: 60)

Yet it is also undeniable that understanding the form of the paintings can provide deep insights into culture and cognition.

Seeing a work as art is also quite compatible with seeing it as something else, and viewing an object in isolation does not of itself make it into an art object. However, placing objects in isolation, as in an art gallery, or in sets, as in ethnographic displays, has at times created the space for discourse over whether something is or is not an art object. And because art has been so inextricably interconnected with the market, the dialogue has been entangled both in an economic and in a cultural value creation process. The South Australian Museum's 1986 exhibition *Art and Land* provides an excellent example of the discourse over Aboriginal art as art. It also illustrates just how challenging Tuckson's action was, nearly 25 years earlier, when he installed Aboriginal art for the first time in the Art Gallery of New South Wales.

*Art and Land* was an exhibition of toas from the Lake Eyre region of Central Australia. Toas were direction signs that marked where people had gone, but they were also engaging and diverse minimalist sculptural forms. On this occasion, anthropologist Peter Sutton and historian Philip Jones decided to exhibit the objects not as ethnography but as art, by the simple expedient of giving each its own space in a well-lit display with a minimum of accompanying information. The protagonist who took them to task was an art historian, Donald Brook (1986), who argued that the way they were displayed in itself was a form of appropriation, since it contradicted the intention of the producers.[15] Although adopting a different and, on the surface, opposite position from Tuckson's, Brooke too appears to have been bound by the categories of his own culture. The acceptance of art works into the Western gallery context is not simply a belated recognition of their universal attributes. It can be a far more radical step that challenges the Western category itself and shifts the definition of art: exhibiting toas as art was part of that process. That is why the inclusion of non-European art continues to generate such opposition: it insists on a different kind of concept of art that threatens to disrupt pre-existing values. At the same time, Jones and Sutton provided, through the accompanying book (1986) and in the debates that surrounded the exhibition, more contextual information on toas than had been available until then. As Luke Taylor pointed out in reviewing the debate, the error is in the polarization of views: in seeing works as either art or ethnography.

> Our theory of art should not divorce the analysis of aesthetic forms from a consideration of social context; the form of the work is a crystalisation of those values. Rather we should investigate the cultural setting of the artist's aesthetic experience and how this relates to the form of the works and also address the ways such artistic forms engender aesthetic responses in members of other cultures who view the works. (Taylor 1988: 96)

# 9 CONCLUSION

There was never going to be a simple conclusion to this book. The topic I have chosen to write about is one of great complexity and is written in the context of rapid change. It is a book about art and the meta-theoretical issues of anthropology and art history, but it is also a book about the ethics of the colonial encounter and its consequences. It is a book about the importance of time in placing ideas and actions in a context that enables them to be understood; but it is also about the need to escape from the constraints of time and particular temporal orderings of things. The artists who seized on what they referred to as a 'primitive art' as a means of escaping from their place in time have much in common with the contemporary Indigenous artists of Arnhem Land who are using art to escape from the way the have been positioned, by recent intellectual and colonial history, as prior to the present in which they live. The dialogue over art remains an active and contested one.

There is no question that the artists and collectors at the turn of the nineteenth and twentieth centuries played an important role in breaking down the barriers between Indigenous and non-Indigenous art. From the perspective of art practice, their response to the forms of 'primitive art' was an integral part of the process of seeing value in the products of other cultures – and seeing value is a vital moment in the process of developing understanding. The irony was that in finding inspiration in the forms, they saw the aesthetic as being their own. The possibility of exploring indigenous creativity further at the time, and entering into a cross-cultural discourse over form, was blocked by an overly determined theory of form in art which developed out of Kantian aesthetics and which gave too great a priority to disinterested contemplation. Irene Winter captures the core of this process well when she writes

> At issue for the application of a general theory of aesthetics to any non-Western, or indeed any pre-early modern Western, artistic production is whether and to what degree one may distinguish the ideal conditions of a pure aesthetic judgement from the historically contingent conditions by which one makes such judgements. That one cannot pare away sensory perception and affective response from aesthetic judgement seems evident. Other parts of the package, however – such as the necessary elevation of particular classes of artistic production to the status of fine art, as well as the insistence upon contemplation and disinterest – were themselves grounded, I would suggest, both in debate with prior concepts of unity of the beautiful and the good in theology and in developing notions of property, ownership, value and identity current in contemporary economic and social theory.

> The perspective is important in the very construct of 'disinterest' and the 'non-utility' of the work in the discourses of early modernism – an idealist position on the one hand, and one that serves to obscure the enormous social, and even political, utility of ownership and display, on the other (Winter 2002: 4)

The reception of indigenous art following its encounter with modernism could have gone in a very different direction if it had not been caught up in the particular European trajectory, if it were 'grounded' differently. It is always difficult to enter particular historical moments – especially moments of significant change – and capture the way in which the world appeared to people living through those times. The impact of modernism and the challenge of primitive art are almost unrecoverable experiences. The anthropologist Raymond Firth provides a glimpse of the excitement, of exposure to exotic forms when he writes: 'the admission into the graphic and plastic arts of distortion, of change of form from the proportions given by ordinary vision, came as a liberating influence'. And then the anthropologist takes over as he continues:

> It was significant not only for an appreciation of the contemporary Western art, but also for a clearer understanding of much medieval and exotic art. Like Romanesque painting and sculpture which have long captured my interest, the painting and sculpture which anthropologists encountered in exotic societies could be regarded, not as a product of imperfect vision, technical crudity, or blind adherence to tradition, but as works of art in their own right, to be judged as expressions of artists' original conceptions in the light of their cultural endowment. (Firth 1992: 19)

Firth's comments enable us to see the complexity of the engagement with non-Western art and the different positions that were adopted. To Firth it was important to connect the expressive dimension of the art with the ideational, to bring concept and culture into the analysis of non-Western art, just as he understood the conceptual to be an integral component of contemporary Western art. The acceptance of non-Western art was unlikely to happen quickly or in an entirely uniform way. Indeed the historical process has been one of changing attitudes over time to classical art, to Egyptian art, to the arts of China, Africa, the Americas and so on. The process of acceptance has been one of engagement, and of the development of particular histories.[1] The timelag involved after the initial stimulus provided by the appreciation of the formal properties of the 'other' art, is a time when understanding of the work develops. The impact of the form of non-European art on Western art practice may be immediate, based on 'sensory perceptions and affective response'. For a viewer knowing nothing about the significance of the artwork, they are left to be interpreted according to the presuppositions of the time – that African art is analogous to the art of children or the insane, that it is a product of untutored minds that allow for expressive freedom, that its virtues are in its faults or in some presumed closeness to a world of spirits or the world of nature. However, as audiences continue to be exposed to the art and begin to place it in the context of regional forms and accumulate more knowledge about the societies that produce it, some of those presuppositions are likely to problematized. Often it has happened without the direct agency of the artists, because of time depth and lack of evidence in the case of ancient arts or an absence of data in the case of many Indigenous arts. However, the history of fine art institutions is that over the previous century they have become increasingly embracing of other arts.

In the case of Australian Aboriginal art, we can see changes in attitude happening as we look at the way particular artists have responded to the art over time and as we see the language of the artworld change to one more engaged with the art. Margaret Preston's writings about Aboriginal art, for example, moved from an earlier aesthetic response in which the formal virtues of the art were thought to be an unconscious product of a faulty technique to a gradual understanding of the complexities of the art in its cultural context. We can see the rhetoric of the curators of fine art institutions moving Aboriginal art toward inclusion within the fine art category as opposed to exclusion. Tuckson's engagement with Aboriginal art as a curator and artist is clearly an important example, but so too was Theodore Sizer's inclusion of Aboriginal art in the 1941 American touring exhibition of Australian art (Stephen 2006) and, prior to that, Daryl Lindsay's 1943 *Primitive Art* exhibition at the National Gallery of Victoria (McLean 1998). But the interventions continued to be viewed as radical even though their effect was cumulative.

James Mollison's conversion to Aboriginal art in the 1980s was a crucial step in moving the Australian artworld to an acceptance of Aboriginal art as fine art. Mollison was the founding director of the National Gallery of Australia, which officially came into being with the National Gallery Act of 1975, but it had begun to develop its collections somewhat earlier. However, although Australian art and 'primitive art' were among its two initial acquisition categories, Aboriginal art was excluded. The grounds were said to be that Aboriginal art was to be housed in a national museum and that the National Gallery should not compete. At the time, though, no national museum existed and it may be that its inclusion was just too hard – would it have been Australian art or primitive art? Be that as it may, in the early 1980s the Gallery shifted its position and began collecting Aboriginal art as Australian art. In 1987, in an article in the *Weekend Australian* (September 12–13), Mollison compared his Gallery's recent purchase of Jack Wunuwan's *Barnumbirr, the Morning Star* with Michelangelo's *Last Supper*. 'It is very difficult to get over the notion of how encompassing some works of Aboriginal art are,' he said. 'If you wanted a work in which the artist has summed up his whole feelings about an aspect of Christian belief, you have to go to something as complex as Michelangelo's Last Supper,' and went on to say, 'I would think that more Australians have seen Altimira or Lascaux as tourists in Europe [than equivalent bodies of Aboriginal rock art] and it is our hope that through responsible publication of the Aboriginal achievement those histories of world art that start with the Palaeolithic will include Australian Aboriginal art, and the information that the tradition of art is alive to the present day.'[2]

Mollison's comments are interesting in part because he drew an analogy not with contemporary art and not based on a narrow definition of aesthetics but on conceptual aspects of the work and the relationship between form and content. Some people might say on this basis that Mollison evaded the issue as to whether or not Wunuwun's painting was contemporary Australian art. It might be argued following the ideology of the avant garde that if Michelangelo produced the *Last Supper* in the twenty-first century it would not be fine art, it would be art out of its place and time. The example is of course a hypothetical one and no one can know the answer. However, contemporary Aboriginal artists are not producing works out of their time. And they are producing works in the context of interactions with other contemporary artists. The trajectory of their works is influenced by its contemporary context. They are part of the diversity of contemporary Australian art practice. The category of Western fine art, or rather the works that are considered appropriate for exhibition and collection in fine art galleries reflecting an institutional definition of fine art, do not make a coherent story. There are no necessary connections between the works included apart from the fact that they all are the result of the same sedimentary selective processes whose criteria for inclusion change over time. Nontheless, since the category contains works of very different types that overlap in time and space, it provides a resource in which precisely the kind of analogy that Mollison makes across space and time can be productively explored. Yet seeing something in common between Renaissance or Byzantine paintings and some works of Aboriginal art does not make them any closer in time, any more than seeing relationships between the aesthetic effect of contemporary Yolngu Art and Op Art make them part of the Op art movement – the relationships are synergistic.

Contemporary fine art – the fine art of the present – is at a point of intersection with the more general history of art. It is influenced by the agency of artists of the present and the contemporary art market. However, contemporary fine art has until recently been too closely tied to a particular present, the present of the Western avant-garde. There is a tendency to subordinate the complex determinism of the past – which influenced the particular form of artworks in their historical contexts – to selective ideologies of the present, but those particular interactions soon become part of fine art's own history, just as the contexts and motivations of art in Celtic times or the Renaissance, or on the voyages of discovery, are among the determinants of form in art. In many ways the job of art history is to rescue art from its entanglement with the fine art category. And indeed the present in retrospect will be seen to have a similar diversity to the past, when freed from the avant-garde obsession with the cutting edge.

Elsewhere I have suggested that the category of fine art is like the mythical anaconda of the Amazonian rainforest or, perhaps more appropriately, the Rainbow Serpent of Arnhem Land in its capacity to swallow artforms from different places and times and recreate them in its own terms.[3] The fine art category also has something of the characteristics of a ragbag, containing an enormous variety of objects, from different places and times – only allowed in on its terms. Over time its contents grow as other arts are elevated to the status of fine arts in relation to developments in European tastes and the trajectory of European practice and art history. Perhaps surprisingly – though it should not by now be a surprise – I have no problem with accepting the works included in the fine art category as art. Nor do I have a problem with qualitative judgements being applied to artworks. My argument indeed is that a substantive definition of art, of which a cross-cultural definition is one example, is likely to embrace most of the works that are defined as fine art.

The definition of art that I have been using implicitly and explicitly is one that appears to move in harmony with the ragbag collections of objects that have been allowed to enter the hallowed walls of the art galleries. My ragbag may move a little ahead at times. My position in Australia means that it is fuller (ahead of many) in its inclusion of Indigenous art, in particular Australian Indigenous art. It includes the artworks that most people would expect to find in an art gallery because the cross-cultural definition I employ includes aesthetics and meaning as attributes of the objects it encompasses.

However, my definition does not have special exclusionary clauses, for example that while it may be perfectly acceptable for an artist allocated a certain temporal position in world art history to make works explicitly for sale, it is unacceptable for a person allocated a different temporal space. To me this is especially problematic if the artists concerned occupy the same real time-space and could even be represented by the same art gallery and included in the same art exhibition. This becomes even more problematic if the use by one artist of the other artist's work could make it into an artwork![4]

Ruth Philips phrases this very well when she writes of Native American art: 'the scholarly apparatus that inscribes the inauthenticity of commoditized wares [is] a central problem in the way that art history has addressed Native art. The authenticity paradigm marginalises not only the objects but the makers, making of them a ghostly presence in the modern world rather than acknowledging their vigorous interventions in it' (1998: x).

It was brought home to me by a letter written by the Australian Trade Commissioner in New York to the manager of Aboriginal Arts and Crafts limited in February 1977.

> We thank you for your recent letter outlining your plans to penetrate the American Art and Craft market with the sale of your products. We have had extensive discussions with Museum directors, for example the Museum of Primitive Art, and leading importers of art objects from the Pacific in New York. From these conversations it has emerged that the market for your products in museums, private collections and so on would not be feasible. As per your catalogue it appears that you are prepared to manufacture for sale a wide variety of Aboriginal art objects. While these objects are 'Authentic' in the sense that they are made by traditional Aboriginal craftsmen and painters, use as media traditional materials and conform almost exactly to the genuine article, they would nonetheless not be considered 'Authentic' by museum curators. The criteria for an 'Authentic' item is that it must have been made for use and perhaps been used in traditional society and not made for sale. In your letter you mention for example the growth in sales of African art in the United States. However, it must be realised that the items that are being sold are collected from traditional societies in Africa (and unfortunately sometimes stolen) and are not the objects of art that one can buy in the capital cities

and major towns in Africa, which are made for sale to such people as tourists and so on.

And then here comes Catch Twenty Two as far as the producers are concerned.

> We have ascertained from the Department of Aboriginal Affairs that exports of these authentic Aboriginal Artefacts such as objects of archaeological, ethnographical, historical, Sacred, ritual, or ceremonial interest, are generally prohibited. They do of course say that artefacts made for sale can be readily exported.

Clearly the problem here is created by the a priori placing of contemporary Aboriginal art in a special category that separates it off from art produced by non-Indigenous Australians, a category that has much in common with the primitive art of the past.

The greatest irony of course is that most contemporary fine art is produced for sale, and hence the fact that something is being produced for sale is not a sufficient reason for its exclusion from the fine art category. While not all contemporary fine art can be sold as a commodity, two widely held assumptions about contemporary artworks convert many into commodities. Contemporary fine art is partly defined by two implicit criteria that we have encountered often in our analysis: the art is art by intention or destination and the works are produced primarily for aesthetic contemplation, to be judged by aesthetic criteria. The fact that they are produced as fine art works to be displayed as such implies that the maker, if he or she is to earn a living by producing them, is making the works for sale or is, in the case of performance art, for example, being paid otherwise for producing the artworks.

None of this means of course that the prime motivation of the artist is to produce a commodity for sale. There is nevertheless an entanglement in the value creation processes which create fine art between the evaluations of the products as art and the market and prestige systems associated with fine art. The problem with the position from fine art is indeed that too often it is centred on exclusionary criteria – which makes a great deal of sense if one views the category as being subordinate to the interests of the art market and the creation of symbolic capital, but can also appear to be contradictory: works that are made for sale by one set of artists are unproblematically fine art while works made for sale by another group of artists are inauthentic. The fact that something is made for sale cannot be a criterion for inclusion or exclusion of works from the category of fine art.

The debate over whether a work of indigenous Australian art is a work of fine art worthy of a place in a fine art gallery or a work of ethnography is interesting precisely because it reveals the exclusionary and inclusionary nature of the process. What becomes excluded is often the original context of the work, its meaning to the artist, data about the culture of production. To be fair, in most cases this kind of ethnographic information is often present in the catalogue or accompanying digital information – but it is just pushed into the background, and what is foregrounded is the form. That which is excluded enables it to be exhibited in a prestige-gallery space in which it can be appreciated as a work of individual creativity. Inclusion in the space of the art gallery almost becomes the defining moment for the shift in category. And yet in this case I would argue that what is included or excluded has nothing to do with what makes the work an artwork. Physically, the work had precisely the same properties before and after its inclusion. Substantively, it seems that the works included in the fine art gallery are simply works that have been chosen for viewing in a particularly privileged way. The desire to provide exclusionary criteria for works included in the Western category fine art, which separate them off from a more general cross-cultural category of art, is the problem, rather than the creation of a space for privileged viewing. Freed from the historical baggage of the Western canon, the art gallery becomes open to the diversity of creative factors that underlie the production of artworks, and that can be revealed and appreciated by an informed viewing of them as objects.

We might contrast Terrence Maloon's statement that Aboriginal works of art are 'not just ethnographic curiosities' with Djambawa Marawili's 'my paintings are not just pretty pictures.'[5] Both statements are unproblematically true yet can also be interpreted to be fundamentally opposed. Maloon made his statement in opposition to what he interpreted to be an anthropological position that the meaning and Indigenous context of Aboriginal artworks were fundamental to understanding them. I would argue that such a position is in part true, but at the same time I would argue that it is self-evident that people can respond to the form of artworks and gain a great deal of pleasure by viewing them as forms. I would argue further, though, that it is reasonable that information should be provided with the works that enables the viewer to understand the works in their cultural context. Indeed in the case of Western art I have argued that the average Western gallery visitor in general comes to an exhibition with some background knowledge of European art history. Djambawa Marawili's statement is precisely a plea for the visitor to his exhibition to have some knowledge of what the works of art mean to him, the significance they have to Yolngu society. I am of course not saying that every Indigenous artist would adopt such a position. Yet I would say that when an artist does believe the meaning of his or her work to be important, this does not make it into a mere ethnographic object. Indeed in a broader sense the cognitive dimensions of artworks as a particular form of knowledge about the world is perfectly compatible with Kant's original conception of what art is.

Most artworks that are today classified as fine art had at one time another history, just as most work of contemporary artists that are bought by today's fine art institutions are made for sale as artworks. Yet although most contemporary artists clearly desire to sell their work, sale is seldom the primary aim of art production; but nor is production of art for art's sake. Nor do artists see the display of their artwork on gallery walls for individual contemplation as the only context for their artworks. Artists are as much concerned with ideas as with aesthetics.[6]

The intention to produce art for sale to an external market as the primary means of support – that is, to become a professional artist in the contemporary sense of the word – only becomes realizable at a particular moment in the development of Western capitalist societies. In previous eras, the production of art for particular purposes was the primary source of remuneration to the artist: the patrons were the Court, the Church, the merchants and so on. However, simply because it is possible to sell art to be exhibited in a gallery does not mean that all the other purposes of art no longer exist. Art can be motivated by protest, can be intended to occupy a space, to make a statement, to shock people. Art galleries have become in some respects purpose arenas, far from being simply places for the disinterested contemplation of form. If that were their only purpose then no one would be concerned about the burning of a nation's flag on the gallery steps or whether Andres Serrano's *Piss Christ, 1987,* was blasphemous. Art gallery curators would be less concerned that exhibitions had coherent themes, and the question of which art was likely to gain the sponsorship to enable a blockbuster exhibition would concern aesthetic discourse only. Moreover, the boundaries between art and not art are not as clear-cut as people might imagine. People trained in the same art schools can develop careers that go on very different trajectories, often skirting the boundaries between different art categories.

In many parts of the world, in particular of course in Europe and the West, the market for art has evolved over time with changing art practice – hence the continuities have been unproblematic and the problems posed to definitions of art rarely addressed. In north-east Arnhem Land, art has become a commodity in a matter of three generations – hence the change in the market for art has been a dramatic one. However, from the artist's perspectives it has been less than dramatic. The world outside views seventy years of art history as being a relatively short time – though a moment's reflection will show that in that period artists in the Western tradition have moved from expressionism to conceptual art and minimalism through postmodernism and into the present. From the perspective of contemporary Arnhem Land artists, the third or fourth generation, they have never known a time in which making a living as an artist was not a possible occupation. They have grown up as artists in the context of capitalism. But they have equally continued as artists in their own society, using art for the diversity of purposes it has in their religious and social life. They are contemporary Yolngu artists articulating with the world outside, and inevitably entangling in the contemporary art market with its precepts of a still influential modernist concept of what art is. But they are not Indigenous modernists.

Accepting Aboriginal art as Indigenous modernism under the constraints of the modernist definition of art is likely to set the art concerned on a particular trajectory that accepts the modernist conditions for the definition of works as art. It encourages the art to be labelled as 'hybrid' and lose its connection with the trajectory it was previously on – people writing about it will emphasize those characteristics it shares with Western modernism – individual creativity, innovation, formalist aesthetics, the intention to produce art for sale. The art is likely to become first appropriated by modernism and then absorbed into it, rather than providing a challenge to it. The reality is that the history of art comprises a multiplicity of relatively autonomous trajectories, each occupying its own relatively autonomous space-time – and that global history includes the history of Western fine art on its trajectory toward modernism. The works from these different but intersecting trajectories can be brought together in the Western art gallery which, if seen as a particular arena for viewing art works rather than as a hierarchical ordering of cultural history, can become a context for appreciating and learning from the creative practice of artists across space and time. My argument, essentially, is to embrace a cross-cultural concept of art, which simply comprises objects produced by artists acting in the world at all times and in all places.

# NOTES

## PREFACE

1. The debate over art and ethnography was played out in the opening exhibitions at the Museum of Mankind. William Fagg, one of the great advocates for African art, curated *The Tribal Image: Wooden Figure Sculpture of the World*, a survey exhibition of some of the museum's most renowned works of 'tribal' art as part of the opening offering, and other exhibitions placed indigenous arts in their social context, as in *Divine Kingship in Africa* which centred on Benin.
2. As Fred Myers writes of the Pintubi 'For Aboriginal people, the art movement has been a positive experience, in general, but from my experience, involvement in the art scene often seems for whites, to occasion some sort of trouble' (2002: 355).

## CHAPTER 1  CROSS-CULTURAL CATEGORIES AND THE INCLUSION OF ABORIGINAL ART

1. She writes about Smith's foundational text on Australian art: 'The logic of the argument in *Place, Taste and Tradition in Australian Painting* excludes art by Indigenous Australians by virtue of the fact that it is constructed around the model of centre/periphery. As Bernard Smith writes in *Place, Taste and Tradition*, 'this study is largely concerned with the mutations which have occurred in styles and fashions originating overseas as they have been assimilated into conditions … existing in Australia' (Smith 1945: 21)' (Lowish 2005: 67).
2. John Onians' (e.g. 1996) project of world art history is one example, as are the perspectives of James Elkins (e.g. 1999) and Hans Belting (2005); the approaches of many of the authors in Westermann (2005) provide others (see also Welsch et al. 2006).
3. The interaction between Indigenous and non-Indigenous artists has been controversial and in many respects productive (see McLean 1998). Much of the controversy has centred on the art practice of the Latvian Australian Imants Tillers (see essays in Hart 2006).
4. Recent Western art practice has been dominated by the ideology of modernism with its emphasis on changing sequences of form and individual inspiration, and on the personal identity of the artist. Modern art is seen as the culmination of a chain of connection stretching back to the Renaissance and Classical civilization: from ancient Egypt to Australia via Athens. This view comes out clearly in a letter Brett Whitely wrote to Lloyd Rees, shortly before the latter's death: 'I know Lloyd that I will continue to be influenced by you until the day I too, come up to, giving in, and to giving over, and I know someone will pick up something of what I have done, and carry the mantle on into the 2000s, whatever shape and form that will take: so the profound thread, that leads its way back to Leonardo and on through the Millennium to Egypt, that wonderful line, the most precious club in the world, that occasionally gets new members and bids farewell to those whose innings of dreamings, are done' (cited in Hawley 1988).

   Whitely's comments are an excellent example of a view of art practice that emphasizes formal continuities over time and disregards the social and cultural contexts of the works produced. It implies an essentialized autonomous aesthetically motivated formal progression. It subordinates art to a particular definition that in fact has a relatively short history in the West let alone elsewhere. This particular Western art world emphasizes form and universalizes aesthetic judgements. Often the language of art criticism seems highly subjective: it almost takes on the form of a secret language in which esoteric knowledge about aspects of formal and stylistic sequences, knowledge of the canon of great works and familiarity with the characteristics or conventions of the avant-garde, give people the authority to make judgements about the value of artworks (Becker 1982).

5.  The relationship between Western art and 'Primitive' art shows interesting parallels to that between Western art and Oriental art, and similar problems are created if one attempts to incorporate the history of one within the history of the other (see Sullivan 1989: 244–61). As Sullivan writes, 'what has happened in Western art in the twentieth century has brought it, in certain fundamental respects, into accord with the Far East. It is as though the inhabitants of one country, with immense imaginative effort, had succeeded in creating a new language, only to discover that it was the native tongue of another land on the other side of the world' (1989: 256).

6.  Clearly that moment of modernism was the culmination of a particular trajectory that can be traced back through Schiller and German romantic idealism to the philosophy of Kant and Hume, whereby the aesthetics of form was seen as separable from content. During the nineteenth century, fine art galleries increasingly became educators of taste and centres of connoisseurship in which attention was centred on objects as exemplars of their position in a history of aesthetic forms. The criterion for selection became focused on an imagined history of European art as aesthetic forms from classical times to the 'present day'. In the fine art galleries the aesthetic judgement of the curators became and 'remain a central criterion of museum curators in their decisions regarding inclusion or exclusion' (Joachimides 2000: 219). However it has only been for moments in that history that the values of artists and connoisseurial creators have coincided.

7.  Lowish comments on Smith's attitude to Margaret Preston and the Jindyworobaks – a cultural movement that aimed to establish distinctively Australian literary forms – as follows: 'Smith did not approve of their efforts, describing the movement as "nothing more than an invocation to go back to a state of nature" or worse "to return to yams and witchetty grubs, to the spear and the churinga and, finally, to Alcheringa"' (Smith, 1945: 166). Smith describes the work of Margaret Preston, a South Australian artist who adapted the designs and colours of Aboriginal art, as a phase of primitivism and, as such, not a 'basis for a truly Australian art' (Smith 1945: 189). It is only recently that the complexity and depths of Preston's engagement with Aboriginal art has been recognized and appreciated by art historians (see Edwards 2005).

8.  My approach to cross-cultural categories is influenced by Needham's use of the Wittgensteinean concept of family resemblance and in particular the idea of polythetic sets (Needham 1975).

9.  Strang phrases this process well when she writes 'the knowledges acquired through ethnographic enquiry are inevitably integrated and synthesized through the subsequent analysis and therefore emerge in the new understandings that are the product of the research – in other words, the outcome of the research, which feeds into the shared and continuously evolving theoretical frameworks of the discipline, is not in fact merely a product of European "science" but a synthesis of the anthropologist's own forms of knowledge and the forms of explanation, the theories and concepts, absorbed during her or his engagement with a particular cultural context. In this sense individual anthropologists serve as conduits, translating and conveying many kinds of knowledge to a common discursive pool' (Strang 2006: 985).

10. Richard Anderson adopts a similar approach in developing a cross-cultural definition of art and also draws an analogy with the study of kinship (Anderson 1992: 928 and 1990).

11. For economics see Dalton (1969) and for law see Pospisil (1971).

12. Needham uses Sokal and Sneath's (1963) definition of a polythetic set that 'a polythetic arrangement places together organisms that have the greatest number of shared features, and no feature is either essential to

group membership or is sufficient to make the organism a member of the group' Needham 1975: 356). They go on to note that it is likely that any class is not fully polythetic but likely to have some defining feature or features in common. In the case of art I would argue that aesthetic effect broadly defined is likely to be a core feature of the set even if it is not a factor in every member (artwork)

13. I must emphasize that the boundary of the frame is not the Western concept. Establishing the frame does not involve arguing that Indigenous art or Indigenous conceptions of land ownership are the same as Western ones; rather, it places both in a more inclusive frame which encompasses their differences as well as what they share in common. The dangers of arguing that Indigenous art or music is precisely the same kind of thing as Western music is that in broader national or global contexts they will then be subject to legal frameworks based on values and conceptions that originate outside the society concerned and that may be incompatible with indigenous practice (see Coleman et al. (forthcoming) for a relevant discussion re indigenous Canadian music and Strathern 2006 for a succinct overview of intellectual property rights (IPR)).

14. Michael Lambek for example, in introducing Tylor's article included in his Blackwell *Reader in the Anthropology of Religion*, justifies his inclusion as the only nineteenth-century writer in the following terms: 'not only because he was among the more sensible, but because the core of his definition of religion as "the belief in Spiritual Beings" remains congenial to many contemporary thinkers and is indeed almost a part of Western "common sense" on the subject. His characterization of animism remains fruitful and does serve as one means to generalize about religious phenomena of all kinds. Animism speaks today to reflections on the mind/body problem and conceptualizations of the person, to the relations between humans and other species, especially in hunting societies, and to conceptualizations of death and the centrality of both mortuary ritual and sacrifice in human societies' (Lambek 2001: 21).

15. The argument of this book is strongly influenced by Munn's conception of value creation and value-transformation processes. As Munn (1986: 267) argues, the focus on value enables the anthropologist to show relationships between domains that are often kept separate and yet which are connected by people in reality acting across domains and creating value transformations in one context that affect value creation processes in another. In this book I will show how art mediates in value creation processes that operate within Yolngu society in the political and religious domain (see also Morphy 1991), how it is used to create value in external relations in the context of the global art market and how change in the domain of art production can influence value in gender relations.

16. As Nicholas Thomas has written 'The most regrettable stereotype concerning tribal societies is the idea that Indigenous knowledge is dominated by the reproduction and perpetuation of tradition' (Thomas 1999: 36). He goes on to note that innovation was not the result of a fetishization of unique personal creativity but integrated within an ongoing cultural dialogue over meaning.

17. Produced by the surrealists under the auspices of André Breton and published in *Variétés* (1929).

18. This issue has been the subject of a major debate between Fry and Willis (1989) and Benjamin (1990).

19. For a detailed analysis of these issues see Morphy 1991.

20. The scales of the works are likely to be different today. Most Yolngu barks headed for the fine art market are a metre or more in height and far exceed the dimension of an initiate's chest. However, the larger work may include the body painting within it or the body-painting design may be reproduced in a more elaborated form. Yolngu have always produced designs to different scales, contracting to the circumference of a bamboo-stemmed pipe and expanding to the variable sizes of sheets of bark or even to the dimensions of a ceremonial ground.

21. Myers discusses this issue in depth for the Pintubi artists of the Western Desert. He writes that the paintings 'emerge out of a way of life and set of practices that have changed but that continue to inform and shape Aboriginal social life in Central Australia' (Myers 2002: 23).

## CHAPTER 2  THE HISTORY BEGINS

1. This section is based on the account in Matthew Flinders's published journals (Flinders 1814).
2. This is summarized from Morphy 2004: 17–18, where the sources can be found.
3. For a detailed discussion of this era of Yolngu history see Egan 1996.
4. A broad perspective on Thomson's contribution to anthropology and his engagement with Aboriginal society is provided in Rigsby and Peterson 2005.
5. Women occasionally dance with spears in ceremonial contexts and men frequently will use baskets and digging sticks for similar purposes to those of women. There are a number of specialist baskets and bags that will be exclusively used by men – for example the tightly woven 'biting' bags that are used as containers of power. Men occasionally make digging sticks and some men have specialized roles in the making of sacred baskets.
6. Thomson, in his unpublished field notes in the Melbourne Museum, noted the importance of rights in designs and gave as an example the designs on a *bathi*: 'So zealously are the proprietary rights in these rangga patterns guarded that their infringement causes fighting... And great gifts were paid for the *bathi* carrying cherished patterns. There is no doubt that serious trouble and blood feuds of long duration have their foundation in this manner. Thus a man who saw another carrying a basket bearing his *mintji* will not speak at once, but he carries word back to his people and killing by magical or other means is resorted to' (September 30 1936).
7. This distinction is well described by Thomson in his article on smoking pipes. 'The simplest are very plain, unadorned, and purely utilitarian. Such objects are referred to more or less contemptuously as '*wakkingu*' [wakinngu], which really means 'uncouth', 'unrefined', in contrast to the highly decorated specimens upon which much time and skill has been lavished' (Thomson 1939a: 87). He continues on the following page to write 'it is the practice in Arnhem Land to dedicate fine or valued objects of material culture to the totems of his clan, which does render them sacred, so that they are then said to be *yarkomirri* [yäkumirri]— with names... The conventionalised *mintji* [miny'tji] or patterns which belong exclusively to the totem, and to the clan that claims it, may now be painted or incised upon the object' (ibid.: 88).
8. The best descriptions of Yolngu everyday material culture remain Thomson's (1939a and b, 1949). Hamby (2001) provides a detailed historical and ethnographic account of Yolngu fibre arts.
9. Early on, a few elaborately decorated *bathi* ended up in museum collections. In recent years Yolngu have neither offered nor produced *bathi* for sale. In many ways they are like *kula* valuables in the Massim, highly valued objects within the Yolngu world that leave an almost irreplaceable gap when they are taken out of use and circulation. They are valued not simply because of what they represent or their physical form but because of their history and their connection to people who made them and used them in the past. This may also be part of the explanation as to why objects that are like them are not made for sale – they might devalue the ones in circulation even though they do not possess quite the value of the older objects. Another factor may be that their market value may never be sufficient to compensate for the labour required in their production and the scarcity of the raw materials used.

## CHAPTER 3  BARK PAINTING AND THE EMERGENCE OF YOLNGU FINE ART

1. Today hollow-log coffins have joined bark paintings as the main form of expression of fine art from Yirrkala. In the 1970s these were not made for sale anywhere in Arnhem Land, though the mortuary poles of the Tiwi of Melville and Bathurst islands had gained widespread renown. People did, however, make miniature hollow logs for sale – scale models a metre at the most in height. Difficulty of transport may have been a significant factor. In the 1980s full-size hollow logs were produced in small numbers for sale. The turning point, however, was probably the *Aboriginal Memorial* of 1988. The *Aboriginal Memorial* was conceived of

by the then art advisor at Ramingining, Djon Mundine. It comprised a series of 200 hollow-log coffins to represent each year of the European colonization of Australia. The memorial was eventually acquired by the National Gallery of Australia and has had considerable impact (see Jenkins 2003). It has familiarized people with the idea of hollow-log coffins as an art form. Interestingly, although no artists from Yirrkala participated in Mundine's project, they have developed the art of hollow coffins more than other Yolngu communities.

2. Many of the bark paintings collected by Thomson from north-east Arnhem Land are shaped as if they were painted on the human body with components included that would have been painted on the legs and shoulders as well as on the chest. The paintings are in a sense illustrations of body paintings. However, this perspective may reflect a Eurocentric view of them. As was shown in Chapter 2, the paintings themselves are autonomous objects that reflect the structure of the body of the ancestor, and one of their contexts or canvases is the human body. Another would be a ceremonial dilly bag, another would be the wooden 'body' of a sacred object. The paintings in a sense are the ancestral mark and part of the conception of the ancestral being.

3. These ideas are developed in detail in the chapters on Manggalili iconography in Morphy 1991.

4. There are, however, signs that this is changing and that art galleries are increasingly responsive to Indigenous works in other media, in particular fibre arts that would previously have been categorized as craft.

5. Berndt for example collected a whole series of paintings that represented the artist's spirit-conception stories or the conception story for one of the artist's children. On another occasion, he commissioned a set of crayon drawings focusing on sexual relations, some of which were published in his book *Love Songs of Arnhem Land* (1976).

6. The expedition established a base at three localities beginning on Groote Eylandt then moving to Yirrkala and finally spending time at Oenpelli in Western Arnhem Land.

7. Mountford's main writing on Yirrkala art was his volume on *Art, Myth and Symbolism* publishing the results of the Arnhem Land Expedition (Mountford 1956). The Berndts wrote extensively on Aboriginal art including co-authoring with others two books for general audiences (Elkin, Berndt and Berndt, 1950 and Berndt, Berndt and Stanton, 1998).

8. Ian McLean (1998) provides a relevant summary of this history. Deborah Edwards's 2005 book on the Australian modernist Margaret Preston documents the close relationship between Margaret Preston and a number of Australian anthropologists, including Elkin, Mountford and McCarthy, in asserting the value of Aboriginal art and promoting its use in Australian design. Preston and McCarthy were both closely involved in the 1941 exhibition, which had as a strong theme the potential of Aboriginal art as a source of uniquely Australian design.

9. A few works by Arrernte watercolour artist Albert Namatjira had been exhibited earlier. The paintings were included in part because they were in an introduced medium and style and hence, as watercolour landscape paintings, fitted in the European category of fine art. Interestingly there was some reluctance about their inclusion because they represented a genre of art that could hardly be considered at the time as avant-garde. Today the Arrernte watercolour artists are thought by many to provide a different but equal challenge to the categories of the fine art market as Papunya paintings or Arnhem Land barks (see for example Hardy, Megaw and Megaw 1992 and French 2002).

10. The exhibition of this collection in the AGNSW caused controversy. A number of critics felt that the works should not have been displayed in an art gallery but that they belonged to the ethnographic museum (see Venbrux 2006: 202).

11. Indeed it is likely that both Berndt and Mountford would have shared their ambition of achieving recognition for Aboriginal art by gaining access to art gallery spaces. Tuckson as the deputy director of the AGNSW was better positioned to achieve that objective.

12. It is interesting that Kupka made a particular point of focusing on the individual style of the artist. Quite correctly he felt that the role of individual creativity in Indigenous arts had been neglected and underemphasized. He saw this as a sign of the failure of anthropology to engage with artistic creativity.

13. Indeed Venbrux (2006) shows the way in which Mountford tried to apply Arnhem Land methods of documentation to Tiwi art on a subsequent research visit there in 1954. The art did not fit his previous practice of documentation as it appeared not to be illustrative of clan-based stories. Indeed it appears from other researchers that Tiwi art had developed on a different basis (Goodale and Goss 1971). Mountford's solution was to encourage artists to produce artworks that were illustrative of stories. Venbrux shows how such works have subsequently been incorporated within the corpus of Tiwi art. The Yolngu situation has been different partly because there have not been the discontinuities in art production for the market that have characterized the history of Tiwi art, and Yolngu have engaged strongly in the documentation process over time.

14. Edwards has superbly documented Preston's consistent engagement with Aboriginal art from the 1920s, and emphasized that her 'knowledge of Aboriginal art was not static but fluid and multilayered, altering its dimensions over the four decades she advocated her distinctive form of nationalism' (Edwards 2005: 96). Edwards shows that, although it took a long time for Australian artists to become aware of the richness of Aboriginal arts, discourse about Aboriginal art was a much more significant theme of the period between the two world wars than has generally been acknowledged.

15. The history of these post-war years has been quite well researched, but most of the research remains unpublished. Interestingly, one of the main published sources – but a very poorly researched one – remains Roman Black's *Old and New Aboriginal Art* (1964), a book by an artist that is itself a reflection of the growing interest of the time. Morphy (1987) and Jones (1988) have produced short overviews of the history of the reception of Aboriginal art. The most detailed account of the growing interest in Aboriginal art in the period going up to the Second World War is Sylvia Kleinert's 1994 doctoral dissertation, and Ilaria Vanni's 1999 doctoral thesis provides an interesting analysis of exhibitions of Aboriginal art up to and including those at David Jones.

16. Warner's friendship with Makarrwala is movingly detailed in an appendix to *A Black Civilization* (Warner 1958), and Thomson's with Raywala pervades his writings (see Thomson 2005).

17. McIntosh captures this well when he writes: 'Understanding the meaning of the presence of the Other has obviously been a work in progress for Yolngu ever since the first outsiders appeared eons ago' (2004: 155).

18. The original account of the Elcho Island Memorial analyses the complexities of the event well (Berndt 1962). The opening chapter of Maddock's general book on the Australian Aborigines (1972) also provides great insight into the complexities of the event.

19. Myers (2002) records how Pintubi artists at Yaiyai in the early days of the development of Western Desert 'acrylic' paintings saw themselves partly engaged in an exchange of value with Canberra, the locus of national power. I gain an impression that in the Pintubi case the gift was less strategically directed at the time and not accompanied with specific targeted requests. This may be because the Pintubi occupied a different historical position from that of the Yolngu of Elcho Island who at the time of the Memorial had had a much longer period of settlement life enabling them to direct action toward a more specific external audience.

20. These maps are quite exceptional creations drawn in crayon on brown butcher's paper. They mark the place names along over 1,000 kilometres of coastline and along the river systems within the region. The southern region was indubitably drawn by Narritjin and Nanyin Maymuru, who may have been responsible for the entire map.

21. Doug Tuffin, who saw the paintings being produced, recalled that Narritjin was the sole painter of the final set of petitions. Earlier versions had been produced but had not been in a form acceptable to Parliament.

# CHAPTER 4  DIALOGUE AND CHANGE

1. Like many Yolngu group names this is not a simple one to translate. Djalkiri literally means 'footprint' or 'foundation', and in this context refers to 'foundation people'.
2. Fiona Magowan (2000) emphasizes the power of Indigenous performance in moving people toward dialogue, highlighting the embodied nature of the interaction, but also showing how it can fail if the participants are unwilling to participate in each other's worlds. In this case Ngulpurr took the opportunity to explain to the audience why the particular song was chosen to ensure that the dialogue that developed could be based on content and not just affect. While the aesthetics of Yolngu painting and song performance are vital in engaging people's attention, Yolngu see them as being part of the whole.
3. While Yolngu ancestral beings are often associated with large areas of land and with numerous places on the routes along which they journeyed, certain places are thought of as foundational to their being and to the lives of the people who succeeded them in the land – these are *djalkiri* (foundational) places and are the focal point of the clans' sacra associated with the ancestral being concerned.
4. Cox writing about what on the surface might seem to be a very different engagement of cultural aesthetics with the outside world – the insertion of Zen arts into new contexts – reveals striking similarities with the Australian case. Cox writes about Zen as a 'valued cultural aesthetic [always] connected in some form or another to political discourses and commercial concerns' (2003: 232). Later he writes 'the question for . . . regular practioners is not what is *the* authentic Zen art, but rather what are the Zen arts that are good for selling technology, representing Japanese culture, and encouraging tourism' (2003: 237). By substituting Yolngu for Zen and modifying the objectives a little, the sentence would apply equally well to Yolngu for whom art is a form of action.
5. This was brought home to me first in 1976. I was sitting among a group of men inside a shade painting a coffin lid. They had run out of wood glue and asked me if I could get them some. The shop was shut so I suggested instead that they used orchid stems as they had in the past and occasionally still did. Rather surprisingly, I had a supply of orchids but no glue! My offer was rejected. Maw Mununggurr, an elder of the Djapu clan and the main painter of the coffin lid, said that the glue would make the painting shine more!
6. A similar argument can be made in the case of hollow-log coffins. In the 1970s when I began my research at Yirrkala, hollow-log coffins were occasionally produced as memorials for the deceased. However, full-sized hollow-log coffins were no longer made for sale. Some artists produced hollow-log coffins in miniature, but full-sized hollow logs were considered impossible to transport and market. Circumstances changed in the 1980s when a few north-east Arnhem Land artists began to produce hollow-log coffins for sale. The Aboriginal Memorial of 1988 (see Chapter 2 note 6) also opened up a large potential market for hollow coffins by showing how powerfully they could be exhibited in sets.
7. Elizabeth Coleman captures this feature of Yolngu art well in developing an analogy with musical interpretation. She sees the different versions of the 'same' painting, at least in some respects, as analogous to different performances of the same musical score: 'Within a rule based tradition, certain features of a work become measures of skill or interpretation . . . Virtuosity, for instance, the ability to perform a difficult passage of music without changing tempo, may be a sign of skill because the passage is difficult' (Coleman 2005b: 94).

# CHAPTER 5  VISUALITY AND REPRESENTATION IN YOLNGU ART

1. This is a revised and expanded version first published as a chapter 'Seeing Indigenous Australian Art' in Westermann 2005.
2. Bernard Smith (1960) convincingly demonstrated the relationship between art, science and vision in European cultural history at the time of the Pacific voyages of discovery.

3. This dimension of Yolngu paintings is discussed in detail in Morphy 1991. A superbly documented collection of paintings of the east Arnhem Land coast and sea is published in the catalogue *Saltwater: Yirrkala Bark Paintings of Sea Country* (Buku-Larrnggay Mulka 1999).

4. For a discussion of cross-cultural aesthetics see Ingold 1996, and also Coleman 2005b, Coote 1992, Morphy 1992 and Winter 2002.

5. See Ian Dunlop's film *Djungguwan at Gurka'wuy* (Film Australia, 1990). For a description of the meaning of the painting in context see Morphy 1991: 123.

6. For a detailed discussion, see Morphy 1991, chapter 5.

7. A number of these paintings are illustrated with accompanying essays in *Buwayak: Invisibility*, the catalogue for a 2003 exhibition held at the Annandale Galleries, Sydney in association with Buku-Larrnggay Mulka.

8. Djambawa Marawili provided much of the documentation for this painting to Frances Morphy in March 2006. The ancestral creation of landscape and the mapping component of Yolngu paintings is discussed in Howard and Frances Morphy 2006.

9. Djambawa Marawili to Frances Morphy, March 2006.

10. *Buwayak*: Invisibility.

11. It has been argued that it was this conceptual view of landscape that both prevented European appreciation of much non-Western art and eventually saw it being opened up to Western appreciation through the intervention of modernist aesthetics. Sullivan writing of Chinese art points out that 'So long as people held the view that the accurate rendering of three dimensional objects as opposed to three dimensional space, was fundamental to good art ... there was no hope that the aims and methods of Chinese landscape painting would be understood' (1989: 108). In the case of the Australian modernist artist, Margaret Preston, Edwards has argued that 'the mnemonic function of Aboriginal art and the sense in both traditional Chinese landscapes and Aboriginal imagery of the presentation of conceptual rather than visual truths, were brought together in vigorous accord in modestly scaled, coherent and simplified organisation' (2005: 176).

## CHAPTER 6 STYLE AND MEANING: ABELAM ART THROUGH YOLNGU EYES

1. Vincent Megaw refers to the significance of this in his important article on the Western Desert movement (Megaw 1982).

2. A version of this material was given as the inaugural Anthony Forge Memorial Lecture at the Australian National University in 1998 and was first published in *Res*. Many people have helped me in developing the argument of this chapter, in particular Karen Westmacott, Frances Morphy and Don Tuzin, who facilitated access to the Forge archives. I would like to dedicate this chapter to the generous presence of Cecilia Ng.

3. See Kroeber (1957) and the influential article on style by Schapiro (1953).

4. I have just completed a multimedia biography of the life and art of Narritjin Maymuru with Pip Deveson and Katie Hayne (Morphy, Deveson and Hayne, 2005).

5. Forge's most detailed statement of his position is his introduction to *Primitive Art and Society* (1973).

6. Diane Losche (2001: 160ff) emphasizes the importance of names associated with design elements in Abelam paintings.

7. The classic work on iconicity in Central Australian sign systems is Munn 1973; see also Morphy 1980.

8. '[O]ur dichotomy abstract versus figurative or representational is misleading at the very least in Abelam terms and I now wish to analyse a set of paintings from one village which includes both types in one corpus. My aim is to show how Abelam artists handle the elements of their flat painting style and manipulate the different bits and their relationships to create association and relationships between disparate valued aspects of their culture' (Forge 1973b: 179).

9. The issue of exegesis is a highly complex one in New Guinea art, since it depends partly on what the analyst's focus is and partly on the degree of verbalization about paintings (see O'Hanlon 1992 for a relevant discussion).

10. While Forge's analysis of Abelam art has been very influential, it has also come under considerable criticism. He has been criticized for neglecting the affective dimension of Abelam art (Roscoe 1995), being insufficiently concerned with what art does (Losche 1997), and giving too much emphasis to the question of meaning (Roscoe 1995; Losche 1997). While such criticisms do draw attention to important dimensions of Abelam art that needed to be further explored, they do not in themselves contradict Forge's own analysis. As O'Hanlon (1995: 832) points out with reference to this critique, it is important 'to recognise the multidimensionality of art' where the semantic, aesthetic, affective and purposive dimensions all apply to the same object or event.

11. Narritjin and Banapana's visit is recorded in Ian Dunlop's film *Narritjin in Canberra*, which includes a sequence of Narritjin co-teaching students in Forge's anthropology of art class.

12. Losche's comment is particularly salient since she was writing about her own and Anthony Forge's separate encounters with the Abelam. Indeed, the section heading in her work is *the hybrid moment in fieldwork: Anthony Forge's question*, and, in a way, this entire chapter is about that question. One missing element is the absence of the Abelam from the discussion, though Anthony had entertained visiting Abelam to a feast in the same room in which we looked at the paintings (Losche 2001: 156). One can only speculate on what difference their presence would have made. The other missing element is Anthony himself. This was the paper we always intended to write together.

13. While I would not suggest any direct historical connection between Yolngu and the cultures of the Sepik River, Yolngu have their own indigenous 'ethnographic' tradition, and their mythology and oral traditions link them closely to the people of eastern Indonesia and New Guinea. The annual visits of the Macassan fleet made people familiar with the indigenous cultures of eastern Indonesia (Macknight 1976; McIntosh 1996). Yolngu beliefs about the dead include an island of the dead, 'Badu' which is a semi-mythical land associated with the Torres Strait Islands and New Guinea (Berndt 1948). Contact with outsiders is reflected in Yolngu ritual and art, which includes detailed representations of their way of life and material culture (see Morphy 1998: 212 ff). Mountford's book contains many references to art that reflects Macassan contact (e.g. Mountford 1956: 292, 409).

14. Forge noted this contrast in his first major article on Abelam art where he wrote: 'The relation of art to myth is a much discussed question. In Arnhem Land, for example, art, myth and ritual appear to be completely interlocked and interdependent; but it seems unlikely that one is justified in taking myth to be primary and the art to be just an expression of it. It seems rather as if they were all three different ways of expressing aspects of the same thing in words, in action and visually, none of them being complete without the other, and none of them being the entire expression on their own.' He contrasted the Arnhem Land case (where his reference point is Mountford's work on the Yolngu (Mountford 1956)), with the Iatmul neighbours of the Abelam 'where there is nothing like this integration' and the Abelam themselves: 'With the Abelam the case is much simpler since there is hardly any mythology at all, and none connected in any way with the most important figures, those of the clan spirits *nggwalndu*' (Forge 1966). Narritjin, who was one of the artists who painted for Mountford on his 1948 American-Australian expedition to Arnhem Land alluded to this contrast when, with no prompting, he said: 'We have a story line with meaning that we did for Mr. Mountford.'

15. See Morphy 1991.

16. According to Forge the Abelam interpretation of this was as string bag.

17. The word *balanda* is used as a polite term for white people. Derived from 'Hollander', it entered the Yolngu language via the Macassan traders from South Sulawesi. In this context, it refers to a race of white sea hunters who preceded the Macassan visitors to Yolngu country and are celebrated in ritual.

18. Occasionally paintings are produced that combine Dhuwa and Yirritja designs. These are usually designs of clans closely related by kinship, in particular mother, *ngändi* and child, *waku*. In such cases the respective moieties' designs occur in separate panels and are never commingled.

19. Interestingly Forge referred explicitly to the outsider's perspective he adopted as something that facilitated interpretation, or perhaps rather enabled the analyst to make explicit what to members of the culture was implicit: 'Further, some of the disentangling of the structures from the readily available facts – art works, ethnoclassification, language, mythology – is easy or even obvious to someone knowledgeable about the culture but not of it and hence not endangered by the analysis' (Forge 1979: 286). However, he recognized that this distanced and objectivist stance was not sufficient in itself. While not denying the validity of the insights it produced he went on to note: 'There are, moreover, homologies of form which one's own socialization may make one blind to; there are chains of puns that seem to lead nowhere; there are all the other untidy bits that indicate inadequate fieldwork and defective comprehension. Yet the patterns are there. They relate to each other and to other patterns in other media from the same culture, and their existence, their interrelatedness, their coherence as meaning, and their coming together in behaviour constitute the proof' (ibid.).

20. Narritjin indeed interpreted one of the paintings in relation to a Yolngu story of a visit to the land of the dead. Narritjin said: 'The old people call this one here the spirit people been in New Guinea and the islands' and Banapana added: 'Aboriginal people they go as spirit people to New Guinea. They think all the coconut tree on the beach come from New Guinea.' Narritjin elaborated: 'Yalangura [a Gälpu clan man] travelled all the way to New Guinea by canoe and when he got there they asked him if he was dead or alive. Alive! Well you got to go back to your country and return when you are dead. And when he returned to the mainland he told the story that live people are not allowed to go to there, you have to die before you can go there.'

21. It is not possible here to offer a detailed discussion of the iconography of this painting. However, the meanings of the set of paintings of which this is a part are discussed in detail in the chapters on Manggalili iconography in Morphy 1991.

## CHAPTER 7 ART THEORY AND ART DISCOURSE ACROSS CULTURES

1. Interestingly a point made long ago by Margaret Preston: 'This art is never an attempt at rigid realism, they represent but never duplicate; this last feature is hardly possible, as all their designs are from memory or imagination' (Preston 1949: 11).

2. The National Gallery had been founded in Canberra about the same time as the Aboriginal Arts Board. The founding document was the Lindsay report prepared for the Menzies' government in 1966 and it was finally established by an act of parliament in 1976, under Gough Whitlam's prime-ministership. The Gallery initially had three main foci, World art, Australian art and Primitive art. It would have seemed that Aboriginal art should be able to find a place in one of the latter two categories. However, as a matter of policy, in order not to overlap with other institutional collections, the Gallery had decided at that time not to build up a major holding of Aboriginal art. Whatever the merits of this decision, there was a danger that it could be interpreted to imply that Aboriginal art was not primitive fine art and that it was not a significant part of the history of Australian art. For a while it appeared that Aboriginal art was almost the only art in the world excluded from the Australian National Gallery.

3. Margaret Preston was the first Australian artist to emphasize the synergies between Aboriginal art and art in the European tradition (though she did so in the context of rejecting the European tradition as the primary heritage for a truly Australian art). She wrote that 'Australia has the good fortune to have a native race who paint and draw as they have always done, and with few exceptions look on their [art as] essential[ly] more than merely covering a rock, bark or ground with forms. They feel dimly something they contact in it that they like ourselves vaguely understand' (Preston 1949: 10–11). While on this occasion somewhat obscurely and inelegantly expressed, we see here Preston's approach to Aboriginal art as more than a model for an Australian modernism, alluding to a sharing of the conception of what art is across cultures.

4. Mariët Westermann makes a related point when she writes that 'the distinction between "primitive" art and pre-modern Western art objects in museum collections is not fundamental: no art objects made before the nineteenth century were made to be put into a public museum of the modern kind. Western and non-Western art objects received their differential status in the course of museum history' (Westermann 2005; xiv).

5. The *locus classicus* of this approach is Goldwater 1967.

6. Westermann (2005: xii) interestingly includes in her definition of art objects 'objects made or found by humans, that have the potential to be put into circulation and demand by their visual aspect, not exclusively but at least in part, an aesthetic response to work efficaciously within their culture'. While the immediate reference in Western art history may be to Duchamp's found objects as an exemplar of objects that are perceived to have aesthetic properties but were not made as art objects, in many respects primitive art objects fit well into the category of found object, their culture in this context being that of the finder not the maker. It is the disregard of the intention of the maker that makes them into found objects.

7. The reference here is to the debate generated by Susan Vogel's exhibiting of a Zande hunting net in her influential ART/Artefact exhibition (Vogel 1988). I do not intend here to give any opinion as to whether the works concerned are artworks in the context of Zande, Dogon or Tikopean cultures. It is also relevant to point out in this context that the works may be appreciated aesthetically in both cultures (the indigenous and the European) without their being art objects in both. A Tikopean headrest maybe an aesthetically pleasing headrest to a Tikopean and primarily appreciated as an artwork by a collector of Pacific art (see Firth 1973).

8. As Myers (1991: 30) writes, 'Aboriginal objects are not simply or necessarily excluded by Western art critical categories; they may in fact contribute to or challenge these discourses for the interpretation of cultural activity in productive ways'.

9. Fred Myers (2002) shows a similar situation in the case of the Pintubi artists where the process of movement of the art from one frame to another is seen to be the product of a dialogic process in which the Pintubi are fully involved, rather than a transfer of authority from one group of producers (the painters) to another (the designators).

10. The distinguished art historian Hans Belting makes this explicit when he writes 'As an art historian, I deal with Western art, where the famous old debate on art and ethnology – that is the debate whether ethnographic art needs an art museum or ethnographic documentation ... does not apply' (Belting 2005: 42).

11. Interestingly, Jonathon Hay argues that something synergistic with Western art history has long been a part of the history and practice of Chinese art: 'The long history of self-fashioning by Chinese artists led to a further particularity of Chinese painting: the importance from the fourteenth century on of art historical self-inscription, that is, the artist's practice of locating self in history using the painting's own history as a frame of reference' (Hay 2005: 116).

12. Westermann (2005: xvii ff.) provides an excellent discussion on the potential relationship between the two disciplines.

13. Van Damme 1997:104 develops a closely related argument when he writes, in relation to the development of cross-cultural concepts for art discourse, '...it may be possible to commence by local concepts that have a semantic overlap with the Western term. By displaying the overlap – or tertium comparationis or "family resemblance" – such concepts may then serve as a bridge to another culture's conceptual system and world view. Further exploration of what might be called the artistic and aesthetic vocabulary within a given cultural context may then lead to the delineation of a relevant field of opinion and reflection in this culture's own terms. Moreover in non-Western cultures there may in fact exist concepts that designate such fields – fields that could then be likened to those that in the Western tradition are signified by the terms "philosophy of art" or "aesthetics"'.

14. My book *Ancestral Connections* provides a detailed ethnography of Yolngu art and the reader will find many of the points touched on here developed further in the chapters of that book (Morphy 1991).

15. The Pintubi perspective well expressed by Myers is entirely consistent with Narritjin's reflections on his art: 'Pintubi representations of their own cultural production are deeply entwined with ideas and practices of personhood, cosmology and the ontological articulation of subjects and objects (Munn 1970, 1973). With images said to come from the Dreaming, the emphasis is not on what the painter has done (his or her creativity) but on what is represented, what value that has itself, and the painter's relationship to it. This ontology exotic and intriguing for many Westerners, is not remote from real life and politics' (Myers 2002: 24).

16. Keen (1994, in Chapter 5) shows how one Yolngu group attempted to maintain control over another by not releasing knowledge which its members possessed of the other group's songs, denying that group access to its ancestral inheritance.

17. On one memorable occasion I was asked by a Yolngu friend if I had seen a design of a particular type at an outstation craft store. It was not certain whether the group concerned retained knowledge of a particular clan design since they generally reproduced designs associated with one segment of their territory only. I feigned ignorance!

18. *Wakinngu* refers to the world in its mundane rather than sacred (*madayin*) state, and in this context means that the paintings are not part of the sacred property of any clan.

19. My discussion here primarily is centred on bark paintings, which together with soft wood carvings were the main forms of art produced until the 1990s. Subsequently Buku-Larrnggay Mulka, the art centre at Yirrkala has established a very successful print workshop. Printmaking is largely but not exclusively practised by women artists. Yolngu printmaking is very diverse and includes images from the sacred art of the clans, but also includes pictorial representations of traditional and contemporary life.

20. In this case the situation is complicated by the fact that the Djet story is primarily associated with a Madarrpa-clan place, not a Manggalili one. The fact that Narritjin invented a painting that is primarily associated with another clan's country is unusual, and identifies the story as one that exists at a very public level. In fact in the iconography of the Djet paintings Narritjin uses elements that are shared across a number of Yirritja-moiety clans.

21. Such ontological positions are of course common to many theories about art and integral to many belief systems. Elizabeth Coleman has pointed out to me the interesting parallels between Yolngu and neo-Platonic conceptions of art in which, for example, musical forms pre-exist their composition. They are, in effect, discovered rather than invented or created.

22. Narritjin Maymuru showed great interest in art other than his own, and provided Anthony Forge and me with a rich perspective on Abelam art when Anthony asked him and his son Banapana to comment on some of his collection of Abelam paintings (see Chapter 6).

23. Over time groups die out and the sacra, including the clan designs, are passed on to the groups that take over the land, and in the process of adjustment new sets of sacra are created and new connections between places are created. However, once the adjustments have been made, the new situation is the one that is said to derive from ancestral precedent. The control over knowledge means that disputes over rights in sacra seldom emerge in public even though they may continue to act powerfully beneath the surface. (For a more detailed discussion see Morphy 1988, 1990).

24. Clearly, clan designs do change over time as they adjust to the demographic exigencies and political process. While in the present Yolngu can control the significance of variations in the form of clan designs by allocating them to particular groups and subgroups in the context of agreement among the participants, the further back in time one goes the harder it becomes to make such determinations. Hence while people can readily identify the moiety of most of the earliest paintings collected by anthropologists, they cannot always identify the painting at the level of clan. Thus with painted objects collected by Lloyd Warner from

Milingimbi in the 1920s, present-day Yolngu, some eighty years later on, are reluctant to make attributions about the ownership of the designs on some objects.

25. The term *buwayak* was first applied to this feature of Yolngu paintings by the artist Wanyubi Marika in discussion with Will Stubbs who runs Buku-Larrnggay Mulka art centre. However, it is also recorded in Donald Thomson's fieldnotes to describe the masking of body paintings produced in restricted contexts by smearing the surface before they are revealed to people in public places.

# CHAPTER 8 PLACING INDIGENOUS ART IN THE GALLERY

1. This chapter is based on a paper given at the 2000 conference of the American Anthropological Association in San Francisco, at a session convened by Russell Sharman on 'The state of the anthropology of art'. I would like to thank the discussant Nelson Graburn for his comments and Margaret Tuckson who put me in touch with Richard McMillan, whose UNSW thesis proved invaluable. Nigel Lendon provided stimulating comments on the paper and corrected some of the errors. Christiane Keller provided some useful references. Frances Morphy helped develop the structure of the argument and improved the clarity of expression.

2. A relevant debate took place in 1986 over Art and Land, an exhibition at the South Australian Museum, in which a set of Aboriginal direction signs from Central Australia were exhibited deliberately as 'art' (see Jones and Sutton 1986; Brook 1986; and Sutton 1987; the debate is summarized in Taylor 1988). Susan Vogel's (1991) account of multi-perspective exhibitions of ethnographic objects considers similar issues in the case of African 'Art'.

3. James Clifford (1988) in a chapter titled 'Histories of the Tribal and the Modern' provides an interesting discussion of these issues, though his eventual collapse of the opposition between museum anthropologists and primitive art aesthetes into an 'anthropological/aesthetic object system' oversimplifies the dynamics of the discourse and diverts attention away from the issues that divided them.

4. This definition is similar to others either proposed by anthropologists (for example Anderson 1990: 238, see Welsch et al. 2006: 28) or implicitly by Boas when he writes: 'The emotions may not be stimulated by the form alone but by the close associations that exist between form and ideas held by the people. When forms convey meaning, because they recall past experiences or because they act as symbols, a new element is added to enjoyment. The form and its meaning combine to elevate the mind above the indifferent emotional state of everyday life (Boas 1927: 12)'. Issues of the definition of art are discussed in more detail in Morphy and Perkins 2006: 1–15.

5. In addition to Graburn's (1976) classic edited volume, two excellent collections of essays have been published by Philips and Steiner 1999 and Marcus and Myers 1995.

6. In some respects my position is in agreement with Zangwill's except that I see institutional theories of art as necessary to provide a partial explanation of the particular history of Western artworlds and the political and ideological bases of their construction. (See Fowler 2003 for a vigorous defence of sociological approaches to the study of art.) I also employ a broader conception of what kind of thing art is. Zangwill is concerned with the barrenness of many sociological theories that fail to get beyond interrogating the institutional contexts of art. He writes that '[in his] view, the central issue in the theory of art is an explanatory one. We need a theory that gives a good explanation of why people create and consume art. In an aesthetic theory of art, the explanation of the fact that people make art and contemplate it is that they want to create things that have aesthetic value and they think they find aesthetic value in things. Crucially, this explanation is not just a causal explanation but also a rational causal explanation. It reveals to us what people see in making and contemplating art. It makes art-making and art contemplation intelligible. By contrast, according to production and consumption skepticism, the real explanation of the fact that people make art and contemplate it is not that they want to create things that have aesthetic value or that they think they find aesthetic value in things, although this is what they think. Instead, art has some other social property that really moves them to make and perceive

it. For example, perhaps art reinforces certain social power relations. These sociological explanations thus involve attributing self-deception or false consciousness' (Zangwill 2002: 208).

7. In 1997, for example, there was controversy over the exclusion of some categories of Aboriginal art from the art fair in Basel. David Throsby (1997: 32) wrote that the chairman of the committee said that letting in recognizably Indigenous artworks from Australia would open up the floodgates to primitive, tribal and folk art from around the world. Interestingly, Tracey Moffatt's work was exhibited with great success at the same fair. The following year an even more heated debate broke out over the exclusion of a number of Arnhem Land artists from the Cologne art fair (see McDonald 1998).

8. Richard McMillan (1997) documents the process of the acquisition of the collection and shows it as the result of a complex process of negotiation between the Gallery staff, in particular Tuckson and the director Hal Missingham, the Board of Trustees and the donor or sponsor Scougall himself. As Nigel Lendon pointed out to me, the Indigenous works were still included under the rubric 'Primitive art' at the AGNSW until the 1980s.

9. It is precisely the particular form of such universals that explains why Bourdieu (1984) is so determined not to engage in aesthetic discourse when considering judgements of distinction, and why Gell (1998) argues so passionately for an aesthetic relativism that eliminates the aesthetic altogether as a cross-cultural category.

10. I use this formulation Maloon/Tuckson in places where it is difficult to know whether the views represented are ones shared by Maloon and Tuckson or are simply Maloon reporting his understanding of Tuckson's position. The confusion may be a sign of just how well Maloon represents Tuckson's arguments.

11. Indeed Richard McMillan's 1997 UNSW thesis 'The Drawings of Tony Tuckson' reveals a heated exchange between Tuckson and Ronald and Catherine Berndt over publication of Tuckson's chapter in the book. Reading further between the lines, one can't help think that the somewhat interventionist editorial style adopted by the Berndt's helped to polarize the debate and make the protagonists' views seem more opposed than in fact they were.

12. See van Damme (2006) for a relevant discussion where he distinguishes between Anthropology A (the study of artistic phenomena in human life) and Anthropology B (the study of the arts of specific cultures).

13. In writing a history of this particular period, one is conscious of dealing with a coded language in which the use of words like 'conceptual' is far removed from their ordinary-language meaning, and position the author in a particular way. Tuckson stresses that non-Western art is conceptual rather than representational, and clarifies his view with a quote from Golding: 'The Negro sculptor tends to depict what he knows about his subject rather than what he sees.' Without agreeing with the presuppositions about Negro art, this perspective should on the surface be compatible with an anthropological investigation. The difference may be that the anthropologist wishes to establish first what the artist knows about the subject of his painting by placing art within a context of cultural knowledge, and establish the relationship between knowing and seeing, whereas a particular modernist world-view sees that knowledge as being communicated directly through the art itself.

14. A point made by Marcia Langton in a symposium held at the Art Gallery of New South Wales to mark the opening of the Papunya Tula Genesis and Genius exhibition, in August 2000 (see Myers 2006).

15. This exhibition provides a well-documented contested arena for most of the issues discussed here. Luke Taylor's (1988) article provides an excellent discussion of the main theoretical issues and concerns, and Sutton (1991) provides an extended summary of the debate from his perspective.

## CHAPTER 9 CONCLUSION

1. In a fascinating analysis of the development of German fine art museums in the nineteenth century, Suzanne Marchand argues that 'The rise to prominence of stylistic analysis and ethnological sciences had a transformative effect on aesthetics and museum design and content' (2000: 197–8). She sees a movement

away from a relatively conservative canon centred on classical and renaissance forms to the development of 'a non-normative discussion of art forms, [a]llowing Heinrich Schäffer, to argue in 1925 that Egyptian art was not inferior to classical art but simply the result of a different sort of "seeing"' (ibid.: 198).

2. It is remarkable how much Mollison's awakening echoed the phrases of Margaret Preston some half-century before: 'The art of the Aborigine has been for too long neglected. The attention of the Australian people must be drawn to the fact that it is great art' (Preston 1941a). In the same year she wrote that 'Australia is the only country ... in which rock painting still flourishes as the normal expression of the Aborigines... [The drawing and rock carvings] are realism in a wider sense than is recognized by European art ... [their] inherent vision opens up a new world for the Australian artist' (Preston 1941b, cited in Edwards 2005: 193).

3. See Luke Taylor 1990 for an explication of the rainbow serpent metaphor. The rainbow serpent has the capacity to absorb the bodies of other animals, incorporating their difference into its own body and identity and creating unity in a world of diversity. Interestingly, it does it in part by imposing a particular aesthetic stamp on the world, the shimmering brilliance of the light associated with rainbows and sparkling water.

4. The heated debates over Imants Tiller's use of Michael Nelson Jagamara's work in his *The Nine Shots*, 1985, was generated in part by this perceived contradiction. At the time, many non-Indigenous artists still had problems in accepting Indigenous art as contemporary art, while the 'same' images incorporated in the work of a post-modern artist were unproblematically components of a fine artwork (see Morphy 2006b).

5. Interestingly, Fred Myers uses precisely the same phrase with reference to Pintubi paintings, reflecting a shared position between Pintubi and Yolngu artists (Myers 2002: 22).

6. I would agree with the spirit of Mariett Westermann's cautious definition of an art object as 'objects made or found by humans, that have the potential to be put into circulation and demand by their visual aspect, not exclusively but at least in part, an aesthetic response to work efficaciously within their culture. Such a response induced by sensuous perception, would at least for those experiencing it, make the art object transcend its immediate utilitarian function' (Westermann 2005: xii), though I would perhaps add that this transcendent nature of objects can be indeed part of their utilitarian function.

# BIBLIOGRAPHY

ALLEN, L. A. (1975), *Time Before Morning: Art and Myth of the Australian Aborigines*, New York: Crowell.

ANDERSON, R. L. (1990), *Calliope's Sisters: A Comparative Study of Philosophies of Art*, Englewood Cliffs, NJ: Prentice Hall.

ANDERSON, R. L. (1992), 'Do Other Cultures have "Art"?', *American Anthropologist, New Series*, 94: 926–29.

ATTWOOD, B. (2003), *Rights for Aborigines*, Crows Nest, NSW: Allen & Unwin.

*AUSTRALIAN Perspecta* (1981), Sydney: Art Gallery of New South Wales.

BANKS, M. (1997), 'Representing the Bodies of the Jains', in M. Banks and H. Morphy (eds), *Rethinking Visual Anthropology*, London and New Haven: Yale University Press.

BECKER, H. (1982), *Art Worlds*, Berkeley: University of California Press.

BELTING, H. (2005), 'Towards an Anthropology of the Image', in M. Westermann (ed.), *Anthropologies of Art*, Williamstown, MA: Sterling and Francine Clark Art Institute.

BENJAMIN, R. (1990), 'Aboriginal Art: Exploitation or Empowerment?', *Art in America*, 78: 73–81.

BERLO, Janet C. B. (2005), 'Anthropologies and Histories of Art: the View from the Terrain of Native North American Art History', in M. Westermann (ed.) *Anthropologies of Art*, Williamstown, MA: Sterling and Francine Clark Art Institute.

BERNDT, R. M. (1948), 'Badu, Islands of the Spirits', *Oceania*, 19(2): 93–103.

BERNDT, R. M. (1952), *Djanggawul: an Aboriginal Religious Cult of North-Eastern Arnhem Land*, London: Routledge & Kegan Paul.

BERNDT, R. M. (1962), *An Adjustment Movement in Arnhem Land*, Paris: Mouton.

BERNDT, R. M. (1964a), 'Preface', in R. M. Berndt (ed.), *Australian Aboriginal Art*, Sydney: Ure Smith.

BERNDT, R. M. (1964b), 'Epilogue', in R. M. Berndt (ed.), *Australian Aboriginal Art*, Sydney: Ure Smith, pp. 69–74.

BERNDT, R. M. (1976), *Love Songs of Arnhem Land*, Melbourne: Thomas Nelson.

BERNDT, R. M., Berndt, Catherine H. and Stanton, J. E. (1998), *Aboriginal Australian Art: a Visual Perspective*. French's Forest: New Holland.

BLACK, R. (1964), *Old and New Aboriginal Art*, Sydney: Angus and Robertson.

BLIER, S. P. (1987), *The Anatomy of Architecture*, Cambridge: Cambridge University Press.

BOAS, F. (1927), *Primitive Art*, Oslo: Institutet for Sammenlingnende Kulturforskning (Reprinted New York: Dover, 1955).

BOONE, S. A. (1986), *The Radiance from the Waters*, New Haven: Yale University Publications in the History of Art.

Bourdieu, P. (1984), *Distinction: A Social Critique of the Judgement of Taste*, London: Routledge & Kegan Paul.

Brettell, R. (1999), *Modern Art, 1851–1929: Capitalism and Representation*, Oxford: Oxford University Press.

Brook, D. (1986), 'Without Wanting to Tread on Anyone's Toas', Artlink, 6: 4–5.

Bryson, N. (1986), *Vision and Painting: The Logic of the Gaze*, New Haven: Yale University Press.

Buku-Larrnggay Mulka (1999), *Saltwater: Yirrkala Bark Paintings of Sea Country*, Yirrkala: Buku-Larrnggay Mulka Centre in association with Jennifer Isaac publishing.

Clifford, J. (1988), *The Predicament of Culture*, Cambridge, MA: Harvard University Press.

Clifford, J. (1991), 'Four Northwest Coast Museums', in I. Karp and S. D. Levine (eds), *Exhibiting Cultures: the Poetics and Politics of Museum Display*, Washington, D.C.: Smithsonian Institution Press.

Cole, D. (1995), *Captured Heritage: The Scramble for Northwest Coast Artifacts*, Vancouver: University of British Columbia Press.

Coleman, E. (2005a), *Aboriginal Art, Identity and Appropriation*, Aldershot: Ashgate.

Coleman, E. (2005b), 'Aesthetics as a Cross-Cultural Concept', in E. Benitez (ed.) Before Pangaea: New Essays in Transcultural Aesthetics, *Literature and Aesthetics*, 15(1): 57–78.

Coleman, E. and Coombe, R. J. with MacArailt, F. (in press), 'Broken Records: Subjecting "Music" to Cultural Rights', in Conrad Brunk and James O. Young (eds), *The Ethics of Cultural Appropriation*, Oxford: Blackwell.

Coote, Jeremy and Anthony Shelton (eds) (1992), *Anthropology, Art and Aesthetics*, Oxford Studies in the Anthropology of Cultural Forms, Oxford: Clarendon.

Cox, R. A. (2003), *The Zen Arts: An Anthropological Study of the Culture of Aesthetic Form in Japan*, London: Routledge Curzon.

Dalton, G. (1969), 'Theoretical Issues in Economic Anthropology', *Current Anthropology*, 10: 63–102.

Danto, A. (1964), 'The Artworld', *Journal of Philosophy*, 61: 571–84.

Dickie, G. (1974), *Art and the Aesthetic*. Ithaca: Cornell University Press.

Dunlop, I. (director) (1981a), *At the Canoe Camp*, Sydney: Film Australia.

Dunlop, I. (director) (1981b), *Narritjin in Canberra*, Sydney: Film Australia.

Dunlop, I. (director) (1990), *Djangguwan at Gurka'wuy*, Sydney: Film Australia.

Eagle, M. (2006), 'A History of Australian Art 1830–1930', *Told Through the Lives of the Object*, Unpublished PhD thesis, Australian National University, Canberra.

Edwards, D. (2005), *Margaret Preston*, Sydney: Art Gallery of New South Wales.

Egan, T. (1996), *Justice All Their Own: The Caledon Bay and Woodah Island Killings 1932–1933*, Melbourne University Press.

Elkin, A. P., Berndt, R. M. and Berndt, C. H. (1950), *Art in Arnhem Land*, Chicago: University of Chicago Press.

Elkins, J. (1999), *The Domain of Images*, Ithaca: Cornell University Press.

Errington, S. (1998), *The Death of Authentic Primitive Art and other Signs of Progress*, Berkeley: University of California Press.

Firth, R. (1973), 'Tikopean Art and Society', in A. Forge (ed.), *Primitive Art and Society* , Oxford: Oxford University Press.

FIRTH, R. (1992), 'Art and Anthropology', in J. Coote and A. Shelton (eds), *Anthropology Art and Aesthetics*, Oxford: Clarendon.

FLINDERS, M. (1814), *A Voyage to Terra Australis*, London: W. Bulmer.

FORGE, A. (1966), 'Art and Environment in the Sepik', *Proceedings of the Royal Anthropological Institute for 1965*, London.

FORGE, A. (1970), 'Learning to See in New Guinea', in P. Mayer (ed.), *Socialisation: the Approach from Social Anthropology*, A.S.A. Monographs 8, London: Tavistock.

FORGE, A. (1973a), 'Introduction', in A. Forge (ed.), *Primitive Art and Society*, London: Wenner-Gren Foundation and Oxford University Press.

FORGE, A. (1973b), 'Style and Meaning in Sepik Art', in A. Forge (ed.), *Primitive Art and Society*, London: Wenner-Gren Foundation and Oxford University Press.

FORGE, A. (1979), 'The Problem of Meaning in Art', in S. M. Mead (ed.), *Exploring the Visual Art of Oceania*, Honolulu: University Press of Hawaii.

FOWLER, B. (2003), 'A Note on Nick Zangwill's "Against the Sociology of Art"', *Philosophy of Social Sciences*, 33(3): 363–74.

FRENCH, A. (2002), *The Art of Albert Namatjira: Centenary Exhibition 1902–2002*, Canberra: National Gallery of Australia.

FRY, T. and Willis, A-M. (1989), 'Aboriginal Art: Symptom or Success?', *Art in America*, July: 109–17, 159–60.

GEERTZ, C. (1971), 'Religion as a Cultural System', in M. Banton (ed.), *Anthropological Approaches to the Study of Religion*, London: Tavistock.

GELL, A. (1998), *Art and Agency*, Oxford: Clarendon.

GOLDWATER, R. (1967), *Primitivism in Modern Art*, New York: Random House.

GOMBRICH, E. (1958), *Art and Illusion: A Study in the Psychology of Pictorial Presentation*, London: Phaidon.

GOODALE, J. and Goss, J. D. (1971), 'The Cultural Context of Creativity among the Tiwi', in C. M. Otten (ed.), *Anthropology and Art: Readings in Cross-Cultural Aesthetics*, New York: Natural History Press.

GOODMAN, N. (1976), *Languages of Art: An Approach to a Theory of Symbols*, Indianapolis: Hackett.

GOUGH, K. (1959), 'The Nayars and the Definition of Marriage', *Journal of the Royal Anthropological Institute*, 89: 23–34.

GRABURN, N. (1976), *Ethnic and Tourist Arts: Cultural Expressions from the Fourth World*, Berkeley: University of California Press.

GRABURN, N. (1999), 'Epilogue: Ethnic and Tourist Arts Revisited', in R. Philips and C. Steiner (eds), *Unpacking Culture: Art and Commodity in Colonial and Postcolonial Worlds*, Berkeley: University of California Press.

GRAEBER, D. (2002), *Toward an Anthropological Theory of Value: The False Coin of Our Own Dreams*, New York: Palgrave.

HAMBY, L. (2001), 'Containers of Power', unpublished PhD thesis, Australian National University, Canberra.

HAMBY, L. (2007), 'Thomson Time and *Ten Canoes*', *Studies in Australasian Cinema*, Issue 2.

HANDSMAN, R. (1987), 'Stop Making Sense: Towards an Anti-Catalogue of Woodsplint Basketry', in A. McMullen and R. Handsman (eds), *Key into the Language of Woodsplint*, Washington: American Indian Archaeological Institute.

HANDSMAN, R. and McMullen, A. (1987), 'An Introduction to Woodsplint Basketry and its Interpretation', in A. McMullen and R. Handsman (eds), *Key into the Language of Woodsplint*, Washington: American Indian Archaeological Institute.

HARDY, J., Megaw, J. V. S. and Megaw, M. R. (1992), *The Heritage of Namatjira: the Water Colourists of Central Australia*, Melbourne: William Heinemann.

HART, D. (2006), *Imants Tillers: One World Many Visions*, Canberra: National Gallery of Australia.

HASKOVEC, I. and Sullivan, H. (1989), 'Najombolmi: Reflections and Rejections of an Aboriginal Artist', in H. Morphy (ed.), *Animals into Art*, London: Allen & Unwin.

HAWLEY, J. (1988), *Encounters with Australian Artists*, Brisbane: University of Queensland Press.

HAY, J. (2005), 'The Functions of Chinese paintings: Towards a Unified Theory', in M. Westermann (ed.) *Anthropologies of Art*, Williamstown, MA: Sterling and Francine Clark Art Institute.

HIATT, L. R. (1966), 'The Lost Horde', *Oceania*, 37: 81–92.

HOLMES, S. (1992), *Yirawala: Painter of the Dreaming*, Sydney: Hodder & Stoughton.

HUTCHERSON, G. (1995), *Djalkiri Wanga, the Land Is My Foundation: 50 Years of Aboriginal Art from Yirrkala, Northeast Arnhem Land*, Perth: Berndt Museum of Anthropology, University of Western Australia.

INGOLD, T. (ed.) (1996), '1993 Debate: Aesthetics is a Cross-Cultural Category', in *Key Debates in Anthropology*, London: Routledge.

IRWIN, David. (ed.) (1972), *Winckelmann: Writings on Art*, London: Phaidon.

JANAWAY, C. (1995), 'Art', in T. Honderich (ed.), *The Oxford Companion to Philosophy*, Oxford: Oxford University Press.

JENKINS, S. (2003), 'It's a Power: an Interpretation of *The Aboriginal Memorial* in its Ethnographic, Museological, Art Historical and Political Contexts', unpublished thesis, National Institute for the Arts, Australian National University, Canberra.

JENKINS, S. (2005), *No Ordinary Place: The Art of David Malangi*, Canberra: National Gallery of Australia.

JOACHIMIDES, A. (2000), 'The Museum's Discourse on Art: The Formation of Curatorial Art History in Turn-of-the-century Berlin', in S. A. Crane (ed.), *Museums and Memory*, Stanford: Stanford University Press.

JONES, P. (1988), 'Perceptions of Aboriginal Art: A History', in P. Sutton (ed.), *Dreamings*, Ringwood: Penguin.

JONES, P. and Sutton, P. (1986), *Art and Land: Aboriginal Sculptures from the Lake Eyre Region*, Adelaide: South Australian Museum in association with Wakefield Press.

KAEPPLER, A. (1978), *Artificial Curiosities: Being and Exposition of Native Manufactures on the Three Pacific Voyages of Captain Cook*, Honolulu: Bishop Museum Press.

KEEN, I. (1994), *Knowledge and Secrecy in an Aboriginal Religion*, Oxford: Clarendon Press.

KELLER, C. and Coleman, E. (2006), What is Authentic Aboriginal Art Now: the Creation of Tradition', *International Yearbook of Aesthetics*, 10: 55–80.

KLEINERT, S. (1994), '*Jacky Jacky was a Smart Young Fella*': a Study of Art and Aboriginality in South-East Australia 1900–1980, unpublished PhD Thesis, Australian National University, Canberra.

KROEBER, A. L. (1957), *Style and Civilizations*, Ithaca: Cornell University Press.

KUBLER, G. (1962), *The Shape of Time: Remarks on the History of Things*, New Haven: Yale University Press.

KUBLER, G. (1985), 'On the Colonial Extinction of the Motifs of Pre-Columbian Art', in T. Reese (ed.), *Studies in Ancient American and European Art: The Collected Essays of George Kubler*, New Haven: Yale University Press.

KUBLER, G. (1991), *Esthetic Recognition of Ancient Amerindian Art*, New Haven: Yale University Press.

KUPKA, K. (1965), *The Dawn of Art: Painting and Sculpture of Australian Aborigines*, New York: Viking.

LAMBEK, M. (2001), *A Reader in the Anthropology of Religion*, Oxford: Blackwell.

LATTAS, A. (1991), 'Nationalism, Aesthetic Redemption, and Aboriginality', *Australian Journal of Anthropology*, 2: 307–24.

LENDON, N. (1995), 'Visual Evidence: Space Place, and Innovation in Bark Paintings of Central Arnhem Land', *Colonising the Country*, special issue of *Australian Journal of Art*, 12: 55–74.

LOSCHE, D. (1997), 'What do Abelam Images Want from us?: Plato's cave and Kwatbil's Belly', *The Australian Journal of Anthropology*, 8: 35–49.

LOSCHE, D. (2001), 'Anthony's Feast: the Gift in Abelam Aesthetics', *Australian Journal of Anthropology*, 12: 155–65.

LOWISH, S. (2005), 'Aboriginal Art: Blindness and Insight in the Work of Bernard Smith', *Thesis Eleven*, 82: 62–72.

LÜTHI, B. (1993), 'The Marginalisation of (Contemporary) Non-European/Non-American Art (as Reflected in the Way we View it)', in B. Lüthi (ed.), *Aratjara: the Art of the First Australians*, Dusseldorf: Kunstammlung, Norrhein-Westfalen.

MACKNIGHT, C. C. (1976), *The Voyage to Marege: Macassan Trepangers in Northern Australia*, Melbourne: University of Melbourne Press.

MADDOCK, K. (1972), *The Australian Aborigines: A Portrait of their Society*, London: Penguin.

MAGOWAN, F. (2000), 'Dancing with a Difference: Reconfiguring the Poetics of Aboriginal as National Spectacle', *Australian Journal of Anthropology*, 11: 308–21.

MALOON, T. (2000), *Painting Forever: Tony Tuckson*, Canberra: National Gallery of Australia.

MAQUET, J. (1986), *The Aesthetic Experience: An Anthropologist Looks at the Visual Arts*, New Haven: Yale University Press.

MARCHAND, S. (2000), 'The Quarrel of the Ancients and the Moderns in the German Museums', in S. A. Crane (ed.), *Museums and Memory*, Stanford: Stanford University Press.

MARCUS, G. and Myers, F. R. (eds) (1995), *The Traffic in Culture: Refiguring Art and Anthropology*, Berkley: University of California Press.

MARIKA-MUNUNGGIRITJ, R. (1999), 'The 1998 Wentworth Lecture', *Australian Aboriginal Studies*, 1: 3–9.

MARTIN, J-H. (1992), 'A Delayed Communication', in B. Lüthi (ed.), *Aratjara: the Art of the First Australians*, Düsseldorf: Kunstammlung Norrhein-Westfale.

MASON, O. T. (1988 [1904]), *American Indian Basketry*, New York: Dover reprint.

McCARTHY, F. (1938), *Australian Aboriginal Decorative Art*, Sydney: The Australian Museum.

McDONALD, J. (1998), 'Black Ban: all they Want is a Fair go', *Sydney Morning Herald*, 29 September.

McINTOSH, I. S. (1996) 'Can we be Equal in your Eyes?: A Perspective on Reconciliation from Yolngu Myth and History', unpublished PhD thesis, Northern Territory University, Darwin.

McIntosh, I. S. (2004), 'Personal Names and the Negotiation of Change: Reconsidering Arnhem Land's Adjustment Movement', *Anthropological Forum*, 14: 141–62.

McLean, I. (1998), *White Aborigines: Identity Politics in Australian Art*, Cambridge: Cambridge University Press.

McMillan, R. (1997), *Tony Tuckson's Drawings*, unpublished MA thesis, COFA, University of New South Wales, Sydney.

McNaughton, P. (1988), *The Mande Blacksmiths: Knowledge, Power and Art in West Africa*, Bloomington: University of Indiana Press.

Megaw, J. V. S. (1982), 'Western Desert Acrylic Painting: Art or Artefact?', *Art History*, 5: 205–18.

Merlan, F. (2001), 'Aboriginal Cultural Production into Art: The Complexity of Redress', in C. Pinney and N. Thomas (eds), *Beyond Aesthetics: Art and the Technologies of Enchantment*, Oxford: Berg.

Morphy, F. (forthcoming, 2007), 'Performing Law: The Yolngu of Blue Mud Bay Meet the Native Title Process', in B. Smith and F. Morphy (eds), *The Effects of Native Title*, Canberra: Australian National University E Press.

Morphy, H. (1977), 'Schematisation, Meaning and Communication in Toas', in P. J. Ucko (ed.), *Form in Indigenous Art: Schematisation in the Art of Aboriginal Australia and Prehistoric Europe*, Canberra: Australian Institute of Aboriginal Studies.

Morphy, H. (1980), 'What Circles Look Like', *Canberra Anthropology*, 3: 17–36.

Morphy, H. (1983), 'Now You Understand: an Analysis of the Way Yolngu have used Sacred Knowledge to Maintain their Autonomy', in N. Peterson and M. Langton (eds), *Aborigines, Land and Landrights*, Canberra: Australian Institute of Aboriginal Studies.

Morphy, H. (1984), *Journey to the Crocodile's Nest*, Canberra: Australian Institute of Aboriginal Studies.

Morphy, H. (1987), 'The Creation of Audiences for Aboriginal art', in A. Curthoys, A. W. Martin and T. Rowse (eds), *Australians from 1939*, Broadway: Fairfax, Syme and Weldon.

Morphy, H. (1988), 'Maintaining Cosmic Unity: Ideology and the Reproduction of Yolngu Clans', in T. Ingold, J. Woodburn and D. Riches (eds), *Hunters and Gatherers: Property, Power and Ideology*, Berg: Oxford.

Morphy, H. (1989), 'On Representing Ancestral Beings', in H. Morphy (ed.), *Animals into Art*, London: Unwin Hyman.

Morphy, H. (1990), 'Myth Totemism and the Creation of Clans', *Oceania*, 60: 312–29.

Morphy, H. (1991), *Ancestral Connections: Art and an Aboriginal System of Knowledge*, Chicago: University of Chicago Press.

Morphy, H. (1992), 'From Dull to Brilliant: The Aesthetics of Spiritual Power among the Yolngu', in J. Coote and A. Shelton (eds), *Anthropology, Art and Aesthetics*, Oxford: Clarendon.

Morphy, H. (1994a), 'The Interpretation of Ritual: Reflections from Film on Anthropological Method', *Man*, 29: 117–46.

Morphy, H. (1994b), 'The Anthropology of Art', in Tim Ingold (ed.), *Companion Encyclopaedia to Anthropology*, London: Routledge.

Morphy, H. (1995), 'Landscape and the Reproduction of the Ancestral Past', in E. Hirsch and M. O'Hanlon (eds), *The Anthropology of Landscape: Perspectives of Place and Space*, Oxford: Clarendon.

Morphy, H. (1996), 'Empiricism to Metaphysics: In Defence of the Concept of the Dreamtime', in T. Bonyhady and T. Griffiths (eds), *Prehistory to Politics: John Mulvaney, the Humanities and the Public Intellectual*, Melbourne: Melbourne University Press.

Morphy, H. (1998), *Aboriginal Art*, London: Phaidon.

Morphy, H. (2004), 'An Anthropological Report on the Yolngu people of Blue Mud Bay, in relation to their Claim to Native title in the Land and Sea', Darwin: Northern Land Council.

Morphy, H. (2005a), 'Mutual Conversion: the Methodist Church and the Yolngu, with Particular Reference to Yirrkala', *Humanities Research*, 12(1): 41–53.

Morphy, H. (2005b), 'Style and Meaning: Abelam Art through Yolngu Eyes', *Res*, 47: 209–30.

Morphy, H. (2005c) 'Seeing Indigenous Australian Art', in M. Westerman (ed.), *Anthropologies of Art*, Williamstown, MA: Sterling and Francine Clark Art Institute.

Morphy, H. (2006a), 'Sites of Persuasion: Yingapungapu at the National Museum of Australia', in Ivan Karp, Corinne A. Kratz, Lynn Szwaja, and Tomas Ybarra-Frausto (eds), *Museum Frictions: Public Cultures/Global Transformations*, Durham, NC: Duke University Press.

Morphy, H. (2006b) 'Impossible to Ignore: Imants Tillers Response to Aboriginal Art', in Deborah Hart (ed.), *Imants Tillers: One World Many Visions*, Canberra: National Gallery of Australia.

Morphy, H. and Morphy, F. (2006), 'Tasting the Waters: Discriminating Identities in the Waters of Blue Mud Bay', *Journal of Material Culture*, 11: 67–85.

Morphy, H. and Perkins, M. (2006), *The Anthropology of Art: a Reader*, Oxford: Blackwell.

Morphy, H. and Smith Boles, M. (1999), *Art from the Land: Dialogues with the Kluge-Ruhe Collection of Australian Aboriginal Art*, Charlottesville: University of Virginia Press.

Morphy, H., Deveson, P. and Hayne, K. (2005), *The Art of Narritjin Maymuru*, CD ROM, Canberra: Australian National University E Press.

Mountford, C. P. (1956), *Records of the American-Australian Scientific Expedition to Arnhem Land*, Pt 1, *Art, Myth, and Symbolism*, Melbourne: Melbourne University Press.

Munn, N. (1970), 'The Transformation of Subjects into Objects in Walbiri and Pitjantjantjara Myth', in Ronald Berndt (ed.), *Australian Aboriginal Anthropology*, Nedlands: University of Western Australia Press.

Munn, N. (1973), *Walbiri Iconography*, Ithaca: Cornell University Press.

Munn, N. (1986), *The Fame of Gawa*, Cambridge: Cambridge University Press.

Myers, F. R. (1991), 'Representing Culture: the Production of Discourse(s) for Aboriginal Acrylic Paintings', *Cultural Anthropology*, 6: 26–62.

Myers, F. R. (2002), *Painting Culture: The Making of Aboriginal High Art*, Durham, NC: Duke University Press.

Myers, F. R. (2006), 'The Unsettled Business of Tradition, Indigenous Being, and Acrylic Painting', in E. Venbrux, P. S. Rosi and R. L. Welsch (eds), *Exploring World Art*, Long Grove, IL: Waveland Press.

Needham, R. (1975), 'Polythetic Classification: Convergence and Consequences', *Man*, 10: 349–69.

O'Hanlon, M. (1992), 'Unstable Images and Second Skins: Artefacts, Exegesis and Assessments in the New Guinea Highlands', *Man*, 27: 587–608.

O'Hanlon, M. (1995), 'Communication and Affect in New Guinea Art', *Journal of the Royal Anthropological Institute*, 1: 832–3.

ONIANS, J. (1996), 'World Art Studies and the Need for a New Natural History of Art', *Art Bulletin*, 78: 206–9.

PHILIPS, R. (1998), *Trading Identities: the Souvenir in Native American Art from the Northeast, 1700–1900*, Seattle: University of Washington Press.

PHILIPS, R. and Steiner, C. B. (1999), *Unpacking Culture: Art and Commodity in Colonial and Postcolonial Worlds*, Berkeley: University of California Press.

POSPISIL, L. (1971), *The Anthropology of Law: a Comparative Theory*, New York: Harper and Row.

PRESTON, M. (1930a), 'The Application of Aboriginal Design', *Art and Australia*, 31: 44–58.

PRESTON, M. (1930b), 'Away with Poker Work Kookaburras and Gumleaves', *Sunday Pictorial*, Sydney, 6 April, p. 22

PRESTON, M. (1941a), 'Aboriginal Art', *Art in Australia*, 4th series, no. 2.

PRESTON, M. (1941b), 'New Developments in Australian Art', *Australian National Journal*, 1 May.

PRESTON, M. (1949), *Margaret Preston's Monotypes*, Sydney: Ure Smith.

PRICE, S. (1989), *Primitive Art in Civilised Places*, Chicago: University of Chicago Press.

PRICE, R. and Price, S. (1999), *Maroon Arts: Cultural Vitality in the African Diaspora*, Boston: Beacon.

RIGSBY, B. and Peterson, N. (eds) (2005), *Donald Thomson : the Man and Scholar*, Canberra : Academy of the Social Sciences in Australia, with support from Museum Victoria.

ROSCOE, P. B. (1995), 'Of Power and Menace: Sepik Art as an Affecting Presence', *Journal of the Royal Anthropological Institute*, 1: 1–22.

RUBIN, W. (1985), *Primitivism in Modern Art*, New York: Museum of Modern Art.

SAYERS, A. (2001), *Australian Art*, Oxford: Oxford University Press.

SCHAPIRO, M. (1953), 'Style', in A. Kroeber (ed.), *Anthropology Today*, Chicago: University of Chicago Press.

SEIP, L. P. (1999), 'Transformations of Meaning: The Life History of a Nuxalk Mask', *World Archaeology*, 31: 272–87.

SMITH, B. (1945), *Place, Taste and Tradition: A Study of Australian Art since 1788*, Sydney: Ure Smith.

SMITH, B. (1960), *European Vision and the South Pacific*, Oxford: Clarendon.

SOKAL, R. R. and Sneath, P. H. A. (1963), *Principles of Numerical Taxonomy*, San Francisco and London: W. H. Freeman.

SPENCER, W. B. (1928), *The Native Tribes of Northern Territory of Australia*, London: Macmillan.

STANNER, W. E. H. (1979), 'After the Dreaming', in W. E. H. Stanner (ed.), *White Man Got No Dreaming: Essays 1938–1973*, Canberra: Australian University Press.

STEADMAN, P. (2001), *Vermeer's Camera: Uncovering the Truth Behind the Masterpieces*, Oxford: Oxford University Press.

STEINER, C. B. (1994), *African Art in Transit*, Cambridge; Cambridge University Press.

STEINER, C. B. (1995), 'The Art of Trade: on the Creation of Authenticity in the African Art Market', in G. E. Marcus and F. R. Myers (eds), *The Traffic in Culture: Refiguring Art and Anthropology*, Berkeley: University of California Press, pp. 151–61.

STEPHEN, A. (2006), 'Early Inroads: MoMA and Australia', *Art and Australia*, 43: 582–5.

STIRLING, Sir E. and Waite, E. R. (1919), 'Description of Toas or Aboriginal Direction Signs', *Records of the South Australian Museum*, 1: 105–55.

Strang, V. (2006), 'A Happy Coincidence: Symbiosis and Synthesis in Anthropological and Indigenous Knowledges', *Current Anthropology*, 47: 981–1008.

Strathern, M. (1988), *The Gender of the Gift: Problems with Women and Problems with Society in Melanesia*, Berkeley: University of California Press.

Strathern, M. (2006), Intellectual Property and Rights: An Anthropological Perspective', in C. Tilley, W. Keane, S. Küchler, M. Rowlands and P. Speyer (eds), *Handbook of Material Culture*, London: Sage.

Sullivan, M. (1989), *The Meeting of Eastern and Western Art*, Berkeley: University of California Press.

Sutton, P. (1987), 'The Really Interesting Suggestion… Yet Another Reply to Donald Brook on Toas', *Adelaide Review* 35: 5.

Sutton, P. (1991), 'Unintended Consequences', *Interior*, 1: 24–9.

Taçon, P. S. C., Wilson, M. and Chippindale, C. (1996), 'Birth of the Rainbow Serpent in Arnhem Land Rock Art and Oral History', *Archaeology in Oceania*, 31: 103–24.

Taylor, L. (1988), 'The Aesthetics of Toas: a Cross-Cultural Conundrum', *Canberra Anthropology*, 11(1): 86–99.

Taylor, L. (1990), 'The Rainbow Serpent as Visual Metaphor in Western Arnhem Land', *Oceania*, 60: 329–44.

Taylor, L. (1996), *Seeing the Inside: Bark Painting in Western Arnhem Land*, Oxford: Clarendon.

Taylor, L. (2005), 'John Mawurndjul – "I've got a different idea"', in C. Kaufmann (ed.), *'rarrk' – John Mawurndjul: Journey Through Time*, Basel: Schwabe Verlag.

Thomas, N. (1991), *Entangled Objects: Exchange, Material Culture, and Colonialism in the Pacific*, Cambridge, MA: Harvard University Press.

Thomas, N. (1995), *Oceanic Art*, London: Thames & Hudson.

Thomas, N. (1999), *Possessions: Indigenous Art/ Colonial Culture*, London: Thames & Hudson.

Thomson, D. F. (1939a), 'Notes on the Smoking-Pipes of North Queensland and the Northern Territory of Australia', *Journal of the Royal Anthropological Institute*, 39: 76–87.

Thomson, D. F. (1939b), 'Two Painted Skulls from Arnhem land, with Notes on the Totemic Significance of the Designs', *Man*, 39: 1–3.

Thomson, D. F. (1949), *Economic Structure and the Ceremonial Exchange Cycle in Arnhem Land*, Melbourne: Macmillan.

Thomson, D. F. (2005), *Donald Thomson in Arnhem Land*, compiled and introduced by Nicolas Peterson, Melbourne: Melbourne University Press.

Throsby, D. (1997), 'But is it Art?', *Art Monthly Australia*, November: 105.

Tuckson, A. (1964), 'Aboriginal Art and the Western World', in R. M. Berndt (ed.), *Australian Aboriginal Art*, Sydney: Ure Smith.

Van Damme, W. (1997), Do Non-Western Cultures have Words for Art? An Epistemological Prolegomenon to the Comparative Studies of Philosophies of Art', in E. Benitez (ed.), *Proceedings of the Pacific Rim Conference in Transcultural Aesthetics*, Sydney: Sydney University.

Van Damme, W. (2006), 'Anthropologies of Art: Three Approaches', in E. Venbrux, P. S. Rosi and R. L. Welsch (eds), *Exploring World Art*, Long Grove, IL: Waveland Press.

Vanni, I. (1999), 'Objects and Histories: Representations of Aboriginality in Exhibitions of Aboriginal Objects 1855–1957', unpublished PhD thesis, University of New South Wales, Sydney.

VENBRUX, E. (2006), 'The Postcolonial Virtue of Aboriginal Art from Bathurst and Melville Islands', in E. Venbrux, P. S. Rosi and R. L. Welsch (eds), *Exploring World Art*, Long Grove, IL: Waveland Press.

VENBRUX, E., Rosi, P. S. and Welsch, R. L. (eds) (2006), *Exploring World Art*, Long Grove, IL: Waveland Press.

VOGEL, S. (1988), 'Introduction', in Susan Vogel (ed.), *ART/artefact: African Art in Anthropology Collections*, New York: Centre for African Art and Prestel Verlag.

VOGEL, S. (1991), 'Always True to you in our Fashion', in I. Karp and S. D. Levine (eds), *Exhibiting Cultures: the Poetics and Politics of Museum Display*, Washington, D.C.: Smithsonian Institution Press.

VOLKENANDT, C. (2005), 'Perceptible Boundaries: Aesthetic Experience and Cross-Cultural Understanding with a View to Johnny Mawurndjul', in C. Kaufmann (ed.) *'rarrk' – John Mawurndjul: Journey Through Time*, Basel: Schwabe Verlag.

VON STURMER, J. (1989), 'Aborigines, Representation, Necrophilia', *Art and Text*, 32: 127–39.

WARNER, L. W. (1958), *A Black Civilization*, Harper and Row, Chicago.

WELLS, A. (1971), *This is their Dreaming*, St Lucia: University of Queensland Press.

WELLS, E. (1982), *Reward and Punishment in Arnhem Land, 1962–1963*, Canberra: Australian Institute of Aboriginal Studies Press.

WELSCH, R. L., Venbrux, E. and Rosi, P. S. (2006), 'Exploring World Art: an Introduction', in E. Venbrux, P. S. Rosi and R. L. Welsch (eds), *Exploring World Art*, Long Grove, IL: Waveland Press.

WESTERMANN, M. (2005), 'Introduction', in M. Westermann (ed.), *Anthropologies of Art*, Williamstown, MA: Sterling and Francine Clark Art Institute.

WESTERMANN, M. (ed.) (2005), *Anthropologies of Art*, Williamstown, MA: Sterling and Francine Clark Art Institute.

WIERZBICKA, A. (2006), *English: Meaning and Culture*, Oxford: Oxford University Press.

WILLIAMS, N. (1976), 'Australian Aboriginal Art at Yirrkala: Introduction and Development of Marketing', in N. Graburn (ed.), *Ethnic and Tourist Arts: Cultural Expressions from the Fourth World*, Berkeley: University of California Press.

WILLIAMS, N. (1986), *The Yolngu and their Land: a System of Land Tenure and its Fight for Recognition*, Canberra: Australian Institute of Aboriginal Studies Press.

WINTER, I. (2002), 'Defining "Aesthetics" for Non-Western Studies: the Case for Ancient Mesopotamia', in M. A. Holly and K. Moxey (eds), *Art History, Aesthetics and Visual Studies*, Williamstown, MA: Sterling and Francine Clark Art Institute.

ZANGWILL, N. (2002), 'Against the Sociology of Art', *Philosophy of Social Sciences*, 32(2): 206–18.

# INDEX

*Note: Italicized* page numbers indicate illustrations

Lendon, Nigel 185, 210n8
Lindsay, Daryl 189
Losche, Diane 120, 136, 204n6, 205n12
*Love Songs of Arnhem Land* (Berndt) 201n5
Lowish, Susan 2, 4, 197n1m, 198n7
Lüthi, Bernhard 183

Macassan people 205n13
    influence on Yolngu art 156
    projection into Yolngu ancestry 132
    trade relationship with Yolngu 29–30, 31, 35, 61, 69
McCarthy, Fred 179
McClean, Ian 201n8
McIntosh, I.S. 202n17
McMillan, Richard 210nn8, 11
McMullen, A. 175
Madarrpa clan 45, 104
    ceremonies 100
    diamond design 121, *122*
    paintings 47, 78, 91, 100–1, 103–4, 110
Maddock, Ken 80, 202n18
Magowan, Fiona 203n2
Malangi, David 164
Maloon, Terence 181–2, 183
Maloon/Tuckson thesis 181–2, 185, 210n10
Manatja clan: diamond design 121–4
Mandanjku 162
Manggalili clan 104
    iconography 201n3
    Maymuru family of artists 150
    paintings 98–100, 126, 150–1
Maquet, Jack 13, 143
Marawili, Bakulangay 90, *90*, 91, 100, 103, 105
Marawili, Djambawa 70, 79, 100, 101–4, *101*, *102*, 105–6, *105*, 107, *107*, 158, 164, 193, 204n8
Marawili, Gumbaniya 46, *47*
Marawili, Mundukul *46*
Marawili, Ngulpurr 70, 72
Marchand, Suzanne 210–11n1
Marika, Banduk 77, *78*, 80
Marika, Dhuwarrwarr 80
Marika, Mathaman 74
Marika, Mawalan *52*, *55*, 74, 77, 80
Marika, Roy 65
Marika, Wanyubi 105, 106, *106*, 164, 209n25
markets/marketing 28, 32, 33, 51–2, 54, 57–8, 154, 158, 165–6
    and Australia Council 28
    and authenticity concept 72

dealership system 58
exports to overseas collectors 57
promotion post-Second World War 57–9
Yolngu motivations 59–66
Marralwanga, Birriya Birriya 162
Marralwanga, Namirrki 159
Marralwanga, Peter, 159, *161*, 162, 163
Mason, Otis T. 173–4, 178
massacres/killings
    Gängan 30–1
    Japanese pearler 31–2
material culture, commoditization and trade 177
Mawurndjul, John xiii, 159, 164–5, *165*, 166
Maymuru, Banapana 112, 150, 151, *152*, 153
Maymuru, Bokarra *94*, 150, 151, *152*
Maymuru, Galuma 105, 108, *108*, 158, 164
Maymuru, Mändjilnga 150, 151
Maymuru, Maymirrirr 151, 153
Maymuru, Nanyin 202n20
Maymuru, Narritjin 40, 57, 63, 74, 75, 98, *98*, 99, *99*, *138*, 150–1, *151*, 153, *155*, 158, 202nn20, 21
    on innovation in art 148, 154, 164
    on role of mind in painting 110
    Sydney exhibition 65–6
Maymuru, Narritjin and Banapana: Creative Arts Fellowship awards 111–12
    analysis and interpretation of Abelam paintings 120–39
    teaching visit to Australian National University 112
Megaw, Vincent 204n1
Melville and Bathurst Islands 54, 181
Methodist Overseas Missionary Society 32, 54, 59
    *see also* missions/missionaries
Midjaw Midjaw 159
Milaybuma, David 162, *162*
Milingimbi mission settlement 32, 33, 54, 57, 63
mining/mineral prospecting 64, 66
    negative impact on local population 70
missions/missionaries
    art collections 32–5
    banning of Aboriginal art 58
    effects and influences on Yolngu 31–5, 59–66
    promotion of Yolngu art 57–9
    relationships with Yolngu 27–8, 60–1
    stations/settlements 32, 43, 59, 62, 70, 75, 158
    support for Yolngu rights 60
    *see also* Christianity; churches

regional economic development meeting (Yilpara 2005) 70
seasonal variation 71–2
*see also* missions/missionaries
Nyadbi, Lena xiii
Nyagere *114*

Oenpelli 57, 58, 162
O'Hanlon, M. 205n10
*Old and New Aboriginal Art* (Black) 202n15
Onians, John 197n2
Op Art 92, 190

painting processes and properties
  colour use in design 41, 73, 92, 151, 152, 159
  creation of ceremonial space 80
  cross-hatching 91, 96, 100–1, 159
  emergent iconicity 96–109
  immanence of figuration (*buwuyak*) 78, 105–9, 158–9, 166
  materials and pigments 73–5
  motivating themes/purposes 50–1
  optical effects 92–3
  scale 64, 74–5, 76, 199n20
  shimmering effect (*bir'yun*) 92–6
  techniques 91–2, 96–109
  training 80–1
  universal component 90–1
  use of coloured crayons 51–2, 64, 75
  *see also* designs
paintings
  ancestral dimension 92–3, 96, 109–10, 148, 149–50, 153, 154, 156
  'anyhow' 48–9, 50, 51, 154
  attribution and ownership 41–3, 149–50, 157–8, 163–4
  clan and moiety identification 56–7, 64
  colours and pigments 41, 73, 92–3, 151, 152, 159
  cultural content and context 90–1
  documentation 56–8, 60, 61–2, 150
  as ethnographic material 51–2
  figurative 49, *49*, 50, 76, 78, 96, 104–5, 137
  genres 49, 150, 154
  geometric designs 48, 76, 76–7, 78, 96, 103, 104, 137, 158–9
  iconography 57
  imagery and metaphors 70, 72, 108–9, 136, 137, 211n3
  knowledge transmission use 61–2, 69–70, 110
  meanings and symbolism 17–18, 93–4, 104–9

as morality tales 154, *155*, 208n20
on motor vehicles 41
production rights 45, 154, 157
representation and expression 103
sacred 17, 49, 63, 75, 76, 124, 154, 208n18
style and content 75–6
transformational aspects 92, 96, 104–5, 132, 136–7
transportation 75, 200n1
visible-invisible dual aspect 109, 110
*wakinngu* (mundane) 17, 18, 50, 154, 200n7, 208n18
*see also* bark paintings; body painting; designs; painting processes and properties
Pan-Australian Aboriginal and Torres Strait Islander art award 88
Papua New Guinea *see* New Guinea
Perkins, Hetti xiii
Philips, Ruth 191
Pintubi artists 197n1, 199n21, 202n19, 207n9, 208n15, 211n5
Pospisil, L. 198n11
Potlatch ban 27
Preston, Margaret 59, 178, 184, 189, 198n7, 201n8, 202n14, 204n11, 206nn1, 3, 211n2
Price, Richard and Sally 25
primitive art 12–13, 88, 143
  categorization 176–7
  collectors 173
  and indigenous art 187
  markets 12
  and modernism 188
*Primitive Art and Society* (Forge) 204n5
prints/printmaking 50, 75, 208n19
*pukumani* poles 54

Quai Branly, Paris 1
Queensland Art Gallery 20

*Reader in the Anthropology of Religion* (Tylor) 199n14
Rees, Lloyd 197n4
religion
  animism 199n14
  anthropological definitions 176, 199n14
  as cross-cultural category 7–8, 11–12
  Yolngu and Christian dialogues 64–5
religious art 4
Riley, Bridget 92
Riley, Michael xiii

women
  in Abelam art 118, *118*, 126, 139
  ancestral 40, *40*, *52*, *55*, 77, *78*, 92, 97, 108, 121,
    125, 126, *138*
  artists 50
  artwork restrictions 72
  in ceremonies 200n5
  gender discrimination 137
  participation in artworks 72, 80–2
  roles in Yolngu society 37, 38, 43, 44
  Yirrkala prints production 50
Woodah Island 31
world-art discourse 2–3, 18
Wunungmurra, Yanggariny 57, *123*

Yarrwidi Gumatj clan 125
Yathikpa 100
  dugong hunters 90–1, 105–6, 107
Yilpara homeland 70–2, 158
Yirrawala xiii, 159, 160, 162, 163, 164
Yirritja-moiety 63, 66, 121
  ancestral snake (Mundukul) 70–1
  ceremonies 39
  clan design associations 128
  cross-hatching technique 160
  diamond designs 101–2, 121
  fire connection 90–1
  flood waters 102–3
  *marrayin* designs 159
  mortuary rituals 136
  paintings 159–60, 200n1
  triangular pattern designs 125–6
Yirrkala mission settlement 32, 51, 54, 57, 58, 80
  AGNSW display of artworks 181
  Church panels 63–4, *63*
  oral histories 60–1
Yirrkala School 69
Yolngu art
  abstraction and representation 76, 109
  ceremonial use 61–2, 79
  change and innovations 72–82, 157–8, 164
  commercialization process 27, 59–66
  concepts 17–18, 35, 157
  continuity and change 43–4, 156–9
  and cultural identity 31, 38–9, 41–3, 77–8, 89,
    149–50, 167
  documentation methods 56–8
  history 28–9, 92, 153–4, 156, 157, 164, 167
  interpretation 149
  and material culture 35–44

metaphysics 17, 78–9, 166
  and modernism 88
  outside influences 156–7
  prints/printmaking 50, 75
  as purposive action 35
  sacred/spiritual value 20–1, 43, 76, 200n7, 201n2
  and social change 148
  templates 48, 77
  transformative powers 35–6
  and value creation process 33, 81, 157, 171,
    199n15
  in Western categorization 141–2
  *see also* collectors/collections; markets/marketing;
    paintings
Yolngu art objects 17–18, 45, 211n6
  armbands *30*, 31, 38–9, 43
  baskets (*bathi*) 37, 43, 200nn5, 9
  carvings 48, 51, 61
  digging sticks 37, 39–40, *40*, 200n5
  dilly bags 38–9, 43, 44, 45, 61, 201n2
  paddles *34*, 41
  smoking pipes 41, 200n7
  spears 31, 36, 37–8, *37*, 43
  staffs 40
  *see also* bark paintings; coffins
Yolngu ceremonies 44, 81, 200n5
  burial 38, 81
  *makarrata* 38
  purification rituals 41, 100
  *see also* circumcision ceremony (*dhapi*); mortuary
    rituals
Yolngu material culture 35–44
  artefact embellishment and elaboration 35, 36,
    37–40, 41–3
  ceremonial dance and singing 37, 41, 42, 70–1
  continuity and change 43–4, 148, 157
  craft activities 81
  design adaptation 35–6
  functional specialization 36–7
Yolngu society
  acuity of vision 89–90
  analogue creation 64, 69, 95, 97, 104
  concepts of art 17–18, 35, 157
  conservatism 72, 73
  cultural and economic changes 80–1
  economy and self-determination 28, 32, 69, 70,
    81
  education and training 32, 69–70, 80
  estate area divisions 45
  first European contacts 29–31